France: THE TRAGIC YEARS

France

"If an offense comes out of the truth,
it is better that the offense come
than that the truth be concealed."
St. Jerome

1955

NEW YORK

Sisley Huddleston

THE TRAGIC YEARS

1939-1947

AN EYEWITNESS ACCOUNT

OF WAR, OCCUPATION,

AND LIBERATION

THE DEVIN-ADAIR COMPANY, *Publishers*

For information address The Devin-Adair Company
23 East 26th Street, New York 10, N. Y.
Canadian Agents: Thomas Nelson & Sons, Ltd.
Library of Congress Catalog Card Number: 54–10820
Manufactured in the United States of America.
Designed by Lewis F. White.

Dedicatory Letter

To His Excellency William C. Bullitt
Ambassador of the United States of America.

My Dear Bill: More than thirty years have elapsed since you read to me in Paris your letter of resignation from the American Peace Delegation, and since then everything that has happened has justified your protest against a Treaty which was a betrayal of our hopes, a repudiation of our principles, and a frustration of the purpose for which we fought the First World War. We both realized that the statesmen of Versailles had doomed mankind to a future bloody trial of strength.

Our friendship, which has never faltered from those far-off days when you took your stand for truth in diplomacy, is stronger than ever as we enter the dark era in which the ineptitude and the pernicious untruths of the past decade threaten to overwhelm humanity.

More appalling than follies and errors are lying legends. It would be possible to correct mistakes, however damnable, did we possess the courage to acknowledge them. We prefer comfortable falsehoods, fatal expedients, purblind propaganda; and we are disturbed by testimony which upsets the conventional views.

In our correspondence you remark that there are "few of us left who have some understanding of the whole swing of events since 1914," when Sir Edward Grey dolefully observed: "The lamps are going out all over Europe; we shall not see them lighted again in our time." A bad peace culminated in a Second World War, and a badly conducted Second World War is leading us to a third world war, with the prospect of Bolshevism triumphant on the ruins of our civilization.

You are good enough to call me "an old friend who has always been right." I have, alas, often been wrong, but at least I have tried to see clearly and to state the plain facts.

My birth in England, my twenty years of working association with America, and nearly a lifetime of residence in France, have made me neither altogether English, nor American, nor French, but something of all three. From my coign of vantage, I have, aided by forty years of training in diplomatic affairs, watched not only the heroic efforts but also the blunders, unrealized in Washington or London, committed in our fight against the evil forces that threaten to enslave us.

My position is unique; my post of observation enabled me to look on with some detachment, though often I was in the heart of things; and it is my duty to refute the strange fictions which falsify all our conceptions. I witnessed in France the civil war and the revolution to which we still refuse to give their rightful names, and the effects of the astounding miscalculations of the statesmen, French, English, and American.

After hopelessly shattering Europe, we are now told that the urgent task is to create Europe. But Europe existed before 1914, when I could travel where I pleased without passport, without permission, without formality. Even after

1918, Europe still lived, and I could enjoy the spectacle of happy and prosperous countries. Today, where is the old Europe? Much of it is behind an iron curtain, and is lost to us. The rest lives in fear, subjected to innumerable restrictions, poor, and dependent on charity.

Having smashed every barrier to Communism, having divided country after country, having abolished the sense of justice and of pity, we await, inadequately defended, the coming of the Police State, with the promise of a new liberation when the Continent has become a cemetery.

I try to render one last service, and I am fortified in placing your name in the forefront of a work which is inspired not by hate (deadlier than the atomic bomb) but by the love of our fellows which alone can save us.

SISLEY HUDDLESTON

Troinex, 1952

Other Books by SISLEY HUDDLESTON

IN MY TIME: A Record of War and Peace
PARIS SALONS, CAFÉS, STUDIOS
FRANCE AND THE FRENCH
FRANCE: A Survey of Historical Forces
A HISTORY OF FRANCE
LOUIS XIV: In Love and in War
PARIS: A Little Guide
MEDITERRANEAN BLUE (Windows on the World)
NORMANDY
PEACEMAKING IN PARIS
POINCARÉ: A Biographical Portrait
WAR UNLESS . . .
BETWEEN THE RIVER AND THE HILLS
EUROPE IN ZIGZAGS
POPULAR DIPLOMACY AND WAR

In French
LE LIVRE DE SAINT-PIERRE
LE MYTHE DE LA LIBERTÉ
TERREUR 1944
AVEC LE MARÉCHAL
LETTRES À UN AMI FRANÇAIS

Contents

Dedicatory Letter to William C. Bullitt v
Foreword by Louis Guitard xi
Chapter 1 France and the War 3
2 Phony War 18
3 Armistice 34
4 Legality of Vichy 49
5 Oran 59
6 Montoire 71
7 Accord with Churchill—French Opinion 84
8 Laval Dismissed 98
9 Darlan 108
10 Occupation 122
11 Hitler Strikes at Russia 132
12 Italy Makes War 144
13 America Enters 153
14 Tragedy of Errors—North Africa 170
15 Bird's-eye View of Vichy 189
16 Conversation with Pétain 203
17 Algiers 215
18 Resistance—Real and False 228
19 Return to Paris 241
20 Counterresistance 254
21 How Paris Was Saved 266
22 Liberation and Sequel 284
23 Revolution and Terror *1944–1946* 296
24 Fourth Republic 325
25 The Marshal Dies 347
Illustrations between pp. 168–169
Index 353

Foreword

By Louis Guitard

When, having weathered the grand climacteric, Sisley Huddleston took leave of this world, his fine face had assumed an added beauty.

The years had not bereft him of that spice of bohemianism which gave a quaint touch to his personality, but had stamped his bearing with great dignity. His great height seemed increased by the loss of some of his corpulence. His high forehead, his slightly graying fair hair, his features more pronounced than of yore, his well-kept, bristling white moustache and goatee, his bushy brows all enhanced the beauty of his eyes. Did he speak, they suddenly kindled, his glance grew searching and intent. His eloquent hands would stress the point he wished to make and then, as if the better to gauge the success of his arguments, he would clap his monocle to his right eye, a gesture too instinctive to be affected.

He was eminently sociable, gay, cordial and forthright, lavishing on his guests the treasures of his culture, humor and enchanting fancy. Intelligence and benignity were perhaps his outstanding qualities. He was eager for information, anxious to understand. Moreover, love of his fellow creatures informed his actions and his writings.

His intelligence stimulated an insatiable curiosity, a thirst for knowledge, and made him broad-minded, independent, inimical to whatever threatened to shackle thought. He loathed dictatorship, sectarianism and party spirit. "A free man cannot be a partisan," he would say.

His kindness caused him to be generous, modest, upright. *Humanity* with him was not an empty word, an ideological term. It actually meant to him the multitude of his fellowmen; and because he truly loved them, he was saddened by their follies; injustice sickened him and he rejected war with all his might. Ailing in 1914, he was laid low in 1939 also. He was sensitive, courageous and a firm believer, so that while folly and violence made him ill, he went on fighting for the sanity of the world still hoping for a brighter future.

Did his ardent nature feel chilled in the severe climate of Britain and ill at ease amid its conventions?

On the shore of the Irish Channel where, in 1883, he was born, sailors had fed his childish dreams. He imagined himself "a passenger in every boat that sailed into the setting sun." To Wordsworth he owed his introduction "into the magic land of poetry"; he shared with a friend the delight of reading Keats under the shady trees of a fine park and, at ten years of age, he wrote an essay on Milton.

In early life he held a modest appointment in the Civil Service. Great-hearted and unworldly, he resigned his post as a protest against the dismissal of a friend.

Journalism proved a haven and made him aware of his true vocation. "But," says he, "my real career was on the boulevards of Paris." At last a real passenger in a real ship, he left his native mists for the gentle sun of the Ile-de-France.

The French blood which, according to a family tradition, flowed in his veins, had prevailed.

Salvador de Madariaga, in a book now a classic, has described the Englishman as a strong-willed man, delighting in action and motion, alternating business and sports, to whom liberty means the right to act according to his bent without any alien interference, within the limits of an empire in which he glories; while the Frenchman, a lover of ideas, reason and order, lives "to develop his intellect and the five avenues—the senses—which lead thereto, whose conception of liberty is the right to think as he lists and to say what he thinks." And he adds: "If the French succeeded in molding the world in their own image, it would revolve as smoothly as clockwork. All men would speak French like Mirabeau and write it like Racine. Soul and intellect would shine on earth like a sparkling river: life's every minute would be a scintillating drop of exquisite pleasure to the delight of the soul." Doubtless, it was the glitter of the diamondlike river that fascinated Huddleston and incited him to live on its banks.

His *humanity* drew him to the land of *humanism*. He instinctively understood and loved it. He steeped himself in its history and literature as Voltaire did in Horace.

As one drinks of an old vintage which rejuvenates the heart's blood.

He ranged all over this land he had adopted for his own, delighting in the trivial attractions of a village fair as in the most grandiose relics of the past. "We will not disdain the gewgaws, for they are tokens of human desires and human vanities—that is of human poetry."

When he settled in Paris, he made his home within a short distance of the Latin Quarter, close to Montparnasse where, sporting a wide-brimmed hat and a flowing tie, he consorted with James Joyce, D. H. Lawrence, Hemingway, and other young Bohemians, all talented and cheerfully poor.

When he left the city for the country, he chose Normandy. There, between Giverny where Monet painted his *Nymphéas,* and Cocherel where Aristide Briand hugged his dreams, he bought a three-century-old mill which he turned into a peaceful hermitage, gay with flowers. "To France," he declared, "I owe my culture and in the same way, the whole of modern Europe is indebted to her for she inherited the spiritual patrimony of Greece and Rome. She is the main factor, the one indispensable element of our world. . . . I cannot imagine a more intelligent, spiritual, *humane* way of life than that of the true France." It is indeed his encyclopædic knowledge of France that enabled him to understand the rest of Europe—a compound, according to Paul Valéry, of the races and countries that were, successively, Romanized, Christianized and subjected to the intellectual discipline of Greece.

An international journalist, the Paris Director of the London *Times,* the European correspondent of the *Christian Science Monitor,* contributing articles to a score of English and American publications, writer and traveler, he devoted the greater part of his talent and energy to the cause of France. He believed that the Anglo-Saxon world knew virtually nothing about her. "Even when the Entente Cordiale was at its best," he wrote, "France has never been properly understood," and he endeavored to set forth the multiple aspects of her genius.

Those who have had the privilege of listening to his lectures will never forget them. He spoke *ex-tempore* with the aid of a few casual notes, stressing the points by a few well-chosen instances derived from personal experience. What he really enjoyed was a debate with his audience, once the lecture was over. He countered objections with ready wit:

it was a marvelous display, something like expert swordsmanship.

He was first and foremost a journalist. From Versailles to Geneva, he never missed an international meeting. He became acquainted with all the more prominent politicians who played a part on the European stage between the two world wars. Considering each problem from a purely humane point of view, he strove primarily, to understand his fellowmen. He had the gift of extracting an interview from the most refractory and tongue-tied of his interlocutors. He was also eloquent. "You are a very dangerous man," said a woman who was herself no mean opponent. "Those who read you are convinced that you are right however wrong you actually are." He was clear-sighted. As early as 1919, he sensed in the Treaty of Versailles the seeds of a future conflict. He lost no time in showing up the sophistries of the League of Nations. In 1935, he denounced the so-called "sanctions" as a prodrome of war. On the morrow of the fall of Alfonso XIII he skeptically queried: "Will the Spanish Republic endure?"

He collected, for our delight, a number of his articles in compilations which, added to his other books, show the facility and diversity of his talent: in all about thirty volumes. Whatever he wrote, in English or in French, he typed straightway, and then read over and edited the typescript. Well informed and versatile, he published books on history, topography, travel, autobiography, besides essays and novels. His pen is always alert, be he grave or gay. Arnold Bennett used to say that Huddleston had the gift of making even a page of statistics attractive. He was impulsive, warm-hearted, *humane*. He was wont to say: "I write because I can't help it. It is my vocation. It is a call and I could not refrain if I would. He did write from the bottom of his heart. René Benjamin, who knew what he was talking about, thus praised Huddleston: "When all is said, the more the soul informs a work the loftier and finer it is. Yours is all soul."

The Spanish Civil War marked the turning point in Huddleston's journalistic career and constituted the acid test of his intellectual and ideological integrity. Litvinov, at Geneva, had cleverly sold most of the liberal internationalists and journalists the fiction that the "popular front" against totalitarianism meant only opposition to totalitarianism of the Right—bitter hostility to Germany, Italy and the Franco régime in Spain. Huddleston's honest and logical mind rejected this mischievous fallacy. As a lifelong libertarian, he had, like Thomas Jefferson, "sworn eternal enmity to every form of tyranny over the mind of man," from whatever source derived. He discerned that Soviet Russia constituted as great a threat to the freedom of the human mind and action as did Fascism and Nazism, and did not hesitate to say so.

While recognizing that there was a segment of honest republicanism and liberalism in the opposition to both the old Spanish régime and to General Franco, he discerned that the Spanish Civil War was also an attempt to establish totalitarianism of the Left in a critical portion of Western Europe. This appraisal was the "sin against the Holy Ghost" to the deluded "popular front" liberal interventionists. Huddleston knew that to continue to tell the truth after 1937, as he had done for a quarter of a century before, meant the end of his career as a popular international journalist. But he did not flinch, even though his worst fears as to his personal career were rather more than realized. The scribes of distorted delusion took over and he was left without a wide reading public for the remainder of his life. This book is a final tribute to his intellectual courage and integrity.

It is not folly to predict that, if sanity ever returns in the world scene, Huddleston will be more honored by later generations than those journalists who misinformed the public for more than a decade and contributed so much to the international disasters that came to the world after 1937.

It was to make clear to the American public both the framework and the details of a particularly confused period of recent French history that Sisley Huddleston wrote *France: The Tragic Years.*

Asserting with Aristotle that "the most poignant drama is that which depicts the fall of a man of outstanding virtue and exceptional accomplishment, from the topmost pinnacle of fame to the lowest depths of physical and mental missery," he wondered that the Gaullist revolution should, in the very middle of the twentieth century, thus pillory Marshal Pétain without arousing the reprobation of the whole world. His amazement was the more justified as, in the person of the marshal, it was nothing less than the regeneration of France that his accusers impeached.

Sisley Huddleston reminds us that the politicians whom 1940 found in office, terrified by the vastness of a defeat they had done nothing to prevent, appealed in their dire need to the most glorious of Frenchmen.

Decades before, eminent statesmen and thinkers had reiterated warnings: "France has fallen a prey to a false ideology and is living on quicksands. The Revolution of 1789 was due to a lie with revolutionary principles." Upon this lie was built a system of anarchy and impotence which, on the material plane, furthered private interests at the expense of general welfare, and on the moral plane, secured the tyranny of materialism. Should not a radical reform—political, intellectual and moral—intervene, France is doomed to collapse under the ruins of her régime.

Men widely dissimilar in character and political views such as Clemenceau, Léon Daudet, Joseph Caillaux, André Tardieu, Anatole de Monzie, Gaston Doumergue, extreme republicans at the start of their career, ended by cursing the system which was causing their country to disintegrate.

At its last gasp, the Third Republic acknowledged its shortcomings. At Vichy, on the 10th of July 1940, a fortnight after the necessary and salutary armistice had been signed, Marshal Pétain was entreated, in due form, to elaborate a "new constitution of the French state," guaranteeing the rights of labor, of the family and of the country.

Forthwith, the marshal proclaimed the urgency of a national revolution, specifying its aims: "We need a strong state, willing to establish the limits of its own powers by incorporating into itself the spiritual values and the fundamental units of the family and the workshop. We demand liberties to strengthen the Family such as the reform of the educational system and the laws of inheritance; to fortify labor by corporate organization; we need sane laws in order to shake off the heavy yoke of politicians and anonymous finance; an intellectual and moral reform, opposing energy to facility, the dignity of Labor to sloth, to the licentiousness of youth, its upbringing in hope and faith, and lastly, to the spreading contagion of egoism, devotion to the country." Deafening cheers saluted the old man who thus awakened in his fellow countrymen the memory of their traditions. The youth of France, who were wilting under the dull presidency of M. Lebrun, were stirred to a healthy enthusiasm. "I have not met with a single Frenchman who could say a good word for the prewar government, which is generally held responsible for the defeat," Admiral Leahy wrote from Vichy to President Roosevelt. A great hope was born.

But daily complications had to be straightened out before the undertaking of the necessary fundamental reforms. Every day the occupation brought up painful problems which had to be solved. Marshal Pétain might proclaim and prepare the renascence but it was not granted him to make good. Before the liberation of the French territory, he could not promulgate the constitutional text which he had drafted without the least reference to Fascist or National-Socialistic theories. His enemies made the most of the delay, the sufferings and weariness of the people. They endeavored to confuse the gestation of the national revolution with actual and often painful administrative acts, made unavoidable by the German occupation, and they succeeded.

Pétain's enemies were the helpless politicians, responsible for the catastrophe, whom General De Gaulle, who sought personal power rather than military feats, had grouped around him in London. "The De Gaulle movement is not so popular as the English and American press insinuate," wrote Admiral Leahy in July 1941. "The Frenchmen I have interviewed, even those who most ardently set their hopes on an English victory, have small respect for General De Gaulle."

In order to bolster up his prestige, De Gaulle had no other recourse than to summon to his side those whom a regenerated France would forever have rejected; since the Communists were the irreconcilable enemies of Pétain, he chose them and Stalin for his main support. He declared at Algiers on June 23, 1943: "Not only do I wish for, but insist upon the collusion with Communists." Hitler had taken his measure. When he gave the order to arrest and take to Germany Marshal Pétain and Pierre Laval, he relinquished Paris to De Gaulle. The madman knew what he was doing.

First, we saw the revolution of 1944–1945, the bloodiest France had ever known. Then came the establishment of the Fourth Republic which is naught but the Third at its worst. "If peace consists in reverting to the prewar political, economical and social condition, France will never recover," asserted Marshal Pétain. De Gaulle turned a deaf ear to this warning. Vichy held out a promise. To cater to his ambitions, De Gaulle turned it into treason. In strangling the "national revolution" he replunged France into the filthy and delicious deliquescence which horrified Clemenceau.

"The disease of verbalism," wrote Huddleston in 1941, "has devastated the world. The history of the last twenty years is principally a history of the slogans accepted by the masses and the so-called élite. Many empty, yet noxious, words, while fanning the passions of peoples and dulling their brains, have enabled climbing and often ignorant demagogues to pursue their professional career of personal ambition and general corruption." Thus he answered beforehand the question with which he opens *France: The Tragic Years.* Why did the world remain passive at the sight of "the greatest personal tragedy of our times"? Because the press and radio had joined forces to convince it that De Gaulle was a hero and Pétain a traitor. Dr. Goebbels is not dead. The halo of De Gaulle and the turpitude of Pétain—or the triumph of propaganda over truth!

Sisley Huddleston was a close observer of the Vichy period of history. He gives an account of events which he witnessed and in which he occasionally played a part. Hence, the value of his book.

One might here and there descry a few errors in this honest record and also question certain judgments.

Huddleston would surely have judged Philippe Henriot with more leniency had he, before writing that page which arraigns him, read the frequently prophetic editorials of the minister of information. Besides, Philippe Henriot was shot down not "by a group of indignant Resistants" but on the injunction of the Algiers authorities, by a slayer who, shortly afterward, was himself shot down just as he was getting ready to blow open a safe.

Huddleston's severe appraisal of Admiral Darlan is still more surprising. Yet he is reasonably fair to Pierre Laval, whom he did not like or trust. This disparity of treatment appears to me to be a result of his responsiveness to personal contacts. He knew Laval personally, while he had never met Admiral Darlan. It is just possible that the perusal of the Admiral's letters and private papers, recently published by M. Alain Darlan, might have qualified his opinion.

Let it be enough to draw the reader's attention to these points; far from deprecating the value of his book, they only prove the author's independence. Sisley Huddleston looked upon Marshal Pétain's policy with sympathy; yet he by no means approved all his decisions or those of his ministers. Moreover, he declares that he does not claim to write the final word of history but merely brings his first-hand testimony to history. He only imparts to us the impressions of an honest and well-informed witness.

When, in 1940, his English compatriots fairly fled the continent, Huddleston did not accompany them. "Never was I so deeply moved as at that moment when France lay prostrate in the dust. I felt as though my whole life had come to an end." He declared that to leave would be akin to desertion. He settled in Monaco. Great-hearted as he ever was, he repeated the famous gesture of Savorgnan de Brazza, who became a Frenchman after the disastrous fall of Sedan. He put in an application for his naturalization papers, in order to have the right to share the destinies of France and to help in the work of regeneration.

The bitter recriminations of Churchill, the "hideous mistake" of Mers-el-Kebir, the support yielded by London to the Resistance, excited his righteous indignation. Had England already forgotten that her ally had borne, almost alone, the brunt of the brutal attack? That, abandoned so soon to their own devices, the French forces had heroically protected the British retreat? He exhorted England to remain loyal for the time being, for fear of jeopardizing the future of Europe, which he deemed would have to coalesce under the moral leadership of France; all that weakened the France of 1940 would recoil on Europe when the war was over. Thus he considered all events "from their possible effect on France."

Marshal Pétain rekindled hope in the French people, sunk deeply in the slough of despond; therefore Huddleston gave him full support. When he heard Pétain declare: "The land cannot deceive. . . . There is not, there cannot be a theoretical and chimerical liberty as against general welfare and the independence of the nation . . ." he applauded. In his book on Saint-Pierre, the Normandy village he had made his home and for which he longed in his Monegasque exile, he endeavored, as in a microcosm, to give a general picture of the whole of France. In the *Myth of Liberty,* he denounced the "master words" which, masking mere abstractions, yet ruled the world; he entreated his fellowmen to reject such myths in order to regain spirituality.

In his opinion, the De Gaulle-Pétain conflict jeopardized the good work of regeneration pursued at Vichy, doing more harm to France than the occupation. To the genuine patriots of the underground movement he quoted the words of Edith Cavell: "Patriotism is not enough!"

In 1943, having become the "youngest of Frenchmen," he was summoned to the presence of Marshal Pétain. He has give us an account of the interview. He nursed the hope that in Vichy should be born a humane peace based on "spiritual values so ground under the heavy boots of the invader"; and that Pétain might legally hand over to his successor a nation "united as a single mind." A year later, the hatred of the coalesced Communists and Gaullists gave their answer. He was thrown into jail. A Monaco paper printed the following caption: "A good haul: The Huddleston traitors have been arrested." Some months later, released at the request of England, he again took up his pen to combat the "disastrous propaganda" of the "Resistentialists." The latter condemned Pétain and tried to dishonor him and rob him of his fame as a victorious general in the former war. Huddleston was aghast and protested: "They were Frenchmen, they who slandered their own country in this outrageous fashion. It is not true that France is composed of millions of traitors!"

He protested, jealous of the honor of his adopted country. His own misadventure left him cold. He bore no grudge. Apparently his old cheerfulness had never forsaken him. "We are, I trust, approaching the end of the dark passage. . . . I remain convinced that, in spite of all, the corruption, the fiendish outcome of the war years, more destructive than the A-bombs, cannot last. We shall revert to the principles without which no civilization can survive: discipline, subservience to legitimate authority, to labor, the respect of the human personality, order, the inviolability of the home, the sense of ownership which is but an extension of the personality, solidarity, mercy, justice, grandeur, nobility, sensibility, the belief in God and the soul, the conception of our divine destiny. And France it is who must lead this spiritual Crusade. Her past wills it, her tradition makes it unavoidable. Europe needs France. The world cannot do without her."

It is impossible to doubt the sincerity of such words, but, alas! they come back to us from beyond the grave.

Huddleston was worn out. Why try to cure the blindness of those who do not wish to see the light? He stood almost alone. Many of his friends were no more. Others lived far away, or, like Bullitt, were wandering around the world. They had forgotten the gay evenings of Montparnasse. Gaullist Frenchmen would be criminal did they not avoid him. The loyal henchmen of the marshal were in hiding or in the many jails of the Fourth Republic. Hatred, persecution, or cowardice held sway.

He recalled the lines of Hilaire Belloc:

I fear I shall be all alone
When I get towards the end.
Who will be here to comfort me
And who will be my friend?

It is true that from René Benjamin he received letters overflowing with affection but also with despair: "We are sunk in a horrible, lifeless bog. . . . For glowing hearts it is a disgusting time to live in."

His eyes betrayed his growing desolation. On July 14, 1952, he was struck down like a huge tree that seems sturdy while mysterious influences are sapping its strength. "We die," he wrote as far back as 1941, "because life is not worth living. The war revealed to many the grim truth. They knew that they were no longer alive. They were aware that everything they held dear is doomed. Wherefore should they go on marching since they were no better than unburied corpses?"

Dear Huddleston! you were to William Bullitt "the old friend who has always been right." You are also to us Frenchmen the friend who cannot die. In your old mill at Saint-Pierre, watchful devotion has prepared all things against your return. There you will find your books and your garden just as you left them before you set out on your last great journey. In the village street you will meet the radiant young girl who will say as she meets you: "I knew you couldn't be dead! you who were life itself!" You will also find again, intact and more ardent than ever, our love and gratitude. It is from our traditions that you have drawn your love of France and these traditions which you have fought for, defending them against the erring and foolish, forgetful of their glorious inheritance. On the road to the necessary "National Revolution," you shine as a powerful searchlight to show us the way.

LOUIS GUITARD

Avocat à La Cour d'Appel de Paris

1

France and the War

I HAD returned from Geneva, where the immense Palace of Nations, a magnificent mausoleum, had been erected just before the final collapse of the League, and I listened with growing anguish in my Normandy mill, which was built 350 years ago and has survived many invasions, to the radio announcements. Mobilization had been ordered, and the ominous white placards were on every wall. But, somehow, the French did not take the mobilization seriously. "It will be like last year," was the general comment. In 1938 there had been the anticlimax of Munich, and many people were confident that there would be another Munich.

It is always unwise to cry "Wolf!" When the real danger comes, there is incredulity. As I had passed through Paris, I heard on all sides: "More bluff! There will be no war." In my Normandy village there was the same skepticism, and in the marketplace of Vernon the women were assuring one another that their husbands would soon return.

Their light-heartedness seemed not unjustified. When Hitler slammed the door of the League of Nations and declared that, with the breakdown of the disarmament conference, Germany no longer considered herself bound by the terms of the Treaty of Versailles, there had been no war. When, by a plebiscite in the Saar, where, as I personally ascertained, the vote was free, that territory had returned to the Reich, there had been no war. When Hitler had reoccupied the Rhineland, and Premier Sarraut had trumpeted the brave word that Strasbourg would not be allowed to remain under the menace of German cannon, there had been no war. When the *Anschluss* with Austria, in defiance of treaty engagements, had been proclaimed, there had been no war. When the German population of Czechoslovakia had been ceded, with the territory that population occupied, to Germany, there had been no war. And when, a few months later, Prague itself was occupied and the conglomerate little state had ceased to exist, there had been no war. Why should there be war now?

This was the feeling of the vast majority of the French at the beginning of September 1939. France, under the terms of an old treaty, was bound to fly to the rescue of Poland, but nowhere was there any enthusiasm. The French had no love for Poland, widely separated from them, and the slogan "Die for Danzig?" raised hesitancy in French minds.

They had been assured that Danzig was, indeed, a German city, and that the making of the Polish corridor was one of the greatest blunders of the peacemakers at Paris. There were much larger issues that did not perturb them, notably the issue of whether Germany was to march from bloodless victory to victory until she secured the hegemony of Europe. Since Munich, where peace had been promised in perpetuity, the tone had been pacific in France. The moral preparation for war had been strangely neglected. War was unpopular in France.

Moreover, the foolish films which showed Polish cavalry

in action against German tanks made the average Frenchman laugh at the antiquated romanticism of the Poles in an age of machinery. Poland had refused to allow Russian troops to traverse her territory to aid countries threatened by Germany. France and Poland were far from being friendly, and the task of defeating Germany to save Poland was about the most distasteful project that could have been proposed by the British to arouse France.

That the motive was fictitious was plain to the ordinary man. Today, he knows that the Great Powers cared little about the fate of Poland, or of the Baltic and Balkan States.

It is time to destroy a foolish legend—the legend that the French are a military people, always ready for glorious adventures. In the days of Louis XIV they could dominate Europe by sheer numbers, and Napoleon could march his armies across Europe at a time when France was the largest nation (barring Russia) on the Continent. But that is the historic past. Ever since I have known France—that is to say, nearly all my life—I have regarded her as essentially antimilitarist, moved only by the direct threat of Germany. She is neither a crusader nor a conqueror: she has lost her Empire two or three times without regret. To regard her as the soldier of Europe is a mistake that is persistently made. She was defeated in 1870 and, though French pride will hardly admit it, she would have been utterly lost without her allies in 1914. It was a foregone conclusion that she would succumb in 1940 unless England made a substantial contribution to the land fighting forces from the beginning.

France has an obsession, partly justified, about Germany, because she has, in our time, suffered from German invasion, and Germany is (or was) nearly twice as large as France and far more highly developed industrially. But France would never again of her own free will attack Germany, and the plain truth is that she was drawn reluctantly into the war in 1939. The Foreign Minister, Georges Bonnet, was notoriously opposed to hostilities.

Whatever may be the technical explanation, the declaration of war in 1939 did not come simultaneously from England and France. There was a difference of only a few hours, but it was sufficient to give many Frenchmen the impression that France's hand was forced. Such errors of psychology are of no little importance.

It was impossible for me, sitting in my study, listening to the radio, to forget that only a few days before the attack on Poland, Russia deliberately came to an agreement with Germany to share the Polish spoils. England had also been negotiating with Russia, apparently unaware that Germany and Russia were secretly in accord.

Germany and Russia had rival ideological systems and were professed enemies; yet they did not scruple to make peace at the expense of Poland. England, too, was anti-Bolshevik, yet she hoped Russia would be her ally. Disappointed, she was again anti-Bolshevik for nearly two years, and then, when Germany and Russia fell out, the Bolsheviks were described as brave and trusty allies. After the war ended, it was seen that Russia had absorbed far more than Germany would have absorbed, and a new anti-Bolshevik campaign began. No wonder the ordinary man is puzzled at these changes of policy.

Before the war, there were, as I estimate, at least thirty per cent of the French ready to adopt Communism as their political creed. When Russia was supposed to be anti-German, these Communists and near Communists were an asset in the coming war with Germany, but when Russia became the associate of Germany in August 1939, and Russia had nothing but praise for Hitler who was assailed, as Stalin and Molotov now affirmed, by French and British "Imperialism," a considerable part of the French population accepted the new doctrine, and the French Communists became a serious liability. They threw their weight against the war with Germany, which was tantamount to a war against Russia—that is to say, against Communism—and their chief, Maurice Thorez—who was mobilized—deserted, escaping to Russia. A letter signed by Communist deputies, demanding an immediate conference to discuss peace terms, was sent to the Chamber. Pacifist professors, writers, and other "intellectuals" issued a manifesto in favor of peace.

The Communists had, individually, all the normal Frenchman's dislike of Germany, and of such movements as Nazism and Fascism, but the volte-face of Stalin in joining hands with Hitler could only increase the doubts and hesitations that marked the beginning of the war.

Nor must we overlook the strong pacifist propaganda, perfectly respectable in its sentiment, which had been propagated in France for years. At Geneva, I had listened with surprise to a responsible statesman—Léon Blum—preaching the doctrine of unilateral disarmament in face of a Germany which was notoriously rearming. Virtually all the literature inspired by the war of 1914–1918 insisted on the horrors of the carnage and predicted still more terrible sufferings not only for the combatants but for the civilians.

There were lost illusions. The soldiers of 1914 were told that they were fighting to end war—and the lie was now patent. They were told that they would make the world safe for Democracy—but they had seen the growth of Bolshevism, Fascism, and Nazism. Their lot, it was said, would be easier; their children would be freed from poverty, every kind of social slavery, and fear of the future: but, since 1919, the lot of the ordinary man had been harder than before, and many ancient liberties were abolished. In short, there was general skepticism, and the old slogans had lost their effectiveness. It is difficult to blame the French, especially when we see in Europe the widespread misery and the far greater loss of freedom in every domain which have, in fact, resulted from the last war.

The successive governments were to blame for the material unpreparedness of the French. Demagogy had been triumphant. Political parties no longer urged the people to work but, on the contrary, to play. The forty-hour week, paid holidays, fêtes and commemorations and manifestations, strikes, notably of the sit-down kind in which the workers virtually took possession of the factories, were the order of the day, and abundance of leisure was accorded to all. I am far from condemning this policy in itself, but it was assuredly not the moment to preach indifference and idleness. The troubled condition of Europe, with the advent of Hitler, the civil strife in Spain, the growing antagonism of Italy after the abortive sanctions, and many other premonitory signs, should have made politicians exceedingly wary.

I had examined the reports on the French army and the air forces in 1938, and I had been appalled by the inadequacy of France's preparations. I had no reason to suppose that any real attempt had been made to overtake Germany in tanks and aircraft. Anyone who was aware of the facts was bound to conclude that France was in no position to resist an attack.

Worse still, perhaps, was the propagation of fear by the governments. In 1914 there were, it is true, refugees: I had myself helped to care for them. But populations were not exhorted in advance to fly from the wrath to come. In 1939 we were all bidden to migrate. Instead of staying wherever we might be, carrying on the best we could, we were encouraged to desert even before the invader arrived. For months my own village had been overcrowded with refugees—before the war began! Evacuation was the new command. Evacuate! Evacuate! I can imagine no worse policy than this official spreading of terror.

We were told, too, that poison gas would be let loose; we were all furnished with gas masks, and shelters were hastily dug. Surely this was no spirit in which to face the trial;

nothing was more calculated to depress the population than the sensationalism of the governments in 1939.

In England, Mr. Chamberlain had declared that war would mean the end of civilization, and his cry was repeated in France. A strange way of fortifying the courage of the peoples! One cannot expect them to rush joyously, or even to march gravely, into war when they are warned that the consequences will be utter destruction, and that there would be neither victors nor vanquished.

These and many other doleful forebodings came to me in my study. There was with me a middle-aged Frenchman, a relative of mine, from Paris. He burst into tears. "It is the end of everything!" he cried, and to console him I could only assure him that things were never as bad as they seemed to be—and as they had been painted by government spokesmen—and that perhaps the war would never start in real earnest. God forgive me my lie! I knew better. I knew that, once the wheels of the Juggernaut begin to turn, nothing can stop them until they have ground us in the dust.

In 1919 I had stood in the Galerie des Glaces at Versailles, watching the plenipotentiaries appending their signatures to the treaty which was designed to bring peace but brought a sword: Clemenceau, Lloyd George, Wilson, a long procession of men whose intentions were honorable but whose performance was damnable. It was obvious that the conditions were too harsh or not harsh enough, too lenient or not lenient enough: either Germany should have been crushed beyond hope of resurrection or, more wisely, the war over, there should have been an agreement on terms which would permit Europe to live in peace.

Fair-minded and informed historians now agree that the main responsibility for both Hitler and the Second World War must be sought in the vindictive treaties which followed 1918—treaties which flagrantly violated the terms of both the Armistice and President Wilson's Fourteen Points. The League of Nations had the power to revise the treaties and promote peace, but it acted rather as an instrument under Franco-British domination to preserve the *status quo* which, in time, produced Hitler. Any peaceful efforts he made to secure treaty revision were summarily rejected. Therefore, pledged to revision, he proceeded to carry it out by bluster and force, the only methods open to him to fulfill his promises. All this has been presented with elaborate documentation by the eminent American diplomatic historian, Professor Charles C. Tansill, in the Historical Introduction to his impressive book *Back Door to War.*

In the courtyard of the Versailles palace I met one of the German plenipotentiaries, the obscure Herr Bell, or was it the obscure Herr Müller? I asked what he thought of the treaty, and he replied sadly: "It will be so different twenty years hence." Foch too, with prophetic wisdom, said that it meant another war in twenty years.

Exactly twenty years later we were preparing for the war which was to wipe off the map nine or ten nations in Europe brought under the domination of Russia, which was to ruin for generations several hitherto Great Powers, devastate enormous tracts of territory, number its dead by tens of millions, and place in captivity, their fate unknown, many millions more. The old morality was despised, there was not even a pretense of justice, human life was held cheap, and concentration camps, labor colonies, unspeakable prisons were established on an unprecedented scale. The ordinary liberties, without which life is not worth living, were denied to an incredibly large percentage of the human race. Can civilization be said to have survived? And if the pessimist in 1919 might foresee twenty years of uneasy peace, today not even the optimist can foresee with certitude a single year of peace, and he is obliged to invent the euphemism "cold war" to describe the world's plight.

What had happened in those twenty years? I shall not repeat the story of my book *In My Time*, but as I went from conference to conference, and in the intervals lived in Paris or Geneva, I may sum up very briefly the causes of the war in 1939 from the French viewpoint.

First, there were demographic reasons. Germany and Italy and Poland—and of course Japan—were overpopulated, while France was relatively underpopulated, and yet the rulers of those countries encouraged natality to bursting point. "We must expand or explode," said one dictator, and the other called for more "living room." Strange that France should now fall into the same snare, and demand births, and pay heavy bribes for births, and believe that salvation lies in quantity and not in quality. While the German population was increasing, Clemenceau made the cynical remark: "There are twenty million Germans too many."

At the same time there was a development of industry and commerce, deadly competition among the nations in every domain. The economic penetration of Germany in the Balkan countries, in particular, alarmed economic rivals. A world-wide scramble for raw products, notably coal, iron and petrol, created violent antagonisms. Chemicals were controlled by huge consortiums. High finance entered the lists, and the strangest combinations were effected.

The sense of grievance under which Germany labored was real, and I for one pleaded from 1919 onward for a comprehensive revision of the postwar treaties, not a piecemeal adjustment which betrayed our weakness while earning no thanks from Germany. Rankling more than material losses was the moral injustice of the "war guilt" clause which attributes the sole and exclusive responsibility of the 1914 war to the German people. The American historians Harry Elmer Barnes, Sidney Bradshaw Fay, and William L. Langer, after careful examination of the documents, have reached a very different conclusion.

France's obsession with the German menace grew when she was abandoned by England and America, who had offered her a security pact in return for the dropping of her demand for a detached Rhineland and then ran out on their bargain. America refused to join the League of Nations she had helped to organize. Availing herself of the fact that preposterously impossible reparations were not paid, France illegally occupied the Ruhr in spite of British protests. The devastating German inflation resulted.

The MacDonald plan of disarmament, belated as it was, was torpedoed by the French, and Germany later walked out of the League. Hitler's proposal or bluff of drastic disarmament was contemptuously disregarded. Barthou began his scheme of encirclement of Germany, and, to complete it, brought the Russians to Geneva. I was at that time accredited to the League, and I marked its speedy degeneration: it became a hotbed of intrigue, a convenient platform for propaganda which, in spite of the pacific terminology employed, tended to divide the world and made directly for war.

The policy of England vacillated. Hitler inevitably arose out of the chaos and confusion of Germany; the British concluded a naval pact with him and generally seemed to favor his rise to power as a checkmate on Soviet Russia.

Italy, as well as Germany, had grievances. Faced with overpopulation, she considered that promises of colonial expansion made to her during the First World War had not been fulfilled. Mussolini's vigorous effort to form a four-power pact for peace was rejected by Britain and France. At the Stresa Conference in 1935, I, like most of the observers present, had the impression that a free hand was tacitly accorded her in Ethiopia. The subsequent application of sanctions, abortive because everybody was willing to supply Italy with petrol, was a deathblow to the League. The subsequent French refusal to accept an Italian ambassador drove Italy into the German camp, caused her to withdraw her protection from Austria, and so permitted aggressive German enterprises.

In my opinion, one of the major mistakes of the 1919 treaties was the breaking up of Austro-Hungary with a sledgehammer. All the Balkan States became vulnerable and offered a standing temptation to the Great Powers. Sooner or later, Germany or Russia would endeavor to take possession of them.

Before beginning her economic drive in the Balkans, Germany marched her troops, in 1936, into the demilitarized zone of the Rhineland. This was Hitler's tremendous gamble. He did not afterward bluff, as we were too inclined to suppose, but on this occasion he actually bluffed. There was then no substantial military strength behind his reoccupation of the Rhineland. Indeed, he ordered the troops, if they encountered resistance, to retire. France did not have the vigor and courage to act alone: the British would not support her. The French newspapers played down the incident, one of them humorously announcing, "Germany invades Germany." It was true that Germany entered her own territory, but the point is that she did so in defiance of the Treaty of Versailles. She challenged the Allies, and the Allies did not take up the challenge. Hitler's prestige rose enormously.

I pass over the Spanish civil war, in which there was a sort of half-hearted rehearsal for a European war, Germany and Italy helping General Franco, Russia and England and France opposing him: it was a preliminary line-up for the future struggle. To make a choice of sides was indeed difficult, and perhaps the strictest possible neutrality would have been desirable. It was unfortunate for France, five years later, that nearly half a million Red Spaniards were allowed to remain on her soil. It had become evident (as I was constantly reminded at Geneva) that Russian diplomacy was not averse to provoking war in Western Europe, a general clash under the sign of "collective security"—that is to say, "collective suicide"—from which she would remain aloof, hoping to extend Communism on the ruins of Europe.

In 1939 Germany incorporated Austria. This was the *Anschluss* which, even if desirable, was forbidden by the Treaty, but poor little Austria, reduced to a big capital without a body, was not, as we used to say, "viable," and she was no longer protected by Italy. I had pointed out the consequences of forcing Italy into the arms of Germany to a British minister, but when I told him that the balance of Europe would be upset he shrugged his shoulders and replied: "We won't cross our bridges before we come to them." Well, we had come to one of them, too late to cross it. I recall my conversation with the leaders of the Little Entente (Czechoslovakia, Yugoslavia, and Rumania) whose only idea was to prevent the return of the Hapsburgs to Austria. "Their return would be the best guarantee against the *Anschluss,*" I argued. "We prefer the *Anschluss* to the Hapsburgs," replied Titulescu, echoing Beneš. But the *Anschluss* meant, sooner or later, the destruction of the Little Entente countries, faced with Greater Germany.

Austria was no sooner swallowed, without effective protest by France and England, than it was the turn of Czechoslovakia, the key to Central Europe. I had always regarded the making of this composite State as an absurdity. Hitler could rightly claim that the three and a half million authentic Germans known as the Sudetens had no place in this hodgepodge of peoples of which only seven out of fourteen millions were Czech. In demanding their return to Germany, he was again, under the loudly proclaimed doctrine of the right of peoples to self-determination, within his natural rights, as Lord Runciman, sent on a special mission, reported.

By this time the succession of easy conquests by Germany, which could have been avoided by a timely revision of the treaties, alarmed France and England. Chamberlain seemingly decided that, if there was to be a trial of strength, it must be on larger issues, and he flew to Berchtesgaden to listen meekly to the ultimatum of Hitler. We now know that Chamberlain's rather supine surrender to Hitler in September 1938 constitutes Britain's chief responsibility—and a serious one—for the coming of the Second World War. Books on the German resistance to Hitler, especially in army circles, by Hans Rothfels, Allen W. Dulles, and others show that, had the British and French cooperated with these movements, Hitler would probably have been overthrown in the autumn of 1938 if he had insisted on going to war over the Sudeten problem. Responsible secret missions of German officers and diplomats went to London and placed this information before the British government. But no positive action was taken on this great and crucial opportunity. Chamberlain gave in at Berchtesgaden, Godesberg and Munich, war was avoided, and the plot of the German generals and their supporters came to naught. Hitler gained in prestige and power during the following months, and when Britain challenged him in August 1939, the anti-Hitler forces were relatively impotent.

It is easy today to criticize the surrender at Munich, but it was loudly lauded as a victory for peace in 1938, and the French Parliament almost unanimously approved Daladier's agreement with Hitler on his return.

Prime Minister Daladier was in doubt as to how he would be received at Paris. Would France show herself chauvinist, would she express anger at his capitulation? He was pale and frightened at the crowds which had assembled. But at once he was aware that he had done an exceedingly popular thing and that the French were by no means disposed to fight Hitler for the Sudetens. He was cheered as a conquering hero. Here was sufficient indication of the true temper of the French. Whether we deplore their attitude or approve of it, it is plain that they were ready to welcome peace at almost any price.

They were troubled when they learned that Chamberlain, without the knowledge of Daladier, had entered into a solemn engagement never to fight against Germany again. That engagement, so soon to prove worthless, seemed to leave not only Poland but France herself outside British concern. It was necessary, therefore, that France at the earliest possible moment should sign a "good neighbor" pact with Germany, and this was done in the Salle de l'Horloge at Paris in December 1938. Alas, we have learned how valueless are the most solemn pledges in modern diplomacy. In that same Salle, I had reported, a few years before, the signing of the Briand-Kellogg Pact outlawing war as an instrument of national policy.

In March 1939 Hitler made his first miscalculation: in violation of his promise to make no more claims, he invaded Czechoslovakia proper and slept in the Palace at Prague. Hitherto, he had been arguably in the right, though he had employed might: now he appeared to be definitely in the wrong. He might be pardoned his impatience to recover the Rhineland, to bring the Austrians into the German fold, to protect the Sudeten Germans in Czechoslovakia; but he had little excuse for his virtual annexation of Bohemia.

In England, there had been a marked desire for an understanding—even collaboration in certain circles—with Germany: but now there was a sudden stiffening of attitude. It was realized that probably nothing except force would stop Hitler. Had England seized this occasion, when Hitler was so clearly perjured and criminal, she would have been justified. But she did not act. She merely issued a solemn warning that "next time" she would act. And, anticipating that the blow would now fall on Poland, she rashly exhorted Poland to stand firm, and pledged her armed support.

Historians will find it strange that the real declaration of war—or at least the decision to make war—should have been based on prospective German action at Danzig. After having acquiesced in repeated drastic aggressions on the part of Hitler, Britain and France decided to go to war over what was probably the most reasonable and justified of all his major demands in the international field after 1933. Leading British statesmen had criticized the formation of the Polish Corridor as probably the worst error of the postwar treaties, and some of them had suggested a revision far more drastic than Hitler's demands in 1939. Even Winston Churchill had said, in April 1933:

> Many people would like to see, or would have liked to see a little while ago—I was one of them—the question of the Polish Corridor adjusted. For my part, I should certainly have considered that to be one of the greatest practical objectives of European peace-seeking diplomacy.

The Danzig question was already practically settled. Although there were anomalous conditions in the Free City of Danzig, it was governed by a German senate with a League high commissioner, and it would inevitably have fallen completely under German control. Poland was then on good terms with Germany. At the League, when somewhat trivial complaints of German encroachments on Polish or League prerogatives were brought forward, I watched Colonel Beck's (the Polish foreign minister) cynical and rather disdainful amusement.

Germany expressed her desire to have an extraterritorial road and a railroad across the Corridor, a most reasonable request in itself. In return for the incorporation of Danzig in the Reich, she offered a Polish Free Port, the conclusion of a 25-year nonaggression pact, and an acceptance of Polish frontiers. There may have been further matters for negotiation, but in the framework of a general European conference, given good will on all sides, there was every prospect of complete success. The trouble was that England could no longer believe in the good faith of Germany. England relied on France to hold out until a coalition could be formed to fight. Germany was so cocksure—as on paper she well might be—of her power to humiliate Poland without any effective intervention of France and England, that she needlessly rushed the negotiations with Poland, making demands that Poland could not accept, such as the instant dispatch of a plenipotentiary who must take or leave the terms offered.

As for Russia, while England was counting on her to fight Germany, she was secretly preparing a pact with Germany for the division of the booty. I cannot understand why the Foreign Office and the Quai d'Orsay were surprised by her last-minute treaty with Germany, for rumors of what was impending reached me in the spring of 1939. The Russian game was obvious: she would welcome a new war in the West, providing she could keep out of it, for, as one of her diplomats frankly said: "The U.S.S.R. was born from the first war, and a second would end in the Sovietization of Europe." So, a week before the invasion of Poland, Russia dramatically ditched the Allies by coming to an agreement with Hitler.

Both sides were too far advanced to retreat without loss of face. Yet France hesitated. She prayed for Mussolini's intervention, as in 1938, but the conference he proposed Britain and France would accept only on the agreement to withdraw the German troops which had already entered Poland. It was certain in advance that Hitler would never consent to a withdrawal. So England, whether she wanted it or not, was fully committed and nothing could stop a war which had been envisaged under vastly different conditions.

France was more reluctant. Georges Bonnet, the foreign minister, undoubtedly desired peace. The deputies were, in private, opposed to war. They lamented in the lobbies. The government hesitated. English statesmen—Churchill among them—vehemently warned them that if the Entente did not now hold, then France would be deprived of British support and would be left alone to face Germany.

Echoes of the pathetic cabinet meetings reached me: the terrible responsibility of launching France into a conflict for the sake of Poland was realized, but the terrible responsibility of deserting England was no less grave. Some ministers consoled themselves with the belief that Germany was, after all, bluffing; others foresaw a series of defeats for France, and even the flight of the government from the metropolis, but somehow, sometime, final victory; but most of them were confident in the strength of the Maginot line which they believed could hold out indefinitely. Nobody was persuaded of immediate success while, as for genuinely helping Poland—so far away, and heaven so high!—it was out of the question. Reluctantly the decision was taken.

It was necessary to demand credits from Parliament. They were asked not openly for war, as in the original draft, but in a new version "for the purpose of fulfilling engagements resulting from our alliances," and finally the demand was euphemistically framed, "engagements resulting from the international situation." It was agreed not to allow a debate, and in fact only two parliamentarians tried to speak. There are those who maintain that the constitution was violated and that Parliament should have voted an official declaration of the entry of France in the war.

The equivocation is now forgotten; the war, the débâcle, the occupation, the liberation, the years of destruction and of misery have passed; and if I recall these facts, it is by way of defense of the French people, who entered the war doubtfully and whose anger at the hour of their collapse in 1940 was, not unnaturally, directed at the ministers of the Third Republic.

2

Phony War

THERE were eight months of respite, in which neither France nor England could properly be said to be actively engaged in war, and during those eight months neither Pétain, an old man of 84, who had long abandoned any real command, nor Weygand, only ten years younger and therefore well past the normal age limit, had the smallest responsibility for what had happened or was to happen.

It is a matter of astonishment to me that the politicians and the generals who proved to be so inadequate in every respect should, by a last-minute shuffle, when everything was lost, have contrived to throw onto the shoulders of these two superannuated men, whose careers had been glorious, the onus of the defeat. They were brought in by Paul Reynaud, who at that time represented them as capable of saving a desperate situation. They were convenient scapegoats for the blunders of the army and of the government over which they had had no control.

To support the charge, the very qualities they remarkably

displayed in the 1914–1918 war are described as defects in the 1939–1940 war. It is true that Pétain as a soldier (but he had not really been a soldier for many years, and was entitled to his glorious retirement) had always been wisely cautious, weighing carefully all possibilities, and in this he had been an excellent foil to Foch, whose fault was a reckless audacity which had often cost France so dear. But Pétain was also tenacious, calculating, and efficient, and had thus won the greatest and most decisive battle, that of Verdun, of the 1914–1918 war. Nothing could be more ungenerous, more than twenty years later, to discover that he could not perform miracles and that, therefore, his past services were not meritorious. Surely, an octogenarian can be allowed to sleep on his laurels. To attribute to him all the political and military mistakes from 1920 to 1940 and to exculpate the parliamentarians and younger generals is a most monstrous manifestation of bad faith.

The assertion that Pétain and Weygand were fossilized may or may not be true: it is beside the point. Reynaud was not obliged to use them any more than Mr. Roosevelt was obliged to recall General Pershing. He was not obliged to bring them from their well-earned retirement to retrieve —or to attempt to retrieve—the blunders of others.

It has been well said that military men are inclined to prepare the next war in terms of the last war. Thus Foch, thinking in terms of Napoleonic warfare, considered that the bayonet was the proper weapon to carry the day in 1914, while Pétain believed in the continuous front defended by artillery. The whole conception of the French in 1939 was based on the experience of trench warfare. They built the Maginot Line, multiplied defensive fortifications, precisely when Hitler was reckoning on the new mobility which mechanized and motorized armies would make possible. In France, there was a young Colonel (Charles De Gaulle), a disciple of Pétain, who caught up with the latest ideas, though he associated them with a professional army. He was indeed the fitting exponent of the new theories which would make of warfare an "art." But it was for the politicians to give him his chance, and they, following routine, nominated as Generalissimo, Gamelin, who did not attach much importance to aviation or tanks, and who was wedded to the notion of a stabilization of the front.

Successive war ministers (Daladier long occupied this post) should in any case have seen to it that the factories worked at full speed in face of the immense accumulation of material by Germany. The army had been cut down by the one-year-service law; it was badly trained; its morale was poor. To declare war without a reasonable prospect of winning is a dreadful gamble with the destinies of a nation.

In May 1939 General Gamelin had agreed with the Polish General Kasprzycki that, in the event of a war in which Poland was attacked, the French army, three days after mobilization, would launch a series of attacks to harass Germany, and fifteen days later would begin an offensive on a grand scale.

In fact, the preliminary engagements were mere skirmishes. The French armies, behind the Maginot Line, rendered no service to Poland, which was overrun in a fortnight without receiving any aid, even in the shape of promised bombings. We now know that the idea which prevailed in 1939 that Hitler's army was a completely mechanized behemoth was a myth. As the American historians, Langer and Gleason, have recently pointed out, "Of the hundred divisions they [the Nazis] put into the field against Poland only three were mechanized and none completely motorized." But even the rudimentary *Wehrmacht* was much more than a match for the archaic equipment and strategy of the Poles. The country which Molotov described as "The hideous invention of Versailles" was wiped off the map, despite its brigades of cavalry and its thirteen infantry divisions massed to march on Berlin. Neither England nor France, who went to war for Poland, could do anything to save her, and today, after the defeat of Germany, we have not restored her political independence, her religious liberty, or her territorial integrity.

I spent some months in Paris or in my Normandy village and was more and more dismayed. Evidences of disorder were everywhere. Troops, as they marched, imitated the cries of sheep, humorously suggesting that they were being driven like lambs to the slaughter. Certain contingents which I saw were totally undisciplined, and the reserve officers could not control them. There were inconsiderable requisitions of automobiles, camions, and horses, left to rust or starve, respectively, in the field. From the factories, which should have been working at full speed, specialists were sent to their regiments, and the countryside was depleted of farm workers. Although I had abandoned journalism, I had kept a little pulpit in a review, and I remember a letter which I wrote to an important newspaper in which I recorded my impressions. There were five million Frenchmen under arms, but there was serious lack of organization. In the village, overcrowded with soldiers, some of them not even in uniform, the Parisians, who were already refugees, were exceedingly doleful. As time went on and nothing in particular happened, life became more normal. The conception of a bloodless war gained ground. "Drôle de guerre," said the French; "phony war," said the Americans. The suggestion that there should be rationing was scouted. "We can't begin a war with bread cards," it was said, although it was apparent that supplies would run short. The fatal facility which had marked French politics, the belief that things automatically arrange themselves, was prevalent in every domain.

Apart from the initial skirmishes, the front, in the shelter of the Maginot Line, was apathetic. Most of the soldiers never fired a shot throughout all the first winter. They called the calm a "false armistice," and there was some fraternization between French and German troops. The Germans encouraged this state of torpor, displaying placards: "Don't begin the war. We won't fire first. Why be killed for England?"

The soldiers grumbled. Had they been dragged from their homes for uncomfortable months in a mock war? The psychological effect of these conditions was disastrous. There might be arguments for war, there might be arguments for peace, but there were no arguments for a situation which was neither war nor peace. To allay the discontent, games were provided, there were appeals for footballs, spectacles were promoted, "foyers" were founded, radio sets were installed. A queer war indeed! I frequently heard repeated a phrase attributed to Goering: "We'll let their war rot"—rot in a sort of stagnation. If no move was made by either side, the soldiers could not stay forever facing each other, and sooner or later they would be sent home.

After the German-Russian declaration that Poland was dissolved, any obligations toward that State had ceased to exist and, therefore, France and England were alone responsible for the continuation of the war. There then began intensive peace propaganda in France. Many people really hoped that the war would end in a compromise. I knew better: for England and France to disband their forces would be to place themselves at the mercy of Germany and would render any resistance to subsequent Nazi demands impossible. Moscow associated itself with Berlin's suggestion, and Communist chiefs, in tracts and clandestine interviews, spoke of the "Imperialist" war imposed on the French government, and the "treason" of Daladier. The "ideological links" between Nazism and Bolshevism were stressed—after all, they were both opposed to "Imperialistic Capitalism!" Russia agreed to furnish petrol, cotton, phosphates, chrome, and other material to Germany, and to purchase supplies for her in neutral countries, thus rendering the blockade ineffective. Emissaries, more or less authorized, were sent to Holland and Belgium to facilitate an accord. In short, an atmosphere was created in which a vigorous pursuit of the war was hardly to be thought of, and matters were allowed to drift dismally.

Then came a diversion. It is not generally recognized today how near were England and France to a declaration of war on Russia. Russia had set up a dissident Finnish government on the frontier and attacked the little country of three million inhabitants. Now Russia, the associate of Germany, was detested by two thirds of the French, and "brave little Finland" won all our sympathy.

The League of Nations, condemning Russia as the aggressor, expelled her from membership. The British and French, in the winter of 1939–1940, drew up a plan for armed intervention against Russia in favor of Finland. The aim was to aid Finland, check Russian expansion, and to cut off the supplies of iron ore which were coming to Germany through Sweden and Norway. The French even planned to bomb the Russian oil fields in the Caucasus. The expedition to Finland was to start in March 1940, and the bombing of the Russian oil fields was set for March 15. But the Scandinavian countries protested the plan to send Franco-British troops through their territory, and this delayed the expedition until Finland was compelled to surrender after a gallant defense. As a matter of fact, the British had already sent to Finland a considerable supply of military airplanes and arms.

What a narrow escape! How different would have been the duty of obedient citizens, who must not form opinions for themselves or cherish sentiments which are not authorized, had Finland not been forced to surrender a week or two before France and England were ready to intervene! It must be confessed that the ordinary man, who has not the nimbleness of wits to change sides as quickly as some of his ministers, may be pardoned for being puzzled when, in a few weeks, we first find that Finland is a gallant nation and then a pro-Nazi country; when we must first regard Russia as an admirable potential ally, and then a despicable potential enemy, and then again a noble nation gloriously defending our cause, and finally a country peopled (to employ the language of Mr. Churchill) by bloody baboons! Opportunism has never overlaid principle so often and so completely as in this struggle since 1939. In France, where laws might be made retroactive, it became necessary not only to attune one's mind to the orthodoxy of the day, but also to contrive to be in accord with the orthodoxy of the morrow.

The French Communist organizations, suspected of sabotage, had been dissolved, and now the Communist deputies who did not renounce their political credo were deprived of their mandate. Many of them were tried by military tribunals and condemned to five years' imprisonment; while Syndicalists, Anarchists, and Pacifists were placed in internment camps.

The defeat of Finland was the defeat of Daladier, who had boasted of the aid he had given—without result. Nevertheless, though I will not be tempted to write a *chronique scandaleuse,* it was notorious that Daladier and Reynaud had long been at odds, and that their rivalry was stimulated by ambitious ladies. Daladier was represented as feeble, although he was nicknamed Taureau (the Bull), while Reynaud was the advocate of *énergie accrue*. In political circles there were grave doubts whether "increased energy" was desirable, and it was currently prophesied that, after two months of Reynaud, Flandin would be called upon to make peace. The misgivings about Reynaud were expressed in a doubtful Parliamentary division. He received 268 votes for his policy of *énergie accrue,* against 156 negative votes and 111 abstentions—a clear majority (which was disputed) of one vote only. Could he really hope to govern, to change the military methods hitherto pursued, when half the Chamber was opposed to him, or at any rate refused to express its confidence?

Reynaud's first move was to make any peace overtures impossible by the issuing of a joint Anglo-French declaration forbidding separate negotiations. Now, for the first time, was France definitely committed to the pursuit of war to the end.

Where the blow would fall could not be foreseen. The attitude of Italy was still uncertain. Ciano favored a pact with France; Mussolini, still smarting under the sanctions imposed at the behest of England, was faithful to the Axis. There were dreams of a new Salonica, for memories of the last war lingered. The Allies counted the number of divisions in Turkey, in Yugoslavia, in Rumania, and in Greece —nearly 100 divisions in all. I pause to comment on the policy of Yugoslavia, since it closely resembles in some respects the policy of France after the occupation, a policy which was approved for Yugoslavia but criticized and even regarded as treachery in the case of France. Yugoslavia, it was agreed, should remain friendly with Germany and Italy and even send them supplies, until the time was favorable to declare for the Allies. The French High Command envisaged an attack on Russia from Syria, airplanes firing the oil wells of the Caucasus and sinking oil ships in the Black Sea. A scheme to destroy Rumanian wells was considered. Incidentally, I should mention that I read numerous statistics which purported to prove that Germany could not carry on the war very long for lack of petrol. I wonder where governments obtain the erroneous information on which they base their false deductions!

It was, however, in the North that the new theatre of war was opened. The French and the English felt obliged to prevent the deliveries of Swedish ore through Norway, and, as Lord Hankey has pointed out, laid plans for an aggressive expedition even before the Nazis. Unfortunately, Hitler, moving more rapidly, forestalled them, occupying Denmark and the Norwegian ports, with the approval of Stalin. After some futile fighting, the British and the French were compelled to withdraw. This was disastrous, especially as Reynaud, in a long-remembered speech, had prematurely proclaimed that the *route du fer* (the road by which Germany obtained iron) was closed forever. Not only had the policy of *énergie accrue* failed lamentably, but the taste for adventure was, as far as the French were concerned, utterly lost. Although the possibility of a German attack through Holland and Belgium was foreseen, France had no plan of cooperation with Belgium and dared not take up positions that might provoke the lightning. On the 9th of May, Gamelin was virtually dismissed by Reynaud, but on the 10th the German armies, after a respite of eight dreary do-nothing months, were set in motion, and as Gamelin had no suitable successor he was, unhappily for him, requested to stay.

Some commentators have seen in the dismissal of Gamelin and the German attack a relation of cause and effect. It is improbable that this was the case. The German plans had long been prepared, and it is clear that a formidable *Blitzkrieg* could not be improvised. I would call attention to the strange conditions in which France was called upon to sustain the shock: morale was poor after a period of stagnation, the greater part of the army was massed behind the Maginot Line, feeling was far from unanimous either in the Parliament or among the people, for the prime minister and the generalissimo were both in disgrace. These things are not, of course, the main causes of the catastrophe, but they are contributing causes. The issue was joined under the worst possible conditions for France.

The conflict, from the beginning, went against France. There has been considerable dispute about the war matériel at the disposal of the French and British. During the War, it was assumed that the Germans possessed overwhelming superiority in air warfare and mechanized equipment in 1940. While, due to the genius of General Heinz Guderian, the Nazis had mastered the technique of mechanized warfare better than France and Britain, we now know that they possessed no vast advantage in mechanized equipment over their opponents in the spring of 1940. They won in their invasion of the West because they knew better than their enemies how to use such equipment and based their breakthrough strategy upon this superior wisdom and strategy. In short, the Nazis defeated Britain, France, and Belgium through better and more up-to-date strategy rather than by staggering ascendancy in mechanized equipment. Even Daladier has belatedly admitted this to be the case.

The first German bombings virtually wiped out the Belgian and Dutch airfields. The Germans had a whole arsenal of new devices. Troops were parachuted or carried by gliders. Rubber boats were in readiness to traverse canals, rivers, or flooded regions. Stukas plunged *en piqué* on the terrified columns. But, above all, the Panzer divisions, led by the brilliant General Guderian, struck panic in the hearts of the French soldiers. One French officer, before committing suicide, mailed a postcard to the prime minister: "My men are brave, but one should not send men armed with rifles to stop tanks." When all allowance is made for the French habit of finding traitors, it is acknowledged that many of the French shells did not explode. Nothing is so contagious as fear, and there was great disorder in the French ranks. I had many talks with officers who had fought courageously—especially artillery men—and they were very bitter about some of their fellow officers, most of whom were reservists. In one garrison town that I know, nobody was left to command when the Germans appeared, sweeping all before them, and the men, after vainly awaiting orders, decided to disband. I would not say a word which would appear to reflect on the heroism of the mass of French troops—many individual deeds of valor were indeed performed, and many desperate stands were made—but cohesion was lacking, and the hopelessness of resistance to a far superior, better armed, and better led army was quickly realized, and soon there was a general rout.

On the 16th of May, the *Jour de la Grande Peur,* The Day of Wrath, it was reported at Paris that the French army was destroyed and a great bonfire was made of the archives at the Quai d'Orsay. The road to Paris was open to the Germans.

The German objective was not, however, Paris: there was a much more important objective, which was nothing less than the encirclement of the British and French troops which had been imprudently rushed into Belgium. Either they should have taken up their ground on prepared positions, before the German onslaught began, or they should have fallen back for a counterattack. Hitler made many mistakes in the later conduct of the war, but it must be conceded that the German strategy in 1940, directed by such great generals as Von Manstein and Guderian, was extremely effective.

The French regarded the Maginot Line as impregnable and, therefore, went to meet the oncoming Germans in Belgium, where they fell into a trap.

Hitler's idea was to break through in the centre, and from the German viewpoint it was brilliantly executed. The French saw the army of Von Bock in Holland and Belgium, the army of Von Leeb facing the Maginot Line, and the army of Von Rundstedt and Von Manstein ready to strike through the Ardennes. Although Sedan and Longwy constituted the veritable pivot of the French defense, the sector was relatively neglected. Von Rundstedt, Von Manstein, and Guderian smashed their way through and were, before the French even realized the danger, in the rear of the troops in Belgium.

The French made three principal mistakes—the first was to push up into Belgium, instead of waiting to meet the shock; the second was to immobilize so many men in the eastern sector; and the third was that of failing to anticipate the northern thrust of the Germans bent on surrounding the British and French.

The British army, comparatively small, was cut off and, if it could not reach the sea in time, would be annihilated. Churchill took over the government in England, and Chamberlain disappeared from the scene. The only question for England was whether her army could get away. In short, barring a miracle, the battle of France was lost by the 17th of May.

How could the miracle be effected? Reynaud, thinking of the first war, remembering the veneration felt for Marshal Pétain and the esteem in which Weygand, the admirable lieutenant of Foch, was held, called them to his side. Certainly, if prestige could have saved the day, if their recall could have inspired sufficient confidence to rally the troops for a desperate effort, these were magical names. But the matériel situation was too hopeless to be redressed by the mere utterance of magical names. The skeptics asked what two aged men, the marshal well past his eightieth year and the general well past his seventieth, could possibly improvise in conditions with which they were unfamiliar, with an army encircled or in panic and with no fresh resources.

Weygand, in a spirit of self-sacrifice, accepted the thankless task, hurried back from Syria, where his duties had been diplomatic rather than military, and at a minute's notice took over from Gamelin. One would have thought that, whether he succeeded or not, France would have been deeply grateful to him. Instead, after the Liberation, this brilliant soldier was kept prisoner for years and an attempt was made to brand him as a traitor, before, at last, all accusations against him were dropped. As for Pétain, who was then, in spite of his years, still serving his country as French ambassador in Spain, where General Franco might well be tempted into the German fold, he too obeyed the call of

Reynaud. He was deaf as well as old, and it was not reasonably to be expected that he could, in fact, do anything. His rôle was simply to act as a sort of banner. If his presence, as vice-president of the council, led to an improvement of the situation, the government would have a large part of the credit. If the worst happened, as was now probable (for an armistice was already contemplated), the old soldier might obtain more favorable conditions for France than the government which had fought against Germany.

In strong contrast with the subsequent slandering and denunciation of the victor of Verdun, was the language of praise employed in 1940. Reynaud was dithyrambic. With Pétain and Weygand beside him, they must, he said, win: they must win because they were the stronger.

My own feelings were mixed. I could not help indulging in the faint hope that some improvement in morale would result, though my reason told me that morale alone is no match for tanks and airplanes. But, at the same time, I could not but be sorry, and even feel a sort of shame, that the two best French soldiers of the First World War should be uselessly involved in a débâcle with which they had really nothing to do.

Bad as matters were when Weygand took over, they were made worse by his inability to impose his command on the British. Both Lord Gort and General Ironside considered the battle lost; the backs of the British were already to the sea; on all other sides they were encircled. Therefore, at all costs, they must get away as quickly as possible. The army was indispensable for the defense of Britain, as were British airplanes. They must not be thrown away quixotically. I held the decision to be just, though painful. It was all-important to live to fight another day. But, in all loyalty, it should have been recognized that the retreat of the British from the Arras region toward the coast robbed Weygand of the last base for a counteroffensive and made the downfall of France inevitable.

Hitler might easily have prevented the escape of the British, but he called off his troops and airplanes, hoping that the English would, if he did not press them too hard, make peace. The escape from Dunkirk was, nevertheless, one of the most dramatic feats of the war. What appeared impossible was accomplished; thousands of heroic deeds were performed. But let us see it in perspective. The British defection, however right and necessary, was the knock-out blow to France and Belgium.

It is sometimes pretended that the capitulation of the Belgian troops influenced the British decision—the contrary is the case: the British decision was taken before that of the Belgians, and the British troops were already fighting their way to the port. It would be generous too to remember that the French troops, themselves doomed to captivity, gallantly covered the retreat of the British.

In 1940 almost everybody in France deprecated any criticism of the British or of the Belgians. Humiliated, we felt that we could cast no stones at others. The disaster was too crushing to be greatly lightened by foolish recriminations. But Reynaud, in the hysteria of the moment, branded the Belgian king, Leopold III, a "felon." To most of us, Leopold's capitulation seemed unavoidable. His ministers were the first to perceive that all was lost, and announced their intention of leaving. They would have liked to be covered by the king, and they proposed that he should accompany them. To this Leopold replied: "My duty is to remain with my army and my people. I may be able to spare them some suffering. In a few days France will fall. England will hold out. But Belgium will for a long time lose her independence. It would be easier for me to fly . . . to await the end of the war in safety. My duty commands me to stay."

This conversation took place on the 25th of May, and the Belgian army held out for several days more.

The resolution of Leopold III to share the plight of the Belgians was infinitely harder to make than that of his ministers to live out the rest of the war in comparative safety; yet it was the king who was blackened and the politicians who were praised. We were to see the same drama in France where, once more, those who, moved by a sense of pity for the French people, decided to stay with their country when they might have decamped, were treated with contumely. There was a strange reversal of values, in which successful flight was esteemed of higher merit than courageously sharing the distress of one's country.

It is all so pitiful that we should surely try to think of each other with some kindliness. I am sure that in 1940 the French did correctly appreciate the course of events. They saw that the evacuation of the British army at Dunkirk was a necessity and they bore the British no grudge. They were proud to help the British to escape from the German trap and, though they deprecated the British talk of "victory" at Dunkirk, they did regard the operation as a magnificent *tour de force*. They understood that what could be saved should be saved. But it follows that England, in her turn, having been forced to leave the battlefield, should cast no aspersions on France, who was now alone, her armies separated, without the means to stop the triumphant foe. That France would succumb was certain. Whereas the British could live to fight another day, the French were doomed to final defeat on their own soil. In this dire misfortune they were in no mood either to blame others or to be blamed by others.

There should have been a decent silence in high places, in default of a penitent *mea culpa*. There should not have been unjust denunciations, recriminations, accusations. It was not the time to look for scapegoats, to shift the blame from one pair of shoulders to another. General Corap was blamed, and then General Gamelin, and then the king of the Belgians—and so the sorry business of putting the blame, whether deserved or not, on others went on, until eventually Weygand and Pétain, who had so little to do with the débâcle, who had been called in to stop the rout when it was too late, were denounced as the authors of France's misfortunes.

3

Armistice

WHEN it became evident that the tide of battle would roll over my corner of Normandy, where it had rolled many times in history, I decided that we could not run the risk of being made prisoners by the Germans. Yet, I deemed the general encouragement of flight the worst of the follies of the war. Invasion is an evil, but even worse is the desertion of town and village. The work of the fields and of the factories must be carried on, the communal life must not cease. Many of the miseries which fell on France may be directly traced to the general exodus.

Something like ten million of the inhabitants of the North encumbered the roads. Pillage was universal. The refugees who arrived in more or less deserted villages took with them whatever they thought might be useful, although they abandoned most of their booty a few miles further on. We must think kindly of these poor folk, homeless, tired, harassed, without the smallest idea of their ultimate destination, often without the necessaries of existence, for food was scarce; but the mentality of the refugees was unsocial, and the damage they wrought is incalculable.

The refugees made use of every kind of vehicle, from perambulators and handcarts to broken-down trucks drawn by horses and even oxen and ramshackle motor buses. They were obsessed with the notion of transporting at least their bed and a few pots and pans. Thousands of them were on foot, and were soon exhausted. They became entangled with the troops, impeding their passage, communicating their fears, and drawing down on them the air attacks of the Stukas. Some of them died by the wayside. Women gave birth in ditches, and were left without the most elementary care. The confusion which prevailed over large sections of French territory was probably unprecedented. Never had I imagined such scenes of human suffering.

The French administration broke down completely, and the huge crowds of citizens, who would have done far better to remain in their homes whatever befell, were left to their own devices on the long dusty roads.

Is it to be wondered at, in these wretched circumstances, which were certainly not the work of Marshal Pétain, who had just been called to the purely ornamental and honorary position of vice-president, that all men with bowels of compassion began to wonder how an end could be put to the one-sided hostilities? For an army to stand firm against all odds, to allow itself to be killed to the last man, is one thing: to involve whole populations in destruction is another.

I had hesitated whether to make for the Swiss frontier and take up my abode once more in a country where I had worked for many years, or to go southward. It so happened that I had an apartment in Monaco, which seemed out of the reach of the invader. We felt, my wife and I, our solidarity with the French, a reluctance to leave them in their hour of trial, and although technically Monaco is not France, it is an enclave in French territory.

It was, therefore, from that tiny principality that I watched the last act of the tragedy. It was there that I was kept acquainted with the course of events, both officially and privately. Many books have since been written on the last days of a free France, and years later all who had played the smallest rôle related their versions of the resignation of Reynaud, who found himself overruled by his cabinet colleagues, and of the perfectly legal and quite regular transmission of powers to Pétain by President Lebrun. There are in the plentiful *mémoires* of the parliamentarians little incidents which are both picturesque and probably true, and words are recalled which may or may not be exact, or may or may not bear the interpretation placed upon them. So many wild and meaningless words are spoken in such doleful circumstances, and so many phrases can be invented eight or ten years afterward! Nevertheless, I affirm that the whole story was, in substance, well authenticated at the time. Everybody wrote sincerely in 1940, with a singular indifference to the presence of the Germans, who did not actually interfere with the operations of Parliament. There was, undoubtedly, a desire to continue the political game, there were intrigues, combinations, personal calculations. The parliamentarians were well aware of the reactions of the public, the overwhelming demand for the cessation of hostilities, and, with few exceptions, the cabinet, the deputies and senators were in accord with the people. Anyone who disputes the defeat today, or who pretends that there was not a universal clamor for surrender, has a short and false memory.

Weygand, whose forces had been vastly diminished, was the first Resistant, and he pushed his resistance to the verge of suicide. There were now not more than forty divisions opposed to the tremendous armies of the Germans, supported by thousands of tanks and innumerable airplanes.

So convinced were the ministers of the futility of any further effort that they went to Notre Dame, Freethinkers though they were, to pray for a miracle. The public, well aware of the antireligious character of most of the ministers, could only believe that there was nothing more to be done when the government appealed to God and the Virgin Mary to stop an enemy that the government and the army could not stop.

Psychologically, the official visit of Reynaud and his colleagues to Notre Dame was a blunder. Though Reynaud gave assurances that the government would stay in Paris—for in 1914 the departure of the government had been mercilessly mocked—the evacuation of the ministers was decided on the 8th of June after they heard a report from Weygand. There have been two contradictory accusations against Weygand: the first is that he counseled the evacuation, the second is that he advised the principal members of the government to remain in Paris where they would be made prisoners like the Roman senators who were captured sitting in their curule chairs.

General Dentz, who subsequently died in a prison of the Liberation, was ordered to remain as governor of Paris, though without an army, and it was agreed that Paris should not be defended.

On the 14th of June the Germans entered the capital without fighting, and everybody agreed that it was wise to avoid the destruction of the wonderful city. The reception of the Germans was not hostile. Molotov, as usual, sent his felicitations to Hitler.

It is interesting to note that when, on the 5th of June, Reynaud reformed his cabinet, he appointed to a minor post Colonel De Gaulle, to whom was given the temporary title of general.

As early as the end of May, Weygand had intimated that, if he could not hold the line of the Aisne and the Somme, the question of surrender would have to be considered. He had, of course, little hope of holding the line, and when, at Briare, there were consultations with Churchill and Eden

(11th and 12th of June), the problem of an armistice was discussed. Churchill did, indeed, suggest guerrilla warfare, but it was pointed out that guerrilla warfare in a country like France would serve no useful purpose and would merely mean the devastation of France. Weygand plainly intimated that the war was definitely lost. Churchill could offer no help, either in men or in airplanes. The British prime minister intimated that no vain recriminations would be made if an armistice was sought. Reynaud decided to turn to America for aid before deciding on this. President Roosevelt's reply was, naturally, in the negative. France was thus completely isolated.

The offer of Churchill to form a Franco-British Commonwealth, citizens of both countries enjoying a double national status, was startling, but it came too late—or too early. I hope some day the ideal will be taken up again; in 1940 it looked like a snare: it seemed to mean that France should place her empire under British control, and even an Anglophile like Reynaud rejected the offer.

Weygand explained once more his position. He was a soldier and he would obey orders. Though his men were exhausted and outnumbered, he was ready either to continue the struggle or to cease fire. The responsibility rested on the government, not on the army.

The quarrel between Reynaud and Weygand was, and is, on the relative functions of the army and the government. The government did not want to be held responsible: if fighting had become impossible, then the army should capitulate in the field, leaving the government free to repudiate the action and to continue in office, if necessary outside the metropolis. An armistice would, on the contrary, involve the government: it would be a political act. Weygand's reply was, of course, that if he capitulated he would be court-martialed and the army discredited. It is surely strange that those who had denounced the capitulation in Belgium should regard it as a proper solution in France. The contradiction is flagrant. Weygand thought only of the prestige of the army, Reynaud only of the prestige of the government. The practical result would be, broadly, the same whether capitulation or armistice were decided upon.

But no; there were advantages in an armistice: the government might discuss conditions which, perhaps, would not be unfavorable or unacceptable. In this dispute, I confess, my sympathies were on the side of Weygand. The government had begun the war: the government should end it. And besides, the armistice might halt Germany, would, perhaps, permit the formation of a government that would interpose itself between the invader and the population and might prevent a total occupation and the appointment of a Gauleiter in France. In the sequel, it was proved that to have consented to an armistice with France was one of Hitler's major blunders. He would, from his viewpoint, have done much better to continue his advance through southern France to the Mediterranean.

This controversy as to whether capitulation would have been preferable to an armistice appears futile today. Much was, undoubtedly, saved in 1940 both for France and for England by the armistice.

The first important intervention of Pétain comes at this point. The honor of the army was dear to him. Let the politicians have the courage which the situation demanded. "Whatever happens," said the new vice-president of the cabinet, "I won't leave France. If there is no government in France, there will be disorder. We can't simply deliver the French people over to Germany. We must not kill the soul of France."

That was surely a dignified attitude—to refuse to run away and constitute abroad a mock government which could govern nothing and nobody. Many of the politicians, appalled at the mess, would have liked to go into exile, first to escape the wrath of the people, second to avoid the risk of being captured by Germany, and third to enjoy the title without fulfilling the duties of office.

In Bordeaux, the ministers again discussed the question of coming to terms with Germany before the whole of France was overrun.

Camille Chautemps, an astute parliamentarian who had been prime minister and was of a compromising nature, suggested that they should neither capitulate nor accept an armistice. Why not simply, as a first step, ask Germany what would be her conditions? Thus, if the conditions were acceptable, they could demand an armistice. If they were unacceptable, then they were not pledged to anything and could continue the struggle. It was not, however, clear how the struggle could be continued, for the French army as an organized body was by now nonexistent. The idea of shutting up a few regiments in Brittany was rank nonsense, while to establish a government in North Africa would certainly draw the Germans after them.

One of the worst absurdities brought forth by critics of the French armistice has been the assertion that, if the government had gone to North Africa, the honor and glory of France would have been preserved and, perhaps, even victory won. There were only a handful of inferior French troops in North Africa at the time, they had inadequate equipment and munitions, none of it up-to-date, the Nazis could have intercepted any efforts to supply this area with men and munitions of war, and they certainly would have pursued the French through southern France and Spain and destroyed any French army or government in North Africa. As a matter of fact, before the armistice, the French government sent several of the leading French experts on air warfare to North Africa to report on the outlook for the continuation of the war from the African base. Without exception, they reported that the situation was hopeless for any such desperate project.

Fourteen ministers voted for Chautemps, six voted against; that is to say, Reynaud was placed in a hopeless minority. He might, however, had he chosen, have reconstructed his cabinet and have tried to carry on. He decided, wisely, I think, to throw in his hand.

Now, in resigning, it was his privilege to name his successor. President Lebrun was still in office, and would undoubtedly have accepted the recommendation of Reynaud. He might have designated Chautemps. It was, in fact, logical that he should choose Chautemps, since it was the proposition of Chautemps which had been accepted.

But Chautemps was no idol of the public. He was an able politician, but he was better in committee meetings and in the lobbies than in appealing to public opinion. It was not such a man who was now needed. Moreover, the Germans would not have been impressed by him. In the task of obtaining the best possible conditions, someone of a larger stature was called for.

Further, it is to be doubted whether any politician, thinking of his future, would have accepted the ungrateful job of facing the Germans.

There was only one man available—the marshal. True, he was old, but his renown would help the French public to swallow the bitter pill of defeat. If the glorious old soldier, who was venerated, came to the conclusion that an armistice was necessary, then the public would be grateful to him for pleading their cause. It cannot be denied that the terms he obtained were far lighter than those imposed on Belgium. The Germans are a military nation and, accordingly, they had a genuine regard for distinguished military men even among their adversaries. They would negotiate more generously with the hero of Verdun than with a civilian.

Now, I wish to make it quite clear that Reynaud, in preferring Pétain to Chautemps, did so in the conviction that Pétain's first duty, the duty for which he was specifically chosen, was to conclude an armistice.

There could be no other reason. Pétain had, after the report of Weygand, subject to fuller information, expressed the opinion that an armistice was essential. In fact, it would have been far better to ask for an armistice before the French army (some two million had already been taken prisoner, and others had thrown away their rifles in full flight) was utterly destroyed. An army which, though beaten, was still in being, would have proved valuable for bargaining purposes. As it was, there was no longer an army. In designating Pétain, Reynaud showed that he had then, if not now, a full appreciation of the truth.

Had it not been so, had he really considered Pétain a potential traitor, knowing that Pétain stood for an abbreviation of the war, it would have been blameworthy on his part: in nominating the marshal as his successor, he too would have been guilty if the armistice was criminal. To put Pétain in supreme control, well knowing his intentions, made Reynaud his accomplice. He was, of course, absolutely persuaded that there was no other way open.

Pétain was, therefore, asked by President Lebrun to form a cabinet. Someone has suggested that the immediate production of a list of ministers shows that the choice of Pétain was not unexpected and was, therefore, the result of a *complot*. This is the sort of poisonous nonsense that has been talked. For days before Reynaud resigned, it had been apparent that Pétain would be asked to fulfill the most painful of all tasks for an old soldier whose career had been crowned, more than twenty years before, by the greatest victory of the war. It would have been easier for him to decline the dubious honor. For him to accept it showed a rare spirit of abnegation. And that, forewarned, he should have his list ready (as every politician called to the Élysée has his list ready) demonstrates how seriously he undertook his task. The list was provisional and was, in fact, considerably revised. It was composed in no partisan spirit: there were on it Monarchists, Socialists and Christian Democrats, men of the Right and men of the Left.

On two points France stood firm, that she would not cede her colonies but would defend them against all comers (surely a legitimate resolution), and that she would never allow the fleet to be used against England. Time after time the representatives of the marshal assured the British on these points. Instructions were at once given that the fleet should be scuttled rather than risk capture by the Germans. Think what a difference it would have made had the Germans added the French fleet to their own! Had France given up the fleet, then the Germans would, indeed, have been formidably equipped. On the other hand, France could not surrender her fleet to the British: that would have been tantamount to a refusal to negotiate, and the wrath of the Germans would have been visited on France.

It was the Spanish ambassador, De Lequerica (with whom I enjoyed friendly relations)—a man who rendered unobtrusively great services to France and to the Allies—who was asked to approach the Germans. The only Frenchman who was really prepared to fight to the last ditch was Georges Mandel, once the right-hand man of Clemenceau, who seems to have contemplated a *coup d'état* and to have entertained, at least for a moment, the idea of arresting Weygand and Pétain and of establishing a new government in North Africa.

On the 17th of June the marshal made his famous speech informing the public that he made to France the gift of his person, in the hope of attenuating the misfortunes of his country. He would ascertain on what conditions the fighting could be ended. His heart bled for the millions of refugees on the roads. He hoped that, after a frank talk between soldiers, Germany would show no severity and that France would preserve her honor.

I listened to this discourse, as did almost everybody in France, in deep affliction, but I too considered that an armistice was a lesser evil than annihilation. Not for a moment did any reasonable man question his decision. Every day, the Germans were advancing, without encountering opposition, deeper and deeper into France. The public was indignant when a number of parliamentarians tried to escape in the ship *Massilia.* Laval, in a memorable phrase, said that you cannot serve your country by leaving her in her distress, thus echoing, probably without his knowledge, the words of Renan after 1870. "You cannot carry your country on the soles of your boots," he reminded those who wished to fly.

The French know their own history sufficiently to dislike *émigrés,* whether they be Monarchists or Republicans, for they have suffered in the past from the bitterness of *émigrés* who returned in the wagons of foreigners. That their instinct was right is clearly demonstrated by the ruthlessness of the returning *émigrés* in 1944.

President of the Chamber Herriot, President of the Senate Jeanneney, and even Reynaud, who might have been willing to serve under Pétain as the French ambassador in Washington, were for the marshal, or at any rate not actively antagonistic. Virtually all the parliamentarians in 1940 agreed that nobody had any chance of standing up to Hitler after the defeat except Pétain. The whole of France and particularly the soldiers (I spoke to many officers who had done their duty, who were exceedingly angry, and were ready to shoot "traitors," by which they meant those who had so badly conducted the war) put their trust in Pétain. An immense sigh of relief went up. It was a sigh indicating shame, horror, regret, but it was chiefly a sigh of relief. In the days that were still to elapse before the armistice became effective, the constant complaint was that matters were not moving fast enough. It is, of course, true that, once the decision was taken, the *dénouement* could not come too quickly.

The next day, the voice of Colonel (temporarily General) De Gaulle was heard in France from London. Who was De Gaulle? It should be borne in mind that very few people had ever heard of him.

Occupying a minor post in Reynaud's government, he had left for London in the airplane of General Spears, the British liaison officer, and he was at that time in no way whatever qualified to speak on behalf of France. I am not criticizing his action: his patriotism is above reproach. But to suppose that the French people would listen to him, precisely at the moment when they were heartily glad that the end of their miseries (they could not foresee other miseries) was in sight, was mere folly. We must put ourselves in the place of the French, and not look at events from the viewpoint of London or Washington. Military men cannot run off from their country, fulminate against their own government, and expect that they will arouse much sympathy. In the most orthodox fashion Pétain had been invested with full authority.

Later, when the name of De Gaulle was in everybody's mouth, it was easy to forget that, in 1940, he was a deserter in the same sense as Thorez. The armistice was not yet concluded, and the duty of De Gaulle was to rejoin his post. He was not even a member of the new cabinet. He was not, as a soldier, authorized to make declarations. He might very seriously damage the negotiations with Germany, to the detriment of France.

Possibly, he was obeying the voice of his conscience in raising the standard of revolt and in setting himself up, with his handful of followers, in a foreign country as the head of a rival government.

I am simply pointing out the exceptional character of

the appeal of De Gaulle, from his place of safety, over the head of the marshal, over the head of Parliament, over the head of the people. To whom did he address himself? Doubtless to the army and army chiefs. Now, whatever were his patriotic motives, it was evident that the insubordination of De Gaulle, authorized by the British government on whom he was dependent financially, could not be passed over without condemnation. All sorts of issues were involved. If every soldier is entitled to disobey his superiors, if every man is to consult his own conscience, his own intelligence, his own interests, even his own sense of patriotism, there is an end of discipline and even of government. And, indeed, much of the anarchy, the chaos, the lawlessness of these dreadful years in France can be traced to dissidence.

Whether the results, a few years later, of propaganda by radio from abroad and a guerrilla warfare at home compensated for the violation of the fundamental principles of society, is a question it is hard to answer. It should be said that France does not recognize the right of conscientious objection, and those who feel themselves obliged to refuse their military duties are heavily punished. Now here was "conscientious objection" of an unprecedented kind. It was the objection of an officer, who normally should set a high example, to the decision, whether right or wrong, taken by President Lebrun and the presidents of the two houses (for they had agreed to the nomination of Pétain, well knowing that, in his opinion, France could not continue the war) and supported by the overwhelming majority of Frenchmen.

The move was so incredible that the public tried to explain it by the suggestion of collusion. It was said by scores of people that Pétain and De Gaulle were in full agreement, and just as the marshal sent Weygand to Africa to prepare an army which would renew the war at a favorable moment, just as he sent Admiral Darlan to welcome the Americans, just as he sent General Giraud to command an army which was, when the Americans landed, still faithful to Pétain, so he sent De Gaulle to London to deceive the Germans, to play, as it were, the English card, while he finessed in France. Pétain was the shield and De Gaulle the sword. The hypothesis was accepted generally for the greater part of the occupation. Would to God it had been true! In any case, it was impossible to regard De Gaulle and the *émigrés,* without mandate, representing only themselves, without the smallest democratic basis, as a government to be obeyed.

Nor, in listening to the radio message of De Gaulle on the 18th of June, did I find any denial of the defeat. On the contrary, he tried to explain it. France had succumbed to enormous mechanized forces; the tactics of the Germans had caught the army chiefs napping. That was the substance of his discourse. He declared—precisely as Pétain would have declared—that the last word had not been spoken, that a lost battle, on no matter how gigantic a scale, was not necessarily a lost war, and that the French empire and the British ally were still in the field. A perfectly proper opinion, an admirable sentiment which assuredly did not differ from that of the marshal, who was less free to proclaim it than De Gaulle. Only on the ground that De Gaulle was commissioned to make speeches that Pétain was unable to make while wrestling with Germany, did De Gaulle's attitude seem, to the bulk of the French in 1940, at all justified.

The preservation of French unity, then as now, was the paramount duty in face of the enemy.

The terms of the armistice (certainly far more generous than "unconditional surrender") were harsh enough, but they might have been worse. Hitler was careful not to treat France as he had treated Poland. He took a longer view. He had some vague notion of drawing France to his side. At the beginning, at least, the German soldiers, well disciplined, behaved with courtesy. Hitler could not, however, refrain from giving a theatrical cast to the signing of the armistice. Just as the French (and their Allies) chose the Galerie des

Glaces at Versailles for the signing of the Treaty in 1919, because it was there that the German monarch assumed the title of Emperor in 1871, so Hitler insisted that the armistice should be signed in the same railway wagon at Rethondes in which the armistice was accepted by the Germans in 1918. The moral is plain: the whirligig of time brings its revenges; and a German victory in 1870 had been followed by a German defeat in 1918, to be followed in turn by another German victory in 1940, to be followed by another German defeat in 1945. Military defeats and victories are ephemeral things. They solve nothing and, until the world resolves to renounce the recourse to arms, there will be no solution to the fundamental problems that afflict mankind.

In marked contrast to French conduct in 1918, the Germans actually endeavored to soften their victory by flattering speeches: they praised the "heroic resistance" of the French, their "brave adversary," and tried to persuade the French that there was nothing humiliating in their terms. As the war continued with England, they insisted on occupying the French coast. They remained in Paris. They occupied most of the industrial parts of France. There was a line of demarcation, which could not be crossed without their permission. But they left southern France to the French government. The French could keep their ships and their colonies—a remarkable concession. Had they not done so, the marshal, in fulfillment of his promise to England, would have rejected the terms. He had, he believed, saved French honor.

In view of the falsification of recent history, I am bound to note that the armistice was not, in reality, the work of Pétain. President Lebrun was still in office, and it was at a council meeting under his presidency that the German terms were unanimously accepted. Yet nobody dreamed of inculpating President Lebrun. The whole blame fell on the aged marshal whose responsibility for the unhappy events was not remotely comparable to that of his predecessors.

4

Legality of Vichy

MEANWHILE we had installed ourselves in our Monaco apartment. It was by pure accident that, a few years before the war, I had bought the furniture and fittings of a little flat overlooking the blue Mediterranean in the tiny principality. I learned to love the anachronisms of that miniature kingdom which was at once French and not French, which pretended to independence though dependent on France for its principal minister, its police, its military protection, and, in large part, for its population. On the rock to which one climbed by broad steps stood the ancient castle of the Grimaldis. There we were back in the Middle Ages. The square before the Palace was defended by obsolete cannon, and heaps of rusty iron balls reminded us of sieges and assaults of long ago. I was on excellent terms with the minister (a Frenchman), the bishop (a Frenchman), the police commissioner (a Frenchman), and with other notables of the principality, including the chief officers of the prince's household. Below the rock lay the modern town of Monte Carlo, frequented by a cosmopolitan crowd and clean, neat, well-kept, bright with flowers nearly all the year round. Sunny terraces, handsome buildings, gardens, gave it an appearance which contrasted strangely with the grimmer citadel. In the world-famous Casino, in the ornate rooms with their green tables, impassive croupiers perpetually informed the gamblers that *"rien ne va plus."*

There were about a thousand Monegasque voters, most of whom held some post or other in the administration or in the Casino. The rest of us—about twenty thousand in all—were of all nations, the French predominating, the Italians mainly occupied in shopkeeping, the English forming a small but influential colony, the Americans even less numerous. The houses are built tier on tier, using one above the other and reached by steep streets or broad steps. In spite of the air of luxury and the wealthy visitors, the bulk of the inhabitants are neither rich nor poor. They are, on the whole, elderly folk, without occupation, enchanted with the amenities of life in this pleasant spot. One could spend a great deal of money, or one could live very modestly. At that time —1940—there were, side by side with the luxurious establishments, plenty of cafés where one could enjoy a substantial meal for eight or ten francs, wine included. Today, the same kind of meal would cost 400 or 500 francs.

Some time before the war, the editor of an important newspaper came to see me and counseled me always to keep a considerable amount of money in my possession. I followed his advice, realizing that bank accounts might be blocked or that I might be cut off from all revenue. Thanks to this precaution, I felt that we could, with care, last out for several years whatever happened.

The Gestapo was not allowed to operate in Monaco, unless in exceptional cases; for the idea of Hitler was apparently to make of the little *enclave* an international centre after the war. With this end in view the Germans wished to show their best side. They helped to develop a radio station and they proposed to set up an international bank.

The Jews who could manage to get to Monaco were tolerated by the Germans. The English and the Americans were, generally speaking, not molested.

In short, Monaco was a sort of oasis, neutral territory. But when I arrived, there was a scare. Preparations were being made for evacuation. I thought the policy of evacuation particularly foolish in the south. It was stupid enough in the north, but at least it could be said that the refugees were fleeing before the enemy, whereas in the south they could only fly into the arms of the enemy. Where could they go where they would be better off? I was told that we must be ready to leave at a moment's notice, and we were given labels and numbers and asked to make up small bundles of our most indispensable belongings. When the word was given we were to climb into our allotted lorry and be driven off to an unknown destination. Our domestic animals would not be allowed to accompany us, and were to be left behind to starve or be killed by a veterinary surgeon.

The scare blew over and we were not evacuated after all. Still, a large portion of the population chose to leave voluntarily. And then, on a hot afternoon, there came over the air a raucous voice, rising to shrill hysterics. I listened dumfounded. France was utterly defeated; her armies were in rout; the triumphant enemy was overrunning the country; and, at this tragic moment, when our hearts were heavy, Mussolini launched his declaration of war against a helpless nation. Nothing has ever made a deeper impression on me than that call to arms.

I had been a friend of Italy: much as I disliked Fascism and the tyranny exercised under the new régime. I could not fail to recognize that Mussolini had worked wonders in a country that had been torn by factions and swamped by corruption. We had certainly not been guiltless; we had failed to carry out our promises made to Italy in the First World War in return for her aid; we had failed to accept Mussolini's proposal for a four-power pact to preserve peace, which ranks with Locarno as one of the two leading efforts for European peace between the two wars; we had applied sanctions and risked a world war for the sake of Ethiopia, which at one moment we were ready to partition; we had refused to entertain friendly diplomatic relations with Italy when it was obvious that we were moving rapidly toward a crisis. The Italian people are artistic, laborious, and patient: it was deeply distressing that they should be plunged into war, for which they have no aptitude.

In the course of my duties I had met Mussolini many times. While I acknowledged his remarkable qualities, his capacity for hard work, his great achievements for Italy, his realism, his will power, his magnetism, his theatrical eloquence, I could not but deplore his frequent arrogance and exhibitionism. I remember his meeting with Hitler at Venice. He came, standing four-square in the launch on the canal, to the hotel where Hitler was staying (and where I too was housed)—a perfect picture of bombastic pride, in strong contrast at that time with the timid-looking Führer, whose head was bent and who wore the shabbiest of trench coats.

Various factors led Mussolini to enter the war, though it might seem that he had overwhelming reasons for remaining out of the conflict. Virtually all classes, groups, and elements in Italy believed in June 1940 that Germany had won the war. There was a rather general feeling that, if Italy did not enter before the end had been reached, she would lose all the spoils of war, as well as being unable to take any vital part in the peace settlement. Further, while Hitler actually did not wish to have Mussolini enter the war, the latter felt that, if he did not take part, he would lose all status and prestige as a member of the Axis.

There was no enthusiasm in 1939 or 1940 for a *fighting* war in Italy, not even on the part of Mussolini. The expenses of the Ethiopian war and the intervention in the

Spanish civil war had been heavy, the soldiers were tired of fighting, and the country was war weary. When the Second World War broke out in 1939, Mussolini, after having vainly tried to prevent the outbreak, was glad to assume a policy of nonbelligerency. He also made a vigorous effort to promote the peace moves after the end of the Polish war. Investigation of public opinion at the time by Italian police revealed a very strong popular sentiment for abstaining from the war. Mussolini was well satisfied with this attitude.

At first, things went well for Italy as she stood aside from the conflict. She was able to profit from sale of war materials and increased commercial activity, made possible in part by British encouragement in the hope of keeping Italy out of the war or even gaining her for an ally. Soon, however, the British placed an embargo on much Italian trade, Italy could not get needed raw materials, and the economic situation became more and more grave in the spring of 1940. But there was no enthusiasm for making war on this account. War intentions arose mainly as a result of the rapid German military triumphs and the general feeling that, if Italy was to gain anything from the war and retain the status of a Great Power, she needed to enter quickly. But neither the Duce, the king and Court, nor the populace envisaged a long fighting war. They only expected to be able to step in, collect the spoils from a collapsed France, and take a prominent place at the peace table. They were to be rudely mistaken and disappointed.

Strange as it may seem more than ten years after, the French were far more resentful of Italy in 1940 than of Germany. They could find explanations and even excuses for their defeat by Germany; but for Italy to attack them in their extremity infuriated them beyond expression.

From my window I watched some of the phases of the battle in the South. We were directly under the great mountain fortresses of Mont Agel and the Tête de Chien, whose heavy artillery thundered continually. At the same time, a terrific storm broke. The cannonading and the thunder were indistinguishable one from the other, and we lived in an indescribable pandemonium of noise for days and nights. Across the water the Italians launched their assault on Menton. They thought they would be able to penetrate far into France, perhaps to Nice, without real opposition, before an armistice left them in possession of the part of France they coveted. But they were mistaken. However demoralized the French might be in the north, they were perfectly able to resist and repulse the Italians. Though they knew that an armistice was near, though they now knew that the war was lost, they would at least teach the Italians a lesson. Thousands of Italians were killed in those few days of fighting, while the French lost only a few score men: and Italy barely entered the beautiful little town of Menton.

That Pétain was not only the choice of the French people but of the parliamentarians as a body, there cannot be the slightest doubt. There had been many political crises in France; there had long been a call for a revision of the constitution; and more than once before the war men of all parties had clamored for Pétain as the one man in France who might restore order. He had excused himself on account of his great age. In default of Pétain, Marshal Lyautey had been suggested, but Lyautey had, in the First World War, discovered that a soldier, however eminent, cannot work with the French Chamber, and the experiment had been very unsatisfactory.

From time to time, when things were wrong, when Parliament was particularly discredited, when scandals were shaking the edifice of government, some publicist or other would remember Verdun, would recall the *mystique* of Pétain, would think of his efficiency, his probity, his calm and courage in face of danger. Thus, in 1935, Gustave Hervé, a pamphleteer without authority, but certainly disinterested and undoubtedly anti-German, clamored for Pétain to purify the Chamber. Léon Blum described Pétain as "the noblest and the most humane of our soldiers." Even the Communists were "Pétainists," and Gabriel Péri wrote in *L'Humanité* of his sense of dignity. The Left as well as the Right agreed that he was patient, farseeing, acting at the right moment; and if he was religious, he was not clerical. His gentleness, his sympathy with suffering, were highly praised. The French have, normally, an exceptional respect for old age. In family and in national life they look up to and obey the Father. Nothing could be more disingenuous than the attempt to use the eulogies of Pétain, by leaders of the Left such as Pierre Cot and leaders of the Right such as Charles Maurras, as proof of a conspiracy.

That the armistice was approved by Parliament there can be not the slightest doubt if one looks at the dates. The armistice with Germany was signed on June 22 and with Italy on June 24. Pétain had been appointed by President Lebrun for no other purpose. On July 9, that is to say, seventeen days later, the deputies and senators assembled at Vichy, in the unoccupied zone of France. They had had time to reflect and to criticize Pétain if they were not in accord. Yet, knowing that the armistice was signed, that the Third Republic had collapsed and was regarded as dead by its most ardent supporters (a military defeat almost invariably means a change of regime), they voted full powers to Pétain, who was not present in the National Assembly. Before the National Assembly met, the Chamber, sitting apart, voted for a revision of the constitution by Pétain by 593 to 3, and it should be noted that the 115 Socialists were favorable. The Senate, in its turn, passed a similar motion by 229 votes to one. The next day the two houses met together. Herriot had pleaded that there should be a rally of the whole nation around the venerable marshal; and Jeanneney, the president of the Senate, attested his veneration for Pétain, who had made the "gift of his person" with extraordinary nobility of soul. The text proposed that full powers be given to the government of the Republic to promulgate acts, over the signature of the marshal, embodying a new constitution of the French State. The rights of labor, the family, and the nation were to be safeguarded. The constitution was to be ratified later (i.e., after the war) by the people and applied by the assemblies it would create.

There is no doubt that the Assembly, in voting this text, which abolished the old Republic and enabled the marshal, as head of the State, to frame a new constitution, accurately interpreted the wishes of France at this time. The assembly was a perfectly legal body: nobody questioned its authority; and it is difficult to see how the supreme position of Pétain could have been more clearly expressed. I repeat that the deputies and senators, duly elected by the people, were acting *after* the defeat and *after* the armistice. No fewer than 569 voted for, 80 voted against, and there were seven abstentions. Those 80 have since discovered that they were opposed to the marshal. In point of fact, many of them framed a still more radical measure, giving the marshal the mission of concluding a peace treaty! They were opposed because they did not think the resolution proposed went far enough. It ill becomes them to pretend to greater patriotism than the rest, that is to say, than the overwhelming majority. Everybody was content to take shelter behind the authority of the marshal.

Now the whole case against Pétain, as it was presented later, was that he was a usurper, that his government was illegal. The contention is completely baseless. If ever a government was legitimate, it was that of Pétain. It was broader based than that of Churchill, who had taken the reins from Chamberlain. It was broader based than that of Roosevelt. It was much broader based than most of the governments that had succeeded one another under the Third Republic.

It should also be recalled that De Gaulle, who had no

claims to represent France, had already raised the banner of dissent in London. Yet, nobody in Vichy mentioned De Gaulle, or dreamed that he, self-appointed, was the head of a legal government. Whether one approves his action or not, he was certainly not a government. Nobody owed him any allegiance. Even among those who fled France, for good or bad reasons, there were few Gaullists. Some went to America, where they were plainly anti-Gaullist. The French colony in London was opposed to De Gaulle and was openly Pétainist. De Gaulle, at the end of three months, managed to muster about 3,000 adherents, and the numbers spread very slowly until an Allied victory was in sight. The army in North Africa, which joined the Americans when they landed, remained loyal to Pétain.

Colonel Passy, one of De Gaulle's principal agents, admits that the Resistance movement in France was nonexistent until the end of 1941. I mean the Resistance movement that acknowledged De Gaulle, for there was, long before, a Resistance which awaited the suitable moment and the word of command from Pétain to declare itself. The Gaullists would not have been displeased—at any rate some of them—to force France into a military alliance with Germany in order to prove the culpability of Pétain and the Vichy government, and so demonstrate that they were the only true Frenchmen. As for sympathy with England, it was far deeper in the France of Pétain than in the ranks of the Gaullists in London. It was notorious that there was no love lost between Churchill and De Gaulle. It has been said on good authority that, when De Gaulle was brought to London, Churchill remarked rather petulantly and contemptuously to those who had produced the General: "Is this the best you could do?" The witty remark of the British prime minister went the rounds in France: "The heaviest cross that I have to carry is the Cross of Lorraine"—the Cross of Lorraine, symbolic of the Massacre of Saint Bartholomew, was the sign adopted by De Gaulle. The French generals refused to place themselves under his orders, and the sailors interned in England indignantly refused, for the most part, to join him.

The spirit of the Resistance was, in 1940, best embodied in the Legion, purely Pétainist, that was formed, consisting of former combatants. I am particularly aware of their sentiments because I was asked by a colonel who never ceased to fulminate against the Germans to act as secretary of a section in southern France. I felt obliged to decline the offer, for I did not feel justified in taking up any official position, but I was in close touch with many of the members of the Legion and can testify that Pétainism was compatible with the most ardent patriotism.

Now, whether the choice of Pétain was good or bad, whether it would have been better to refuse to have any relations with the invader and allow a Gauleiter to give orders without discussion, is beside the point. The only point that really matters here is that, in fact, the marshal was given a legal mandate by the Assembly. Neither he nor the generals, admirals, and officials who obeyed his orders can be regarded as traitors or judged for acts which were perfectly legal in 1940–1944 and were retrospectively branded as illegal and criminal in 1944–1945 by a government which had then no basis in law and was self-constituted. Whether Pétain fulfilled his mandate well or badly, he was certainly made the head of the State in a completely legal manner.

Events have taught the French that lack of discipline and disobedience may often be dubbed virtues, and those who practice them may sit in judgment on the foolish citizens who are disciplined and obedient. That way lies anarchy.

5

Oran

It is not my purpose in this book to criticize any person or country. As we approach the series of tragic mistakes of the Allies in their treatment of France, I wish to make it quite clear that I intend to utter no censure, but only to explain. I write in the hope of contributing to mutual understanding and charitableness. It is obvious that England, and afterwards America, took certain deplorable steps which it would be wrong for me to gloss over, but these were often due to misinformation, and I have no doubt that they appeared to be justified when seen from the angle of London or Washington. Yet, it is only fair to consider the French case, altogether different from that which it was represented to be, and still woefully ignored. In the heat of the battle, ignorance of the truth may be properly excused, but there is no excuse today for any failure to establish or to accept the truth.

Nothing can be more painful than the spectacle of persons—or nations—whom one loves equally in angry opposition. Great as was my grief at the collapse of France, I was even more dismayed by the lack of comprehension in England.

It is surely not unfair to say that, if the fate of France should have been foreseen by everybody—as it was certainly foreseen by me—it was the inevitable consequence of the gravest faults in England as well as France. Many tales came to me of the nonchalance of the British authorities and the British public in the early stages of the war. When the British made their remarkable escape from Dunkirk, leaving the French to face the Germans alone, there were bathers on the beaches of Southern England who looked up with surprise at the return of the shattered army. Such unpreparedness, such underrating of the task they have undertaken, belong to the British character, which is temperamentally incapable of looking far ahead. But the disaster of Dunkirk should have brought not only an intimate consciousness of England's peril but a vivid sense of the plight of the French.

Instead, there was born of the danger a violent outburst of wrath against the French. In England, France was accused of having let down her ally; and there was no appreciation of the possibility of a comparable feeling in France. Such recriminations were deplorable: the plain truth is that Germany was far too strong for England and France combined in 1940.

That England should be alarmed at the possibility of the French fleet falling into the power of the Germans was natural. Were the French fleet put at the service of the enemy, the odds against England would be greatly increased. Time after time, British spokesmen, including the ambassador to France, including Churchill himself, insisted that they would acquiesce in any decision, would keep their sympathy with the French, would bear no resentment, on one condition: that the fleet were not surrendered.

Time after time this assurance was given. I made it my

business, as an old diplomatic correspondent, to ascertain the sentiments of the new government, and I was satisfied that France would never betray her ally by delivering up her warships. I did not hesitate to express my conviction in letters and articles which I contrived to send through Portugal. It was insulting to doubt the word of honor of the old soldier who had been placed in command.

Time has shown that his word was to be trusted. His definite order to the plenipotentiaries was not to yield up the fleet. Yet, despite the repeated pledges, England remained suspicious. I do not know by what measure she judged the marshal. Mild or severe, the conditions of the armistice did, in fact, exclude any surrender of the fleet. Rightly or wrongly, the instructions to sink the ships rather than surrender them or allow them to be captured by the Germans were subsequently carried out. On this specific point, properly regarded as of the highest importance, Vichy did not fail.

Had Pétain been in the smallest degree hostile to the British, had he wished to "collaborate" with Germany, had he been a "traitor" to France, nothing would have been easier than for him to obtain far better terms from Hitler by using the bargaining counter of the French fleet. Yet, neither in 1940 nor in 1942 did the thought ever traverse his mind. It seems absurd to defend him from such a charge.

The problem hardly lends itself to retrospective speculation. Both Churchill and Hitler later recognized the folly of the armistice from the German viewpoint. Hitler lost a tremendous opportunity in halting his forces at the Pyrenees, and, on the whole, the armistice proved to be exceedingly profitable to the British.

Yet, there were forces in 1940 which seemed positively to desire French collusion with Germany. The marshal was compelled to defend himself against pressure from two sides—the pressure of France's enemy and the pressure of France's ally. If it was logical that Germany should try to woo the French, it was incomprehensible that England (and the Gaullists) should endeavor to push them into the arms of Germany. An outcry was raised that Pétain was contemplating the surrender of the fleet, when it was quite clear that he was not.

France had been guilty of no hostile act against England. The French fleet was helpless, lying out of the reach of the Germans at Oran—or, as it was called in France, Mers-el-Kebir. There were anchored at Mers-el-Kebir the two battleships *Dunkerque* and *Strasbourg* of 26,000 tons, older vessels such as the *Provence* and the *Bretagne,* an airplane carrier, the *Commandant Teste,* and half a dozen destroyers. On the 3rd of July, at two o'clock in the morning, they were commanded to join the British fleet, to sail to British bases, or allow themselves to be conducted to Martinique or the United States. If they refused these propositions, they must scuttle themselves within six hours.

Admiral Gensoul replied that he could not accept an ultimatum of that sort from a foreign power: he had already declared that in no case would the fleet fall to the enemy. At four o'clock, Admiral Sommerville, acting on instructions, opened fire. The British ships included the *Hood* of 42,000 tons, the *Valiant,* the *Resolution,* and the *Ark Royal.* The *Bretagne* was quickly sunk and the *Dunkerque* damaged. The *Provence* was grounded. The *Strasbourg* managed to get to Toulon, together with three destroyers. More than a thousand French sailors were killed. On the British side the figure has been put as high as 2,000. On the 5th of July there was another attack on the wounded *Dunkerque,* and 200 sailors were killed. The military justification for this butchery of seamen serving an unfortunate ally is hard to find. I understand that Sir Dudley Pound later expressed the view that, without this aggression, the French ships might well, in due course, without compulsion, have joined the British. However that may be, the protest of Pétain was dignified, but the sentiment in France was one of high indignation. To suffer at the hands of the Germans was one thing: to suffer from British assaults was another.

My correspondents informed me that there were divided counsels in government circles. Admiral François Darlan, particularly angry at the naval losses, was all for reprisals. The navy had never been defeated as had the army; French pride in the fleet was unshaken; and it was difficult to understand why the British should have inflicted this deadly wound. Had the affair of Mers-el-Kebir been planned by the Germans to make a breach in the Franco-British alliance, it might well be considered as another victory for Germany.

England may have been misinformed for a time about the intentions of the French; and General De Gaulle was completely out of touch with French sentiment. I considered it my duty to express my conviction in a number of messages that the fleet would never be given up to the Germans. Naturally, whatever I could say carried no weight, but I was not mistaken, and official corroboration was not wanting.

I will confine myself to a few facts. On June 19 the First Lord of the Admiralty, Mr. Alexander, and Sir Dudley Pound paid a last visit to Admiral Darlan at Bordeaux. They expressed their concern at what might happen to the fleet, though realizing the need for an armistice. They did not demand the delivery of French ships to England, but they were properly alarmed at the possibility of the Germans making demands that would, perhaps, be fatal to England. Darlan declared that, if the armistice clauses contained any claim to the fleet (as the Allies, in 1918, had claimed the German fleet, and as they, in this war, claimed the Italian fleet), the French would refuse even to discuss the matter. Whatever I shall have to say later of the conduct of Darlan, he was a proud seaman, who considered that, if the army had been defeated, the French navy had come out of the ordeal with honor. In no case, he assured the British, would the ships be placed at the disposal of the Germans or employed against the British. That was an engagement of honor, which was repeated by Admiral Auphan. The fleet would remain French—or it would be destroyed. In fact, standing orders were at once sent to the fleet to scuttle any ship that was in danger of falling into enemy hands.

President Lebrun was still in office, and he sent a confirmatory telegram to the English king—"I would remind Your Majesty of the assurances which have been given by my government to the British government that the French fleet will never be used against Great Britain. I trust these assurances will suffice to keep the government of Your Majesty in the path of friendship in which my government hopes to walk."

One would have thought that no doubt could be entertained of the loyalty of the French, but De Gaulle, on the London radio, reproached the French government for "delivering intact" the fleet and the aviation to the enemy for use against the British. After Mers-el-Kebir, he knowingly falsely affirmed that the French government had agreed to yield up the fleet to the enemy, and that the enemy would have employed the ships against England or against the French empire. "I declare, without circumlocution," he concluded, "that it is better that they should have been destroyed."

Thus he persisted in his misrepresentation of French intentions, he approved the destruction of the French ships by the British at Mers-el-Kebir, and he preferred the sinking of the fleet to the extremely remote danger of its capture by the Germans.

It is rather shocking from the French point of view that a French soldier in London should publicly announce his satisfaction with the action of the British. And it is paradoxical that he should have permitted French admirals to be condemned, after the Liberation, for having exactly the same preference as he professed, and for ordering the destruction of French ships in 1942 to prevent their seizure by the enemy.

I cannot omit the reply of the marshal in his message of July 10, 1940:

> A new trial has been inflicted on France. England, breaking a long alliance, has attacked unexpectedly and has destroyed French ships immobilized in a port and partly disarmed. Nothing foreshadowed such an aggression. Nothing justifies it. Did the British government believe that we would deliver our warships to the Italians and the Germans? If it believed such a thing, it was wrong. . . . France, defeated after heroic combats, deserted yesterday, attacked today, is now alone in face of her destiny. She will find fresh reason for stiffening her courage, and preserving her faith in her future.

I do not see how the marshal could have said less: we should be surprised and thankful that he did not say more. The attack on the French fleet was, I believe, a hideous mistake, and now that the natural excitement of the war has died down, surely it does not demand a great effort of imagination to understand the tragic position of France. She had suffered the worst fate that can befall a nation, she had been beaten in the field, she had been compelled to conclude an armistice, she was occupied by the enemy, and now, to fill her cup of bitterness, her unconquered navy, which she had refused to cede to her adversary, was attacked by her ally, in spite of every possible assurance she could give. Moreover, the attack, she could not but suppose, had been encouraged by the false information given by one of her own generals.

How could the attack be regarded as anything other than an act of hostility? How could it win support in France for De Gaulle? How could it fail to provide propaganda for Germany and encouragement for the few but active Frenchmen who were ready to range themselves on the German side in the hope of obtaining more advantageous conditions? No wonder that the marshal and the men around him, no wonder that the ordinary Frenchman, felt that France was indeed abandoned when even her friends treated her as a potential foe to be assailed and demolished.

Yet, in these sad circumstances, the marshal spoke in sorrow rather than in anger, and by his moderation did nothing to inflame French sentiment. He still called on the French to have faith in the future of their country, to strain their own efforts toward their eventual liberation. I think it was a happy event for France that Pétain was in command. Supported by his foreign minister, Baudouin, he kept a cool head, determined that no provocation should drive France into a reversal of the alliances.

To me, whose sympathies were at once with both France and England, the Franco-British quarrel at the beginning of a war whose issue was uncertain and whose destructiveness was all too certain furnished an agonizing problem. I felt as must feel a child whose parents, whom he equally loves, are divorcing. Loyalty to one must not mean disloyalty to the other. My adult life had been spent in France, and my roots were in France. My home was in France, my lifelong companion was French, most of my friends were French, my habits were French. Most of my books had been about France and the French, and in thousands of articles I had pleaded for a true Entente, to which plenty of lip service was paid but which was never a reality. The truth is that the two nations are entirely different in temperament, yet, paradoxically, it is on their union, their unreserved cooperation, that the safety and prosperity of Europe may ultimately depend.

What moved me most in the months that followed the débâcle were the constant appeals of mothers who had lost their children in the exodus, husbands who had lost their wives, wives who had lost their husbands, grandparents who had been separated from their families—thousands and thousands of homeless folk cut off from their dear ones and in many cases never to see them again. Day after day, long lists of missing relatives were given over the air, and as I thought of this vast sum of human misery, my eyes were filled with tears. At no time during the dreadful years did I realize so poignantly the meaning of the rout. We are inclined to read statistics of casualties cold-bloodedly. The full sense of the human and individual tragedies does not come home to us. But, as I listened to the daily recital by the radio of these personal afflictions, the full horror of it all depressed me.

In the messages of Pétain, delivered in a voice which trembled with emotion, it was the references to the prisoners in Germany and the refugees in France that were by far the most touching. I felt that here was a soldier, a statesman, who did not think in abstractions, who did not try to detach himself from the miseries of his people, whose heart bled for the innocent victims of international rivalries. The soul of France had to be saved, but the body of France had also to be protected. What would it serve to proclaim that France still lived if the human beings who composed France were driven to despair? To alleviate their sufferings, to aid them in every possible way, was now the primal task.

This human aspect of the question did not always present itself to many of those Frenchmen who had escaped. They were rightly indignant at the fate of the abstraction they called France; but they gave little thought to the real France, that is to say, to their compatriots who were in captivity or hopelessly wandering on the long straight roads. I remember that one of the *émigrés*—safely in America—a woman who, I am sure, is deeply compassionate in normal circumstances—actually called on the British to tighten the blockade of France, because some percentage of the foodstuffs which entered France might go to the Germans. I could understand the hatred for the Germans—even I had to whip up my imagination to remind me that they too, though our enemies, were poor misguided human beings like ourselves—but complacently to demand the sacrifice of the innocent French people to this hatred seemed to me inhuman.

I know that such sentiments were resented in France and did great harm to the cause of the *émigrés* who lived securely in relative physical comfort and presumably had no conception of French difficulties at the moment.

For myself, I could not help feeling that it was shameful to leave the country where I had spent the happiest years of my life, now that France was suffering. Had I been younger, had I been able to help in England or in America, I should doubtless have decided otherwise. It was possible that I could find in France ways of being useful, morally if not materially.

I at once took steps to place my house—a fairly large house—at the disposal of the mayor of my Normandy village, inviting him to lodge there as many refugees as possible. Hundreds of refugees were thus accommodated and, although my house was utterly wrecked and pillaged, although after the war I was compelled to repair and refurnish it, although my papers were scattered to the winds and my most precious souvenirs destroyed, I regarded these losses as of minor importance in the immense holocaust of war.

Incidentally, I might contrast the fate of my home, offered to the French in their need, with that of one of the most beautiful houses in Paris which was owned by a wealthy American lady who had been a great friend of

France during the First World War. Though occupied by Nazi officers during the whole period of the occupation, her house was left in almost immaculate condition when the Germans evacuated the city.

Never have I seen the better side of the French, who are subject to many moods, so clearly revealed as in 1940. They were willing to share everything with one another. They recaptured the sense of their solidarity. If only they had kept that mood to the end, their lot would have been easier than it afterwards became. Perhaps it was too much to expect that their finer qualities would remain uppermost. In my own case, a worthless fellow who had shared the hospitality of my house eventually denounced it to the Germans as "enemy" property, so that it was confiscated and further ransacked, while the mayor was accused by the Germans of concealing "enemy" property—a heinous offense.

I wish I could convey a convincing picture of the loving-kindness of the French people in those months which followed the defeat. Never were they gentler and more considerate of one another than in their humiliation. They were patient, ingenious, full of the milk of human kindness, united, rid of the poison of politics.

I felt myself more than ever attached to the French. All their faults, of which I am well aware, were then more than compensated for by their virtues. It seemed to me that to flee would be a sort of desertion, that I must share the bad days as I had shared the good days in France. I was furnished with papers, heavily sealed and signed, looking more official than any official document I have ever possessed, and it would have been easy for me to make my way through Spain. But I would not go: I felt it my duty to stay on.

Coaling vessels came to take off those who wished to leave and, in the most uncomfortable conditions, in grime and squalor, without the most elementary conveniences, many set off on long and perilous voyages. On the quayside they abandoned expensive automobiles. They left behind them the belongings they had accumulated during many years of residence in France.

There were, however, a few who, like myself, refused to go or who went only after repeated warnings. As we did not appear to be in immediate danger, I addressed to them a circular letter proposing the formation of a society of Anglo-Americans, to mark our affection for France, our unabated sympathy, our unchanged fidelity. The replies I received were not encouraging. Some of the writers declared they had more than enough of their personal problems to solve without associating themselves with those of France. I wrote a letter which was published in the French newspapers insisting on the double loyalty of those who had enjoyed the hospitality of France. And my affinities with the French, in those hours of unimaginable emotion, revealed themselves more and more as the difficulties developed.

If we were to remain, in the vague hope of serving France, as we determined to do from the beginning, it was obvious that we must, if possible, obtain French protection. There was no sense in allowing ourselves to be treated as foreigners and perhaps interned for the duration of the war.

Accordingly, I had a long conversation with the French consul-general, Monsieur Jeannequin, who became my friend: we read together the accords which regulated the relations of Monaco with France. He immediately agreed to take me under his wing, and thus to spare me many discomforts that I might otherwise have suffered. Without this, I was unprotected, for there had been a general exodus of official persons.

6

Montoire

Though I wish to convey the impression that the events in France made upon me, it is chiefly my design to put on record the reactions of the French. I was able to judge these with my special knowledge and training as an old diplomatic correspondent; but what particularly interested me was the untaught spontaneous judgment of the ordinary Frenchman. It may be asked whether the ordinary Frenchman exists and how he is to be identified. I reply that it is never difficult to distinguish between the natural sentiments of the majority—for most people think and feel alike—and the artificial, exaggerated opinions of partisans.

In Paris, there was a small minority who took up special pro-German positions. From the beginning to the end they were in total opposition to Vichy. No greater mistake could be made than to confound the two capitals. The marshal and his government were even more bitterly criticized by the collaborating cliques of Paris, protected by the Germans, than by London or later by Algiers.

There can be no understanding of France unless the distinction between Paris and Vichy is clearly realized. As is doubtless inevitable, the French neophytes of Germany were more German than the Germans, whether because they were mercenary, or fanatical, or were victims of their own wishful thinking. It would be idle to deny that there were in France a number of men to whom the word traitor, in its conventional sense, might properly be applied—men who not merely accepted, with more or less resignation, the presence of the occupant, but who gave the occupant their conscious support, sometimes for ideological reasons, sometimes for misguided political reasons, but more usually from altogether unworthy motives. Yet they were few, a mere handful, though very voluble, and in the southern part of France, where the German pressure was less felt, they scarcely existed.

The ordinary Frenchman was stunned by the catastrophe. He could do nothing except try to pick himself up and continue his life as well as he could. To find a niche, to earn a livelihood, to meddle no more than was necessary with matters that were altogether beyond his control, such were his preoccupations. Yet, he was deeply incensed against the politicians whom he held to be responsible for the disaster. His fury, though contained, was hot against those who had held power, and if they had fallen into his clutches, it would certainly have gone ill with ministers, and even deputies, whose names had been blazoned in the press. With those who had endeavored to fly, whether to England or to America or to Africa, he was particularly angry. To quit the country in her dire distress seemed to him cowardly, a flight from responsibilities incurred.

The same ordinary Frenchman rallied to Pétain not only because Pétain was a venerable figure but chiefly because he had remained in the hope of protecting the French. After all, forty million Frenchmen could not go to England or to

America or even to Africa: they had to stay on, and the idea of staying, of keeping one's feet planted on the soil of France, of clinging at all costs to the *patrie*, was transformed into a duty, an ideal, the highest form of patriotism. For my part, I confess that I shared that conviction and sympathized with the physical love of the Fatherland that is peculiarly characteristic of the French.

France may, indeed, be composed of ideal elements, of historical, literary, spiritual conceptions, but France is essentially the village where one was born, the city where one worked, the very earth which clings to the soles of one's boots and cannot be carried off. The immense, the overwhelming, popularity of Pétain sprang principally from his embodiment of the profoundest sentiment of the ordinary Frenchman.

It was unfortunate that from London perpetual attacks were launched against the marshal, who had certainly done nothing to antagonize England. It was obvious that France could not, for the time being, take overt action against Germany. She was still busy, as it were, sorting herself out. Even had she been organized, had she been able to think of anything except bringing order out of chaos, the reprisals of the Germans would have been dreadful had there been premature revolt. The utmost circumspection was necessary.

Yet it must not be supposed that, even in the earliest days, there was no resistance. The Legion of which I have spoken, grouping ex-combatants under the authority of the marshal, was meant to be the nucleus of a new army. Officers were recruited for this new army, with instructions never to reveal their existence until the hour struck. Munitions were hidden. Youth camps were developed whose final objective was clear. The blindness of the Germans surprised me, for I was acquainted with these and other secrets and many other persons naturally knew of them.

General Weygand went to North Africa to prepare an

army there which would some day reenter the fight—an army which always regarded itself as the army of the marshal. Far from submitting to defeat, far from awaiting the call of De Gaulle, there was immediately in France a clandestine movement of resistance which was sponsored by Vichy.

I have said that the ordinary Frenchman could not consider the British retreat from Dunkirk in the same light as it was considered in England. It left France entirely open to the invader, without British assistance, without any but the most remote prospect of American aid. There was then no suspicion that, later, Hitler would be so mad as to fall on Russia, his current ally, who warmly congratulated him on his success against France. The attacks on the marshal were sorrowfully resented and, in my view, were a blunder. I was informed that certain letters of mine expressing this opinion were brought before the British cabinet, and that it was decided to modify the radio broadcasts, since it could not be doubted that, in fact, the marshal did represent France. This was recognized by the United States, by the Vatican, by Russia, who sent ambassadors to Vichy, and by all the countries not engaged in the war.

Then came Mers-el-Kebir, the crowning blunder, which caused much heartburning in France and might have had the most serious consequences for the future of Anglo-French relations had not the marshal been there to soothe wounded spirits and, while protesting in measured terms, to refuse, in his wisdom, to be forced into irreparable antagonism with England.

But I am happy to record that every grievance was forgotten, and a fresh admiration for England was manifested everywhere when it became apparent that England would never succumb before the menace of a German invasion. At first, the ordinary man had, for a brief space, deemed it likely that England would fall. Now he saw that she was indomitable. He saw that she would never yield and that whatever happened she would listen to no overtures of peace, which could only have been at the expense of France. The old conception of England, firm and invincible, in spite of modern weapons, in spite of airplanes, was confirmed, and as the days passed and England belatedly awoke to the realities of the war, I heard nothing but the most enthusiastic eulogies of British courage. In that hour, England regained the sympathies she had come so near to losing.

To be sure, there were endless speculations on the reasons for the delayed German onslaught on the little lonely island. The French, after their own downfall, had perhaps an exaggerated notion of Germany's might—though exaggerated or not, there was no doubt that Germany was formidable. Hitler was not ready to follow up his victory: he clung to the hope of negotiations; there were, in fact, attempts at negotiations in Spain and in Sweden. The French believed that Hitler was being cleverly stalled off until the bad weather set in; but, in their ignorance of what was actually happening, they acquired the conviction not only that England would refuse to surrender or come to terms, but that Germany, by hesitating, had lost her opportunity of subjugating England. In the dying days of autumn, 1940, the prestige of England stood higher than ever in France.

There were the most extraordinary stories. It would be interesting to inquire into the wild rumors that were propagated. One of the most surprising was related to me by a friend who operated a clandestine post and swore to its truth. He told me with a wealth of details how thousands of small landing craft, mostly rubber boats, had set off for England. They were in sight of the shore; the English were strangely inactive; when suddenly the whole sea burst into flame and devoured the German army in a great holocaust. In vain, I pointed out that such an event could not be concealed; that the radio would announce it. He remained unshaken in his belief—had he not heard it in the messages he intercepted from England? I have seen no reference to the story since that time; and my friend left soon afterwards on a mission in the British service.

We watched with the deepest concern the air battle over Britain, of which Churchill has written so eloquently. England had withdrawn from France such fighters as she possessed, refusing to risk them in the final stages of the struggle, where they would probably have been ineffective, unable to stem the irresistible tide of German conquest, and would have been lost for the new battle that was to be waged for Britain. The French, in spite of their own plight, mostly agreed on the wisdom of the British decision. There were astonishingly few recriminations. Had there been any widespread anti-English feeling, at Vichy or elsewhere, a great deal might have been made of the lack of solidarity at a crucial period. The more I ponder on the events of the years of occupation, the more I am persuaded that, except for spasmodic outbursts of anger in particular circumstances, Anglo-French friendship stood the strain remarkably well.

While the Battle of Britain was proceeding, the population of France was settling down after its wanderings, the workers were seeking to earn a living, the employers were trying to set in motion the wheels of industry, the government was wrestling with immediate problems such as the distribution of foodstuffs. Surely, sufficient attention has not been paid to this human side of the unprecedented *débâcle*. The most essential thing in 1940 and in the succeeding years was to feed the hungry multitude. We are far too inclined to think in terms of politics when we should think in terms of simple humanity. A civilization had broken down. The primordial task was to straighten out the confusion.

The Germans were not helpful. They took whatever was necessary for the maintenance of their huge armies. The incidence of the population had shifted: there were millions of displaced persons in the Vichy jurisdiction who had somehow to be lodged and fed in regions which, even in normal conditions, could not have supported them: and transport was not available. Between the north and the south of France was a separating line that it was difficult even for officials to cross. Districts in the north, such as the Pas-de-Calais, were attached to the German administration in Brussels. France was in danger of being dismembered, and while the liberation of France at some remote date was ardently hoped for, it was too often forgotten by the *émigrés* that the liberation of a cemetery would be useless. The first business of the French was to live, and when I hear all sorts of brave statements today I cannot help remembering that the vast majority of the French were compelled to work in factories that contributed to the needs of the Germans as well as the French. If all those who had, in one way or another, unwillingly "collaborated" with Germany were to be put into prison, few would escape, and France would be one immense concentration camp.

I continually received news from Vichy. I have rarely in my career been kept better informed. Some of the men around Pétain I knew very well. The marshal never tired of repeating that France would never turn against England, while he professed the warmest friendship with America. But there was with him Pierre Laval, whom I had first met as a penniless lawyer in the First World War. He was then on the extreme Left. He had enriched himself and, in a successful political career, had moved Rightwards. His experiences with England had embittered him. He favored a German victory, or at least a compromise in which he might play the part of a Talleyrand. Alibert, minister of justice, was antiparliamentary, anti-Semite, nervous, and impulsive. Du Moulin de la Barthète was intensely anti-German but was associated with the *Action Française*, the Royalist newspaper. Bouthillier was excellent as finance minister. Lucien Romier was an old friend of mine, an exceedingly able journalist whose articles in the *Figaro* were among the wisest I have ever read: the marshal soon made of him his closest counselor. There was Bergery, later ambassador, remarkably intelligent and progressive, deeply interested in social reform. René Gillouin was an ex-professor of philosophy, an inexhaustible source of ideas. Henri Massis, a literary man, was a loyal adviser, pro-English and intensely anti-German. There was Dr. Ménétrel, at the same time a young *protégé*, secretary, and medical attendant of the marshal. Vichy seemed to me mainly a hodgepodge of thinkers rather than of men of action or of practical politicians, and their contradictory ideas rather canceled out.

In addition, there were generals and admirals, with most of whom I was unacquainted. If they did not constitute a very competent team, they were no worse than most of the teams I have seen at work, though their task was greater; and if there were not more experienced politicians at Vichy, it was because the French politicians were mostly in hiding.

Another blunder was made when, on the 23rd of September, 1940, De Gaulle, escorted by British ships, presented himself before Dakar and called on Governor-General Boisson to yield up the colony to him. Apparently, De Gaulle had led the British to believe that he could walk in without a shot being fired. He was repulsed and the British did not follow up the defeat. Now, this was a rash act which could only have been taken in ignorance of the possible consequences. Boisson, without question, in spite of the harsh treatment he subsequently received, was a good and courageous patriot. But it might have been fatal to France and indeed to England, so soon after the armistice, to give the impression that the French would not defend and hold their African possessions and bases. The Germans were already not sure that they had acted wisely in concluding an armistice: they were tempted to denounce it, to occupy Marseilles, the great French port on the Mediterranean, and the great French naval base of Toulon, and thus leap to the defense of the African colonies and protectorates if the French were incapable of holding them. The whole edifice of the armistice, advantageous to England as well as to France, would be broken down. "If you won't or can't protect Africa, we will," the Germans said in effect.

Much more was at stake: the Germans were negotiating with Spain: one of their plans was to traverse Spain, to wrest Gibraltar, not too well prepared for an attack, from the British and so close the Mediterranean. Franco, whatever his sympathies might be (and on the whole he was alarmed at the prospect of an alliance with Hitler), stalled off Hitler in his interview with the Führer on October 23, 1940, by asking what he knew to be an extravagant price. He asked for nothing less than French Morocco, as well as Gibraltar, and also for Oran. I considered then, as I do now, that Franco was astute in putting forward conditions that wrecked all Hitler's plans. For the Spanish demands naturally alarmed Italy, whose pretensions in North Africa were exorbitant. If he granted either of the rival claims, Hitler would have to break irrevocably with France, and somehow Hitler persuaded himself that France might still be a valuable associate if he did not press her too hard.

It is in the light of these considerations that we should regard the famous interview of Hitler and the marshal at Montoire. The meeting has been represented as disgraceful, and it was partly on the photographed handshake of Pétain and the German dictator—the merest formality of political protocol—that an accusation of treason was built up against the marshal. It is, of course, preposterous to suggest that, as the relations of France and Germany then stood, there should be no communication between the victor and the vanquished. According to such a grotesque doctrine, any German leader who has held any discussion with an English, American, or French chief—not to speak of Russian officials—since the defeat of Germany, but while a state of war still officially existed, is guilty of treason. It is too obvious to require the slightest discussion that, when a country is defeated, its only weapon is that of negotiation.

I am not prepared to affirm that Pétain was conscious of all the implications of the Montoire meeting, but certain it is that it turned out to be a clever move. So it impressed itself on me, and only the stupid propaganda which was poured out *ad nauseam* could have made it appear otherwise.

The marshal had sought this interview. It occurred the day following Hitler's abortive talk with Franco, when he was returning, perplexed and disappointed. Which was worth most to him? Tolerable relations with France? Or an alliance with Franco which would give him control of the Mediterranean but would utterly destroy the Italian alliance?

To anyone like myself who has watched diplomacy for most of a lifetime, the significance of Montoire was almost incalculable. I sat down in my study to think out the meaning of the meeting, given a normal degree of diplomatic intelligence on the part of the marshal and his advisers. How different it was from that which would surely be attributed to it by uneducated opinion, which would see in it only an attempt to bring about a reconciliation between victor and vanquished, and would approve or condemn such an attempt at reconciliation, in accordance with the narrowest political views and sentiments!

It has always appeared to me to be the tragedy of our time that the public, in consonance with our professed democratic principles, should presume to exercise a real control over diplomacy while being swayed by emotional sentiments which, in turn, sway the sentiments of those whose business it is to guide the destinies of nations; for it is utterly impossible for the public to grasp the elementary precepts, much less the subtleties, of diplomatic dealings.

Nothing did more harm to the marshal in the eyes of the uninformed masses, whether in England or eventually in France, than the Montoire interview. It was entirely misunderstood. It was not what a vain people thought. It was almost the opposite of that which it was said to be.

All that the marshal could do was to let drop the word Tilsit, with a knowing look, in conversation with his intimates, trusting that their historical knowledge would be sufficient to enable them to see an analogy between his position and that of Alexander I, who pretended to accept the friendship of Napoleon—with disastrous results for Napoleon!

In point of fact, it was not suggested that any conclusions whatever were reached at Montoire. In the communiqués and the commentaries, the word "collaboration" was indeed employed—a word which afterward came to have a sinister sense. Here is an excellent example of a perfectly innocent and elastic word, capable of a variety of meanings from the vaguest to the most criminal, which on account of its false associations must now be discarded—at any rate in France!

What kind of collaboration was envisaged? None whatever. The French are often accused of allowing themselves to be fobbed off with empty words, but on this occasion the Germans were content with an expression that meant absolutely nothing beyond the existing and obligatory relations of a conquered country and the occupant. Pétain accepted the "principle" of collaboration. Nothing more. In fact there had to be, and already was, some kind of *modus vivendi* between the Germans and the French, and for anything more Pétain declared that he could not take an important step without consulting his government and the Chamber—which for obvious reasons could not meet.

Yet for this purely negative result, Hitler was induced to hesitate between his policy of bribing Spain to the detriment of France, and his alternative policy of treating France with relative liberality.

The purpose of the marshal—certainly of his advisers—was to keep Germany out of Spain at all costs, out of the Mediterranean, out of North Africa; and in this purpose he was considerably assisted by the reluctance of General Franco to enter into a bargain with Germany. It is really very simple, and I cannot suppose that any diplomat was deceived. Yet Hitler was deceived, and soon discovered he had been cheated.

To the suggestion that Germany would help France in Africa, the marshal replied that France would defend herself, and had no need of German help.

I marvel that Hitler was so naïve as to be taken in by assurances whose only object was to keep Germany within the terms of the armistice. The truth is that Hitler was not a man of great perspicacity, and if sometimes he acted with remarkable speed, he was often extremely hesitant, as in the critical early months of the Russian campaign. He was flattered and overawed by the meeting with the marshal, whose prestige as a soldier was on the topmost peak and whose presence was imposing by its dignity and air of nobility. In all his dealings with France, Hitler was badly inspired, and in nothing more than in the armistice and again in the interview of Montoire. The war had gone well for him, but it was not yet won; and if he had great vanity, he had also the doubts and timidities of the upstart.

Such was Montoire, a triumph for the marshal, who had played the game with consummate skill, and a diplomatic defeat for Hitler who could not make up his mind whether to crash through Spain or to occupy the whole of France and bar and bolt the Mediterranean. It may have been then that he decided to turn against Russia. So thinks one of Pétain's most ingenious defenders, Louis-Dominique Girard, who boldly proclaims Montoire a "diplomatic Verdun" for the Nazis.

7

Accord with Churchill— French Opinion

In all wars there are so-called "secrets." But in my experience, both in 1914–1918 and in 1939–1945, there were astonishingly few real secrets, even "top secrets," that were impenetrable.

One so-called secret accompanied the meeting of Montoire of which I became aware, but it does not seem to have been disclosed either to the Germans or to the Gaullists. It is even now not acknowledged. The British could hardly reveal it when De Gaulle was in power in 1945, since an accord was reached with Pétain behind the general's back, but that is no reason for concealing it today.

At the very moment that the marshal met Hitler at Montoire, to stop him, if possible, from entering Spain, his secret emissary, Professor Louis Rougier, met Churchill in London. A Franco-British understanding, which entirely swept away any vague suggestion of collusion between Pétain and Hitler, was registered. It may be argued that it was not duly signed—but it was executed. It may be pretended that no official pact exists, but a document with Churchill's annotations exists. It may be hard to find an appropriate name for the document, but it was at any rate a "gentleman's agreement."

Among my informants were two young men who frequently went to Vichy and brought me the latest "secrets." There was, besides, a distinguished French writer who was in the confidence of the marshal and who trusted me. There was, further, a diplomatic correspondent of a newspaper published in Lyons, who was one of my closest friends. In addition, an American newspaper man had taken over one of my posts and he lived in the south. There was a Belgian abbé who played an important political rôle and a Belgian economist who today is one of the principal advisers of the Belgian government. These are only a few of those who brought me or who wrote me confidential information.

I am unable to assign an exact date for the knowledge that came to me. It came piecemeal. Important as the "secret" was, it leaked out in intimate circles. Without any attempt to reconstruct the various versions and different stages of perhaps the most striking story of the war, I will recall that among my earliest notes I find an *aide-mémoire* entitled: "The Reply to Montoire."

"Do you know that Pétain is negotiating at London?" asked one of my visitors.

"I have heard that there are unofficial conversations, but I do not know what has come of them."

"Well, there's a sort of gentleman's agreement. London will call off the attacks on Pétain, and will no longer keep up a severe blockade of France. Coasting vessels from the French ports in North and West Africa will be allowed to bring foodstuffs to unoccupied France."

This English concession was already in operation. A friend of mine who was radio operator on a trans-Mediterranean vessel, whom I saw from time to time, made my mouth water with his stories of the abundance and the cheapness of food-stuffs across the water. Because, at first, the blockade had been total and we had, accordingly, suffered not only through German requisitions but because of the blockade, the relaxation was in itself a proof that something had been done. The British had good reasons for applying restrictions. They properly feared that the Germans, as well as the French, if not more than the French, would benefit by the Mediterranean gap in the blockade.

"And what are the French to do in return for the slackening of the blockade?"

"Very much what they have already agreed to do—not to surrender their fleet, and to bring the French empire into the war whenever it can strike effectively."

"Bring the empire back into the war." That was what the government of Vichy promised in 1940, and it never ceased to prepare for this eventuality. Weygand, who organized the North African army, took the reasonable view that it would be folly to provoke the Germans prematurely, to start a fight that could only mean destruction, since North Africa lacked munitions and arms. To draw the Germans into the French dependencies would be to invite defeat, would lose the fruits of the armistice, and would bar the Mediterranean to England. He summed up his opinion epigrammatically: "If our Allies come with two or three divisions, I will fire on them: if they come with twenty I will receive them with open arms."

Until the French could be of real assistance, they should not reveal their intention, but when they were sure of adequate support, they would "bring the empire back into the war." That was plain common sense.

The story, though Professor Rougier has written at length of his mission, must again be told. There had been contacts at Madrid between Sir Samuel Hoare (Lord Templewood) and François Pietri; there were conversations with Pierre Dupuis, the Canadian minister at Vichy, who acted as a go-between, and Jacques Chevalier, the famous philosopher, with his university friend, Lord Halifax. Principally, however, René Gillouin, one of the marshal's confidants at Vichy (as he afterward told me), had introduced Rougier to Pétain with a view to his serving as a secret emissary at London. Neither the Gaullists nor the Germans were to have cognizance of his mission, and the marshal gave him, as credentials, a simple sheet of notepaper with a recommendation in the marshal's own handwriting.

Rougier arrived in London a few days before the Montoire meeting, saw Sir Alexander Cadogan and, I think, Lord Halifax; and, finally, on the day of the Montoire meeting, Rougier was received by Churchill. The negotiations were almost ruined by a false report in an American newspaper of the conclusion of a separate peace between France and Germany. Alsace-Lorraine had been surrendered to Germany, and Nice to Italy, according to the cable, of which it would be interesting to learn the origin. No wonder that Churchill blazed up furiously when Rougier was introduced. No wonder that there was an acrimonious exchange of reproaches. Why did not the North African troops enter the conflict? Why, replied Rougier, should they doom themselves to extinction? Had not Poland, Denmark, Holland, Belgium, Norway, and France been thrown into the furnace without avail? Why, therefore, North Africa? Why provide another victim, and so draw the German across the Mediterranean? It was not until the mischievous falsity of the news from America was exploded that Rougier could explain the French proposals.

They were eventually drawn up in the shape of a report of the conversations, annotated by the British prime minister. Whatever its value, in the legal sense, it was acted upon. It furnishes, to my mind, indisputable evidence of the disposition of the marshal, and it would have been generous to acknowledge it, as such, at the proper moment.

It was, then, agreed that England would help in the reestablishment of France, on condition that she afforded no help to Germany and, particularly, that she did not hand over her air and naval bases. The "passive resistance" of France was recognized as a form of assistance to England. The attenuation of the blockade was promised. Recriminations by radio would be controlled. No ports in North or West Africa would be surrendered by France. The French forces in the empire would resume the war when the Allies were strong enough to debark in adequate numbers and to equip the colonial troops. As for the French fleet, it would be scuttled if there was any danger of its falling into German or Italian hands, and orders given to that effect annulled in advance any ulterior orders.

Surely in the spirit, and indeed in the letter, whatever slight breaches may be discovered in the course of the following four years, France faithfully fulfilled her engagements; and it is idle to object that the *procès-verbal* does not formally bear the signatures of Pétain and Churchill. France and England had no official relations: for obvious reasons, neither Pétain nor Churchill could announce their accord, but the good faith of the marshal is completely attested, and there can be no doubt of his continuous efforts, under fierce German pressure, to abide by his pledges.

One of the misfortunes of the war is that Churchill distrusted Pétain and disliked De Gaulle. As these two men, with their personal differences but their fundamental accord on France's future, really represented France and the two phases of the French spirit—one calling for immediate and unreflecting action, the other calling for quiet and patient but always confident effort—it may properly be concluded that there was little understanding of France in British governmental circles.

In one of my books on France I have dwelt at length on the paradoxes of the French character: their romanticism, their realism; their spirituality, their materialism; their daring, their prudence; their clamor for equality, their respect of hierarchy, their histrionic gestures and their capacity for sober perseverance. Meredith, with his exceptional insight, has a brilliant passage about the contradictions of the French, who are at once sentimental and logical, often behaving impulsively, and yet keeping their feet on the solid earth, flamboyant yet tenacious.

The double character of the French was never better exemplified than in the Pétain-De Gaulle opposition, though there are many other examples, such as the Thiers-Gambetta opposition. Invariably, in all serious conjunctures, the French instinctively display these two sides of their nature.

In every Frenchman there is a blend of the practical and the ideal, of the reckless and the cautious. Their contrasting qualities form a happy synthesis. There was, for example, in the First War, no greater antithesis than that of the imperturbable Joffre and the audacious Foch, and the French appreciated the merits of both. In the peace years there was another striking contrast—that of the precise Poincaré and the careless Briand, of whom (with some exaggeration) Clemenceau said that while Poincaré knew everything he understood nothing, and while Briand understood everything he knew nothing.

Pétain belonged to the patient and prudent category of Frenchmen, and surely patience and prudence were never more needed than in the years of German occupation. But he was not blind to the virtues of De Gaulle. According to De Gaulle's secret agent, Colonel Rémy, the General in London actually perceived and approved the purpose of Pétain, his former chief, in spite of his fiery denunciations.

I think it was almost impossible for the average Englishman to comprehend either De Gaulle or Pétain, who represented two poles of the French character. Churchill, in spite of his imagination, could not understand that both De Gaulle and Pétain were bound to put France first, though their methods were different.

It should be added that, in the London arrangement, whatever it may be called, it was agreed that the territories which were faithful to Vichy would not be attacked and that they would be justified in repelling an invasion by no matter whom, in order to give the Germans no excuse for intervention. For the French (that is to say, the Vichy government) to have admitted, without resistance, either the British or the Gaullists would not only have been an abdication of the authority which was left to them in the south of France and in the overseas territories, but would have provoked the occupation of North Africa by the Germans—an occupation which it was all-important to prevent. Any invasion by the British, or by the Gaullists with the support of the British, would have been an act of hostility, an unwarrantable attack on an unfortunate ally. The defense of the territories, on the other hand, would not have been an act of hostility: one cannot, even in wartime, reverse the rôles and abolish ordinary logic. And if military necessity is urged as overriding other considerations, military necessity itself demanded that French territories should be respected, lest the Germans should substitute themselves for the French and perhaps drag the French against their will into an open quarrel with the British.

Of course, it could be pretended that the Germans were, in any event, coming in. That was the reason given for the attack on Dakar. It happened to be false. It was agreed that Vichy, on its side, should make no attempt to regain the African territories, at Brazzaville and in Central Africa, which had declared for De Gaulle.

It should also be recalled that, in his agreement with Churchill, De Gaulle had stipulated, or perhaps the English had demanded, that the troops he might subsequently muster should never be used to fight against the French. The possibility seemed remote. It was inconceivable that a new war—a Franco-French war,—should be grafted on the old. If there was, on any pretext, to be fighting against the French —which God forbid!—let it be done by the English, sacrilegious as the thought might be, but not by the French. The horror of horrors is surely civil war.

As for fighting against the British, the marshal continued to protest that never, in any contingency, would he permit France to be drawn into a reversal of the alliances. He sent a message through the Portuguese minister at Vichy; and he also charged De Lequerica, the able and devoted Spanish ambassador at Vichy, to make his position, which was more than amicable, clear to the British government. De Lequerica told me on several occasions of the firm resolve of the marshal to resist any attempt to force him in a fatal direction. I think I can add that the Spanish ambassador was equally determined that Spain should not be led into the German camp against England.

In the light of these facts, which cannot be refuted, and of the testimony of the American ambassador, Admiral Leahy, who has never disguised his sympathy and admiration for Pétain, the distorted presentation of the various incidents of the war, attributing to the marshal anti-English sentiments and a certain readiness to cooperate with Hitler, will not bear examination.

I will not endeavor to distinguish between all the nuances of thought that manifested themselves at Vichy and at Paris. But one or two observations are indispensable. Marcel Déat, at Paris, once a highly intelligent Socialist, who had "evolved" and become the advocate of a single party, and was willing to collaborate with Germany in the construction of a unified Europe, was a polemicist of no mean order. His newspaper did not penetrate into the unoccupied zone, but from time to time, I saw a stray copy.

The attacks on Vichy were more virulent than those of the Gaullists in London, though they were directed from the opposite angle: he considered Pétain as an obstacle to the grand design of Hitler. He went far beyond Laval, who was kept in check by the marshal and by his own temperament, which prevented him, in general, from adopting a clear solution. The danger that Déat, supported by the Germans, might one day supplant Pétain and carry France, officially at least, toward the goal desired by Germany, was ever present. He was the implacable adversary of *attentisme,* of "waiting and seeing." Everything which the marshal supported Déat rejected. Some of his criticisms of the personnel of Vichy were well founded; but it would have been a sad day for France if he had seized power, as was always possible. Anything that tended to weaken the authority of Pétain, faced with such an opposition, was mistaken policy. If for no other reason—and there were many positive reasons—it was necessary that the marshal should stay in the post assigned to him by the National Assembly. For him to withdraw would have been to give France over to a Gauleiter—or a Déat.

Another candidate for the succession, completely at the service of Germany, was Jacques Doriot. Doriot was a man of immense energy. He had been a Communist, a leader of men and, in his day, had been as popular as Thorez is today. Then he had turned anti-Communist, had founded a party to fight Communism, and had a host of adherents. It was inevitable that, as the rift between Russia and Germany widened, Doriot would go over lock, stock, and barrel to the side of Germany in the crusade against Bolshevism. He had been patriotic enough before the German invasion, and most of his followers were undoubtedly sincere when they had enlisted under his anti-Communist banner. They were deeply compromised when their chief turned more Hitlerian than the Nazis, and many of them suffered at the Liberation for having been, years before, members of his party.

The war was a strange war, in nothing more than its ideological character, which actually persuaded normally patriotic Frenchmen to join hands with the enemy who was occupying their country because that enemy, in the course of the combat, became the enemy of the Bolsheviks!

Among other men whom I had known in my time as correspondent at Paris was Fernand de Brinon, who was nominated by Laval as a sort of ambassador representing the government of Vichy at Paris. Unhappily for him, he had a reputation as the champion of a Franco-German understanding. Many other eminently respectable Frenchmen have professed themselves in favor of a Franco-German understanding, including Caillaux, Briand, and (in certain conditions) even Poincaré, not to speak of Flandin and Robert Schuman. There was nothing wrong in the idea of a peace-time Franco-German *rapprochement.* But just because he was the exponent of a policy desirable in itself, he should have held aloof from office when France was defeated. It was, though he did not seem to realize it, his policy, too, which had been defeated. Fixed ideas in politics, which take no account of circumstances, place their victims in untenable positions.

The French have always been fond of secret societies and, some time before the War, there was much talk of the Cagoule and the Cagoulards (Hooded Men). It would be difficult to set out their objectives, except that they were at once anti-Bolshevik and antiparliamentarian. I could never take their plots seriously. The Cagoulards were never more than a mere handful of men who liked to conspire darkly, and the governments, when in difficulties, loved to unearth a more or less harmless *complot.* It was a common custom of politicians to accuse a political adversary of having associations with the Cagoule. As the organizations lacked numbers and weapons, it was merely flattering to them to discover that they had met, under cover of the night, in an old deserted mansion on a lonely moor, to discuss in whispers the overthrow of the régime. Their belated romanticism served no other purpose than to enable the authorities to create a mildly sensational diversion. Eugen Deloncle was the most prominent Cagoulard left in France, and he associated his voice with that of the Germans.

The press of Paris was altogether different from the press of Vichy or of Lyons. In general, the national newspapers, known as *journaux d'information,* remained in the capital and did not close their columns to German propaganda. To them were soon added newspapers specifically subsidized by the Germans, with directors or contributors who had been prominent in the past as advocates of the Franco-German entente. I had known some of them and could only regret that, misled by their ambitions, their singularly warped peacetime convictions, their relations, or their love of lucre, they failed to see the difference between collaboration with the Germans in wartime for the making of war, and collaboration with the Germans, and all other European nations, in peacetime for the preservation of peace.

The *journaux d'opinion,* for the most part, went to the unoccupied zone, where they were much freer. They were naturally compelled to publish the official communiqués, and there was a censorship at Vichy, as in all the belligerent countries. Yet, they did enjoy a certain independence, provided they exercised it with discretion, and it was often easy to read between the lines. The *Temps, Le Figaro, L'Action Française* were among those newspapers which were transferred to the south and supported the marshal. When the purge began at the Liberation, it was ruled that there was no reproach to be made against the newspapers which had left Paris—provided they had ceased to publish at a date arbitrarily fixed toward the end of 1942.

As for the Paris papers, they were automatically condemned, though the ruling implied that Parisians should have been left entirely without newspapers under the occupation. Most of the provincial newspapers in the unoccupied zone were, whatever their attempt to maintain their independence, closed down at the Liberation, and their offices and plants were seized, mainly by the Communists.

To understand the case of the Communist organ, *L'Humanité,* we should recall that Russia, still the ally of Germany, was fulminating against the French and English "Imperialists" at the very time she was annexing the unfortunate countries of the Baltic—Esthonia, Latvia, and Lithuania—which it had been part of British policy to maintain and which were now abandoned by the Germans. Stalin had, likewise, annexed a piece of Finland and, of course, half of Poland, and the other half was eventually to fall into his clutches as a satellite state. He now took Bessarabia and East Bukovina, and Molotov, on his visit to Berlin in November 1940, announced Russia's intentions in Bulgaria and her designs on the Straits in order to secure free access to the Mediterranean. There was also the question of Rumanian petrol, which was invaluable to Germany but which Russia coveted. There is reason to believe that, alarmed by the greed of Russia, who was gathering in the spoils without fighting, and whose object was to push the Western Powers into a war of extermination which would leave Russia the veritable master of Europe, Hitler was making up his mind to demolish his voracious partner by a sudden and short campaign in the following spring, whereas Goering was, more wisely, still urging a descent through Spain to Gibraltar, Casablanca, and Dakar. It will be perceived how Pétain's diplomacy—and I think Franco's—tended to induce Hitler to spare France and to turn his arms on Russia; naturally, the Communists could not forgive the marshal for thus contributing, whether consciously or not, to upsetting the Russian scheme.

In the meantime, the apparent friendship between Hitler and Stalin continued. Hitler had fresh complications to unravel; Mussolini, against the advice of his generals, not wishing to be outdone by Hitler, began his silly war against Greece and was promptly driven back by the Greeks into Albania. In North Africa, too, the Italians were proving themselves to be the soldiers of operetta and were being chased across the desert for 500 or 600 miles by the British.

The Communists, with the adaptation to circumstances which distinguishes them, professing their sympathy with the Germans in France, applied for permission to republish *L'Humanité,* to which the Germans saw no objection—though Vichy did! The French Communists, who were later to pose as the only patriots, were against British "Imperialism," against De Gaulle, against "Capitalism" (which, they seemed to think, Hitler was also), and, naturally, against Pétain. The precedent of Brest-Litovsk was invoked. If the Communists were molested in France, it was not by the Germans at this stage: it was by the Vichy authorities. There was some fear (which was greatly exaggerated) that, with the connivance of the Germans, they might set up a Communist government at Paris and achieve their ends, as the Russian Communists had done after Brest-Litovsk. Whether the Germans would have entered into such a scheme I cannot say, but I do know that there was an anti-Communist phobia in France that, with vague memories of the bloody Commune of 1870, persuaded intelligent men of the possibility of a Red Revolution.

I have now sufficiently revealed the situation, as it actually was, to ask: who but the marshal could have faced it with any hope of success? Who could have maintained the equilibrium, menaced from all sides, but Pétain? For France to throw in her hand was surely unthinkable. To leave whoever would to take command, under the cynical regard of the invader, would have been criminal. To cease all show of negotiation with Germany, to deliver France wholly to a ruthless *Gauleiter* might appear heroic in London; in France, it would have been national abdication. And there were few politicians who would have dared to face the Germans. The politicians had gone into hiding. They were in their funk holes, preaching obedience to the occupant, until the time should come when they could return to power by abusing the man who had saved them.

8

Laval Dismissed

We must carefully distinguish between the policy of Pétain and the policy of Laval. It was perfectly proper and, indeed, admirable to remain in France and to stand up to the Germans. It was right to negotiate, to temporize, to endeavor to protect the French people. What was wrong was to show the smallest zeal in the service of the enemy, to obey even his slightest behests willingly. Often it would have been folly to oppose the Germans flatly, without arms: it was wise to manoeuvre, to play for time, to elude the demands of the occupant when vital interests were at stake. Yet the dividing line between the yes-man (the Quisling) and the patriot (obliged to yield to pressure, to retreat before an irresistible force) was narrow and was exceedingly hard to define.

Now, the marshal represented for the French the spirit of prudent resistance, while Laval, rightly or wrongly, represented the spirit of conciliation.

The clash of two conceptions was bound to provoke a crisis. On a number of occasions, Pétain had expressed his intention of ridding himself of Laval at the earliest opportunity. Some of his remarks were widely circulated, for Vichy had become a sounding board. He had even, I was assured, conveyed to the British his lack of confidence in his prime minister. He felt no gratitude toward the man who had conducted the proceedings before the Assembly with a certain technical skill. On the contrary, the marshal was irritated, feeling that Laval had imposed himself on the government, as he had imposed himself on Caillaux, on Briand, on Tardieu. Had the marshal's hands been free, he would never have chosen the Auvergnat, who was still smarting under the British rebuff in the Abyssinian affair.

It may be that Laval had more or less satisfactory explanations to make as to his intentions, if not as to his conduct, had he been allowed to defend himself in 1945. Suffice it to say that, while the marshal was almost unanimously approved in the early months of Vichy, Laval was exceedingly unpopular—the most unpopular man in France, as he himself was ready to acknowledge.

The cooperation of the two men was rendered the more difficult in that there was not only an undoubted difference in their policies but also in their temperaments. Their training was utterly dissimilar. The marshal was, first and almost exclusively, a soldier, with a highly developed sense of hierarchy. He was accustomed to issue his commands to his immediate subordinates, who would pass them on, until they arrived at the stage of execution. Laval had been brought up in the looser atmosphere of the Chamber, where nearly everything is done by nods and winks and slaps on the back, and all the free and easy relations of familiars, with constant give-and-take, mutual concessions, compromises, and favors. The marshal was cultured, precise, methodical, while Laval was uncouth in manners and in appearance. The marshal punctiliously demanded careful reports, whereas Laval was slap-dash, opportunist, preferring to leave little trace of his activities, employing an astonishing variety of personal agents. When the marshal asked that a decision should be put in writing, Laval complained that papers found their mysterious way to London. The marshal offered to lock secret documents in his private safe: Laval still insisted that, somehow, their contents leaked out through the iron door. The marshal was in personal habits clean and meticulous; Laval wore a soiled white cravat, was without style. The marshal detested smoking, but Laval had, like Briand, a half-consumed cigarette perpetually hanging from his lower gipsylike lip. The marshal spoke deliberately, in careful though simple language: Laval, though ready-tongued, affected a careless speech. The marshal was, in short, aristocratic in his demeanor, and Laval was what was held to be democratic. There never was a more ill-assorted pair. The wonder was that, having by the vicissitudes of the war become political bedfellows, they should have remained together so long.

The messages of the marshal, whatever may have been thought of their contents, were felicitously phrased. They were, perhaps, written for him by literary men—indeed, I knew some of his "ghosts"—but they bore his unmistakable mark. They contrasted markedly with the looser utterances of Laval. It may be thought odd that the literary turn of the marshal made a far greater appeal to the masses than the rambling and often awkward demagogy of his prime minister, but there were several reasons—first, the perfect clarity of the marshal's announcements, second, a certain quality of emotional sincerity. It should be remembered, too, that even the humblest Frenchman has a nice ear for the French tongue. Laval was likely to stumble into shocking errors, to strike false notes. I need give no other example than his notorious blunder (two years later): "I desire the victory of Germany, because . . ." But nobody heeded his explanation that, if Germany was beaten, Communism would be dominant in Europe. It is probable that he did not mean to declare his hope of a German victory over France and England, and that he was thinking only of the struggle between Germany and Russia, but the effect was catastrophic. That amazing blunder could not, of course, be foreseen in 1940, but one was always apprehensive of his clumsiness. Everybody felt his unfitness to act as the second in command to the marshal, but the *élite* was particularly hostile to him from the beginning. He was a politician, seemingly unaware that we were not engaged in a game of politics but in a life-and-death struggle. I had never regarded Laval as too intelligent, despite his rise to political heights; sometimes, I thought him definitely unintelligent, even on a low level—the purely electioneering one—for example, his foolish ten-per-cent cut in wages and government payments on the eve of an appeal to the country. He had, perhaps, a peasantlike astuteness: little more. And the secret of his climb to power lay in his ability to shelter himself behind greater men for whom he was prepared to play the sedulous ape. Even now, it was behind the back of the marshal that he screened himself. The most that can be said for Laval is that, in the international realm before 1939, he possessed greater realism and flexibility in working for the peaceful adjustment of current problems than any other French leader of his time.

The marshal was alarmed at the false interpretation that had been given to the Montoire meeting. It was one thing to deceive the enemy, it was quite another to direct the French people into a path that could lead only to their subservience to Germany. He decided to break with Laval and, at the same time, to break with the promise, real or assumed, of "collaboration."

There were around him men who enjoyed his confidence and who deplored what they described as the servility of Laval in his dealings with the Germans. It was probably more exact to accuse Laval of not keeping the marshal and his fellow ministers informed of his promises and half promises, and of committing France to courses that could not be approved by the Vichy government. He was regarded as anti-British by a cabinet which was, on the whole, pro-British. As he was already designated as the successor of the marshal, who foresaw the possibility of his own demise, it was human, all too human, that he should arouse jealousy. Was he not climbing, not only on the back of the marshal but on the back of the Germans, to a sort of dictatorship, or rather indispensability, by the grace of Hitler and Mussolini? Under the pretext of discussing the return of French war prisoners, the return of the northern *départements* to the administration of Paris and not of Brussels, the relegation of the problem of Alsace-Lorraine to the end of the war, the reduction of the daily German indemnity of 400 million francs to less than half that sum which, at that epoch, was enormous, and, finally, freer communications between the north and the south, between the occupied and the unoccupied zones—under the pretext of discussing these questions, was he not making himself an agent of the enemy? And what new concessions was he offering in return for German pledges on these points? The marshal complained that he was being kept in the dark, and although Laval protested that he was concealing nothing, Pétain's suspicions grew and scarcely required the stimulation of Bouthillier, Peyrouton, Baudouin, Alibert, Admiral Platon, and General Huntziger. Admiral Darlan, the nearest rival of Laval, preferred to remain outside the ring that was gradually closing round Laval.

Hitler was interested in magnifying the policy, as yet nebulous, of Franco-German collaboration. The policy should be consolidated and crowned by one of those spectacular manifestations that the Führer loved. I do not know who originated the proposal of a solemn removal of the ashes of the Duc de Reichstadt, the son of Napoleon, the "Aiglon," from

Vienna to the Invalides in Paris, but the grandiose character of the ceremony, as it was planned, appealed to Hitler's sense of the theatrical. It was to be conducted with Wagnerian pomp. At midnight, the casket of the little "King of Rome," about whom romantic plays had been written, about whom a whole literature turned, was to be conveyed by the dusky light of torches to the great domed tomb with which all Parisians are familiar. At the tomb, Hitler and Pétain should meet, clasping hands in silence as the coffin descended into its last resting place. There and thus would be sealed the reconciliation of France and Germany.

The dramatic *dénouement* of the age-old Franco-German quarrel which had cost Germany, as well as France, so much was fixed for the 13th of December. The marshal's refusal would be regarded as hostile. Yet his acceptance would indeed be a betrayal of France.

Something had to be done, and done quickly. The adversaries of Laval found a ready and receptive ear: the marshal had already made up his mind that Laval must be dismissed. They had no difficulty in persuading Pétain that Laval had suggested the removal of the remains of the Aiglon, in order to commit France definitely, irrevocably, to the policy of a Franco-German alliance, and in order to make the marshal the prisoner of the Germans at Versailles, while a new government, headed by Laval and composed of De Brinon, Luchaire, Déat, Doriot, and others, who were pro-German, would be set up in Paris.

Let me remark, in passing, that, whether any such plot existed in the month of December 1940, the danger was always real of a pro-German government superseding the government of the marshal. Whatever allowance may be made for the possible personal sentiments of the marshal—his conviction that he alone could protect the French population, his anger at the supposed attempt to replace him—his attitude seems to me conclusive proof of his entire lack of sympathy with the invader, proof of his resolve to defend France, at any risk to himself or to the country, against the establishment of a Quisling, that is, a German-appointed government. It required considerable courage to flout the Führer, to wreck the scheme of spectacular reconciliation at Paris, and to arrest the favorite of the Germans.

We can, then, picture the amazing scene in the Council Chamber at Vichy, on the eve of the projected ceremony of Paris. The marshal, white with indignation, in his coldest and most cutting voice, demanded the resignations of all his ministers. Silently they obeyed. Some of them were aware of what was happening: others were astonished. When the marshal had before him the resignations, he announced that he would accept only two of them—those of Laval and of Ripert, the minister of education. Laval, who did not expect such a move, stuttered in consternation. He voiced his reproach, reminding the marshal of the debt he owed, warning him of the consequences of an insult to Hitler. The marshal replied that German propositions, of which he had systematically been kept in ignorance, had been considered by Laval. Laval protested that the marshal had been informed of all transactions, that Pétain was revealing himself as an implacable enemy and was plunging France into an adventure whose end could not be foreseen. The marshal was adamant, and Laval left dejectedly, fearing the worst.

This *coup de théâtre* proves the fundamental difference between the marshal and Laval in their approaches to the terrible problem of Franco-German relations. It is true that Pétain, in announcing it in his icy voice, which sounded on the radio like the snap of the knife of the guillotine, was obliged to attribute the dismissal of Laval to domestic reasons. He could not do otherwise, unless he was prepared to announce open defiance to the occupant and be swept away in a torrential invasion of the southern zone. But the facts are clear; and they surely, even if they stood alone, exonerate the marshal from the charge, incredible in itself, of complicity in the designs of Germany. His views about "collaboration" were made perfectly plain when he took what was undoubtedly a bold and even venturesome stand. He displayed, once more, the spirit of Verdun. Thus far and no farther!

Instead of the Wagnerian inhumation of the bones of the Aiglon by the light of smoky torches in the Invalides, with the marshal and the Führer clasping hands as in an *image d'Epinal,* to celebrate the alliance of France and Germany, there was the barest ceremony, the principle actors being conspicuous by their absence, and the remains of the poor Prince were hurriedly bundled into the vault of the Invalides.

Meanwhile, the discomfited prime minister was dining disconsolately at Chanteclair, the restaurant frequented by diplomats and journalists, uncertain of his fate. He counted perhaps on the timidity of the government of the marshal. But he could not be sure. Strange things happened in revolutionary days—and we were, indeed, in a gigantic revolution which began with the defeat, continued with the Liberation, and has, perhaps, not yet ended. There were, in fact, those who counseled a court-martial at midnight, before the Germans could intervene, a speedy execution of Laval, recalling that of the Duc d'Enghien by Napoleon. Or, perhaps, a timely shot to prevent a prisoner from escaping? . . .

Vichy was virtually in a state of siege. The police had been mobilized by Peyrouton. The army was under the orders of Huntziger. No trains were allowed to leave the provisional capital of France. Every evening, Laval had gone to his home at Chateldon, a few miles out of Vichy, returning in the morning, like a businessman to his office. Now, he was informed that his chauffeur had been arrested. The secretaries of Laval were locked in their rooms and forbidden to stir. The girl typists had been sent to bed. And, presently, Laval himself was placed under escort, conducted to Chateldon, his house occupied by troops and police, and there he was to remain pending further decisions.

Two days later, Otto Abetz arrived in Vichy, with an escort of armed men, to demand the liberation of Laval, and the dismissal of all who had taken a conspicuous part in his downfall.

Of course, Laval had to be released. On his return to Vichy he was loud in insults of the marshal: "a blown-up bladder," "a marionette," "an old fool in his dotage," and so forth. The marshal stood firm: he would not take Laval back into his cabinet. For him, the policy of subserviency to Germany, the policy of repeated concessions, the supposed policy of Montoire was ended, and the dismissal of Laval was the sign and symbol of a new resistance to German encroachments. Why the Germans did not insist on the retirement of Pétain, then and there, is inexplicable. His attitude was just as defiant as that of De Gaulle, and he was in France, while De Gaulle was in England.

Presumably the Germans were still hoping to obtain more from France by relative tolerance, by a certain show of friendliness, by the pretense of leaving some independence to the French than by the harsher methods that had been employed in other countries. They recognized that France was not to be won by coercion—though they never abandoned the weapon of coercion, and made plentiful use of it. They would have preferred that France should enter into their plans willingly. Doubtless, they realized that the deportation or even the withdrawal of the marshal would produce such a spirit of revolt that it was better to temporize. You can do much with bayonets, but you cannot sit on them and, with all his ruthlessness, Hitler was not blind to the need of conciliating the French if he was to build the new Europe for which he hoped.

Nothing that has been revealed since the exciting days of

December 1940, when I was informed of everything that passed at Vichy, has induced me to alter my view, first, that Pétain was a true resistant; second, that Hitler was not willing, in spite of his intense distrust of the marshal, to relinquish, by employing purely violent methods, the possibility of coming to an accord with the French.

It may be that the tactics of the Germans in France were, in some respects, more dangerous than the frank appointment of a *Gauleiter*. For Germany was, after all, the master. The creation of illusions in France, short-lived as they were, unhappily lured far too many excellent Frenchmen into unconscious treason to the higher interests of France and prepared the civil war whose effects are still felt today. "Correctness," relative consideration, immediate material gains and concessions, did more to corrupt the soul of France than the most complete domination. The mistake of Laval was to think that, by petty bargaining, France could be saved. Those who thought like him were outside the realm of reality and were deceived by false hopes. By a deplorable and enormous paradox, it may be said that what in the end saved France was the brutality and the violence into which the long occupation degenerated.

9

Darlan

THE nomination of Admiral Leahy as ambassador of the United States at Vichy, at the beginning of 1941, rekindled hope and joy in France. It was a proof that France was not deserted by America and that eventual assistance might be expected. This new recognition of Marshal Pétain as the only legitimate chief of state, after the armistice, after Mers-el-Kebir, after Montoire, after the dismissal of Laval, endorsed the verdict of the National Assembly and the French people.

My old friend, Ambassador William C. Bullitt, had been recalled to give his report on the French débâcle. His opinion of the marshal's suitability for the terrible task which had devolved upon him was exceedingly high. Pétain was the one Frenchman who could face the Germans with undimmed prestige and an unblemished record of patriotism.

It is significant that Bullitt's successor was one of the most distinguished American servicemen. Servicemen understand one another. Had it been possible, General Pershing, Pétain's old comrade-in-arms, might well have been sent, but the general, himself a national hero in the same degree as the marshal, was unable to comfort and reassure the marshal by his presence because the weight of years bore too heavily upon him. He could only express his unchanged esteem and sympathy with his peer in France. In default of Pershing, the choice of Leahy was the best and the most flattering for the French and their elected leader.

The association of Pétain and Leahy could not help being fruitful. While the admiral remained—and his stay was broken only by the bereavement he suffered in the death of his wife—there was never the slightest hint of a divergence of views on vital matters, nor any question of the devotion of the marshal to the permanent interests of France and the Allies. Admiral Leahy never took the view that, in accepting office at the lowest ebb of France's fortunes, the marshal was betraying his country. It was perfectly agreed that, in employing the only weapon of a defeated nation, namely, negotiations with the enemy, Pétain was protecting the French people, maintaining their unity so far as the occupants and the *émigrés* permitted, seeking a necessary *modus vivendi,* organizing the communal services about which the Germans cared nothing, and preparing clandestinely an eventual but not premature revolt. The relations of America with official France were cordial and confident, and we all saw in the encouragement of the Vichy government a promise of American sympathy which was extremely valuable at that time of dejection.

It is not within my province to comment at length on the remarkable ambassadorship of Leahy. He has himself given a fine account of his stewardship, in which he pays the highest tribute to Pétain and his profound patriotism. I should have thought that his testimony was conclusive. We were persuaded that the powerful Republic across the Atlantic would sooner or later come to the rescue.

Robert Murphy, the active *chargé d'affaires,* was signing

accords with Weygand and placing his consuls, in extraordinary numbers, in North Africa, where a new army was being organized, with the full consent of the marshal, in order to prepare for the 1942 landing. There can be no doubt about the connivance of the marshal, Weygand, Leahy, and Murphy in the measures which finally led to the discomfiture of the Germans. Why should honest Frenchmen, whose only crime was to share the confidence of America in the marshal, have been harshly treated three years later by the returning *émigrés* who had manipulated the microphone from a place of safety?

But, in the meantime, Admiral Darlan had succeeded Laval as "Dauphin" in France, and the change was not as satisfactory as had been hoped. As a Nazi leader observed: "When we [the Germans] asked for a chicken, Laval, after long wrangling, gave us an egg. When we asked for an egg from Darlan, he hastened to give us a chicken."

The epigram must not be taken too literally. It is probably true of Laval, and it contains at once a defense and a criticism of his system. It is exaggerated in respect to Darlan. He did not offer more than an egg when an egg was required, but he was less inclined than his predecessor to haggle with the occupant. The trouble with all bargaining was that whether an egg or a chicken was yielded, it was always at the expense of France. If the Germans took eggs or chickens by force, no Frenchman was to blame; but to consent to concessions which went beyond the terms of the armistice, itself a *Diktat*, was a fault that cannot be estimated solely by the degree of importance of the concession.

Laval had imposed himself on the marshal; Darlan was imposed on him by the Germans. Pétain had judged Laval with severity; for a long time he judged Darlan more indulgently. It was natural that he should prefer the officer to the politician, for he had good reason to hold in abhorrence the politicians who had so large a responsibility for the ruin of France. Accustomed as he was to the more direct dealings of military men, whether they belonged to the army or the navy, he trusted Darlan as he had distrusted Laval.

It is not part of my purpose to represent Pétain as free from error. Who was free from error in France, in England, or in America? He was old and, although perfectly lucid and extremely well preserved both physically and mentally, he could not be expected to display superhuman energy. He looked to others to relieve him of a portion of the burden he could not carry alone.

Louis XIV, in his declining years, when misfortunes fell upon France, receiving an elderly marshal who had failed, consoled him with the sorrowful but kindly reflection: "Monsieur le Maréchal, we are not fortunate at our age."

Democracies are not as comprehending and compassionate toward unsuccessful servants as the old monarchies. Darlan was no more popular than Laval. He was almost unknown to the masses. He had had a distinguished record, but it was not marked by exploits that fired the imagination of the public. He was, in fact, what the French contemptuously call a "career man." His technical capacities were highly regarded. He had, however, risen in rank rather by his activities on land than on sea. He was more of a bureaucrat than a sailor. Much of his life had been spent in the Ministère de la Marine, in the offices of the rue Royale. He had been the favorite of two or three ministers of the Third Republic. His friendship for a prominent Socialist leader was well known. The Radicals regarded him as having sound political leanings.

Perhaps, the marshal was mistaken in thinking that he had replaced a politician by an expert for, in spite of his title, Darlan was a politician.

In my Paris days, I had seen him occasionally. He affected the breezy airs of the sailor, smoking his pipe, employing crude expressions. His reputation was that of a man who was greedy of honors. He was, I understand, well thought of in the navy, and there is no doubt that he thought well of the French navy. Between the French fleet and the British fleet there existed professional rivalry: the French considered themselves superior to the English, and the English were ready to return the compliment. We need not regret an *esprit de corps* that is not unhealthy in itself. It may be that the latent anger of the French navy against the British navy, held responsible for the massacre of Mers-el-Kebir, induced the Germans to give their support to the candidature of Darlan. If so, the consequences of this bloody Franco-British episode—that false initial note in the concert of the war—were indeed pernicious. They were to go on accumulating to the end.

Darlan was an ambitious man, though he was without the substance to clothe his ambition. He aimed at nothing less than supremacy in France. He—and not Pétain—was the real counterpart of De Gaulle.

In the multitude of unwarranted accusations against Pétain, accusations based on mere errors of appreciation, on unfortunate decisions such as everybody made, or on accusations which rested on downright and infamous lies, there has been a singular omission. I will supply it here. I accuse Pétain not of betraying his country but rather of a grave mistake of judgment and political procedure—even, perhaps, a usurpation of authority—in assuming to name his successors. He nominated two men in sequence for the succession, first Laval, and then Darlan.

Even had these two men been infinitely better than they were, had they been far more fit for the post of chief after the demise of the marshal, he had no right to name them as his political heirs. The National Assembly had called Pétain to command, in the utter bankruptcy of Parliament. But it did not designate, and would not have designated, either Laval or Darlan. Neither of them stood on the same level as the marshal. Neither of them was, in the smallest degree, qualified as the leader of the French. The choice of Pétain was virtually unanimous: the choice of Laval, and afterward of Darlan, was desired by nobody but themselves.

The marshal's mistake in nominating successors, however patriotic and well-intentioned, was especially grave in the light of the fact that he had removed the checks and balances of parliamentary government and had established a virtual dictatorship where the law is what the chief of state wishes it to be. This situation might not be so dangerous temporarily, when the chief was a high-minded Christian patriot like Pétain. But it involved great risk if such a man should happen to be supplanted by an amoral, if clever, political horse trader like Laval, or an ambitious military bureaucrat like Darlan.

The marshal's motives in naming successors were surely understandable and honorable. He had long ago outlived the span of human life allotted by the Psalmist. The chances were that he would die before the end of the war. When he was elected, it was believed that his work would soon be accomplished and that, with the cessation of hostilities, Parliament would be free to choose a younger man. But it was now evident that months, years, would elapse before normal conditions returned and, in the meantime, France had for ruler a venerable soldier who, at any moment, might be unable to fulfill his duties.

Now, Pétain was not an octogenarian who refused to envisage the fate of all mortals. He was obsessed by the inevitability of his end, and he thought of the confusion into which France would fall were he to die, as it were, politically intestate. To recall Parliament was impossible; to leave the hopelessly divided team of Vichy to fight out the problem of his replacement was undesirable. Nobody could foresee, in that hotbed of intrigues, in which the Germans would be enlisted in the cause of this or that aspirant to power, what influences would be uppermost. The odds were that the Germans would appoint a *Gauleiter,* and the benefits of the armistice (now acknowledged by every impartial observer) would be swept away. Even worse, the Germans might appoint a Quisling.

Therefore, to cut short all contention, Pétain made his will, in the form of a decree, naming Laval, whom he considered the most capable of carrying on his task, as his successor. When Laval lost his confidence, he rescinded his will, and substituted for it a new testament, naming Darlan, whom he thought the least tainted with sectarianism or vulgar ambition.

So Darlan was promoted, to adopt the language of the French, to the rank of Dauphin, by the grace of Pétain. We may properly blame the marshal on two grounds: first because his nomination of a successor exceeded his moral and, I think, legal rights; second, because the nominations were bad ones.

According to gossip, Pétain was soon undeceived. He saw Darlan as he was: a man who was ready to take his place not out of a disinterested sense of duty, but out of a vainglorious conviction of his own deserts. The monetary rewards at Vichy, from the marshal downwards, were trivial; they appear almost contemptible today; and the marshal, both for public and private purposes, was content with the most modest emoluments. His life was simple: he lived without ostentation in the rooms of a hotel, and he expected his staff to live in almost Spartan conditions. Darlan demanded more both at Vichy and at Toulon.

The voice of Darlan, as it came to us over the radio, was unimpressive. It was high-pitched, without distinction. Doubtless, it is absurd to judge ministers by the accident of their voice but, now that the radio is the principal vehicle of communication of rulers with the masses, it is surely a handicap to be "unradiophonique." Character is conveyed in the spoken word, in the enunciation, in the tone. In the case of Darlan, the effect was disagreeable.

Darlan brought into the cabinet a number of admirals.

Pétain was already surrounded by generals, most of whom had little to boast of in the recent campaign; and now the advent of admirals, at Vichy and as governors in the colonies, admirals who had not been beaten, perhaps because they had few opportunities of fighting, was not greeted with applause.

Among the civilians was Pierre Pucheu, a brilliant technician who had been associated with the heavy industries; later he went to join the forces of General Giraud in North Africa, on the assurance that his services in the Resistance would be welcomed, only to discover that his action against the Communists in France was an unpardonable crime—for which he was later shot. There was Benoit-Méchin, a Germanist of talent, who had written a remarkable history of the German army and sincerely envisaged the fusion of peoples in the eighteenth-century style.

There was, above all, Pierre-Étienne Flandin, a nominee of the marshal, a friend of England. He was brought in to redress the equilibrium. In England, his acceptance of office in the government of Vichy was viewed with great favor. Flandin was the titular head of the French foreign office. He enjoyed good personal relations with influential Englishmen; he had often visited them, and his sentiments were well known. It was, therefore, anticipated that his principal preoccupation would be to reassure the British government of the continuance of the Entente.

He was, however, reproached for his telegram of congratulations to Hitler after Munich when, for a brief spell, we had hoped that peace was to be preserved, not for a year but for a generation. The telegram was indiscreet, especially as Flandin then occupied no official position; but it corresponded to the widespread feeling of 1938. When Flandin, following years in prison in North Africa and in France, was tried after the Liberation, Randolph Churchill, the son of the British prime minister, gave evidence on his behalf and reminded the tribunal that Roosevelt had also sent a telegram of congratulations to Hitler. Nothing can be more unfair than to rake up political incidents, which are quite innocent when they occur, at a later date when they may be made to seem reprehensible. The tribunal was compelled to acquit Flandin but, because of his short association with Vichy, Flandin not only suffered long detention but was robbed of his right to reenter Parliament when experienced statesmen were badly needed in the reconstruction of France.

Secret messages from England encouraged Vichy in its resistance to Germany. Flandin had presently the occasion to make contact with Admiral Leahy. My American informant at Vichy spoke in glowing terms of the good understanding that Leahy reached with him.

Otto Abetz, the German ambassador, persistently refused to recognize the new foreign minister and, after a few months, the position of Flandin became untenable.

Short as his term was, it was helpful in temporarily removing misunderstandings. In the hope of counteracting undesirable elements and promoting needed reforms, Pétain established in January, 1941, a National Council of representative Frenchmen to counsel him and to support him. Despite many obstructions and frustrations, the National Council played an important rôle in the activities of the Vichy government. Through select committees chosen from the Council, advice and guidance were provided for the various political, economic and social reforms during the Vichy régime which we shall describe briefly later on at the end of Chapter 15.

It was a trying year, that of 1941. The rigorous winter, in a France which was without adequate supplies of food, of coal, of every necessary of life, and was stripped of means of transport, increased our sufferings. Moreover, we were compelled to watch helplessly the continued triumphs of the Germans, in Yugoslavia, in Greece, in Crete, and in North

Africa, where the famous General Erwin Rommel had arrived to aid the harassed Italians, whose job it was to force their way to Cairo but who had dismally failed, as they failed in all their military operations. Darlan, essentially an opportunist, sought to curry favor with the Germans by making more and more concessions.

He did not know, when he went to Berchtesgaden to see Hitler in May 1941, that a new phase of the war was heralded by the dramatic flight to England of Rudolph Hess. Various versions were given in France of the spectacular flight. One of them, spread after the attack on Russia, was that he was alarmed at the Führer's plans and, foreseeing the downfall of his country, decided to separate himself from Hitler before the catastrophe. Another was that he had gone mad. I could accept neither explanation. I had met Hess, a tall black-browed figure, some years before and, remembering our conversation, I was convinced of his intelligence, his ability as an organizer, and his loyalty to Hitler. I took him to be the type of German who had an unconcealed admiration for the British, and I could readily believe that, for him, the prospect of a war to the bitter end with England was calamitous. I must suppose that he went to England with the consent of Hitler, in a last attempt to induce the English to come to a compromise before the Germans turned their arms against Russia. It is impossible that Hitler would begin a new war without endeavoring to engage the British in the coming campaign against Bolshevism. That the plan failed, that Hess was repudiated, does not in the least militate against the thesis. Emissaries on dangerous missions must expect to be repudiated if they fail.

Anyhow, on the 10th of May, 1941, Darlan did a most imprudent—not to say impudent—thing: he agreed to help the Germans by according them the very facilities in the overseas bases that the marshal had promised the English he would never concede.

The Near East was simmering in revolt; Iraq had risen against the English, and German airplanes had gone to its assistance, halting on Syrian airdromes, and the British had bombed Beirut, Palmyra, and other towns. The affair was not serious: Hitler was too deeply engaged in other preparations to divert his forces to the Near East; but there was some danger of altering the course of the war if Turkey could be persuaded to join either England or Germany. As a result of Darlan's talks, the Protocols of Paris were drawn up, and these Protocols had the gravest implications. It was no longer a question of a few airplanes in transit, making momentary use of French airdromes, with or without French consent: it was a question of formal agreement by which France definitely pledged herself to aid Germany, in violation of the Churchill-Rougier accord. Syrian war material was to be sent to Iraq; the German *Luftwaffe* was to be allowed to revictual on Syrian airdromes; and the Germans were to use Syrian railroads. Similar facilities were to be given in the port of Bizerte in North Africa. Dakar was to be converted into a German submarine port.

The flagrant breach of the agreement with England was indisputable; the collusion with Germany was undeniable. France had entered on a path that could lead only to alliance with her former enemy.

I hasten to state that the Protocols were never ratified and were immediately disavowed by the Vichy government. Yet the marshal, who was no party to arrangements made behind his back, had been caught napping. His vigilance had been betrayed. He had moments of inattention, in which he left too much to the men around him. Happily, Weygand was more alert. He immediately discerned the peril, and he was no sooner informed of the negotiations than he hurried to Vichy and denounced the admiral. Although his general attitude was against any premature rebellion of the French before the Anglo-Americans were ready, Weygand bluntly declared that, if the Germans tried to avail themselves of anybody's permission to use French bases, he would, whatever the consequences, give the order to fire on them. The marshal refused his consent and signature. The Protocols were dead.

Franco-British relations were rendered more tense by the seizure of French ships suspected of carrying contraband, and Darlan threatened to have French vessels escorted by his warships. As for Syria, De Gaulle poured fuel on the fire when it would have been better for French as well as for British interests for him to have been a peacemaker between Vichy and London. I have no need to remind my readers that, particularly after the First World War, France and England clashed in the Near East. The British have been jealous of French influence in regions rich in petrol or necessary for the transport of petrol through pipelines. Such is the unfortunate fact; and, whatever were the grievances of the dissident French, they would have done well to remind themselves that, from the French viewpoint, they could do only harm to their own country by egging on the English to attack Syria.

Precisely what General Catroux, one of De Gaulle's lieutenants, told Wavell, I do not pretend to say, but that Wavell was told of an alleged Vichy intention to give up Syria, holus-bolus, to Germany, is possible. The story was so unlikely that Wavell was frankly skeptical. The animus of the *émigrés* must have been intense if it led them to direct the British troops against a territory which the British were willing to detach from France. That was the way to lose Syria and the loss would be not Vichy's loss but that of France. Surely De Gaulle and Pétain should have shown solidarity on matters that concerned not merely one side or the other but the country of them both. The question should not have been whether De Gaulle or Pétain could fly his standard in Syria, but whether the flag of France should fly there, as it had done traditionally. I think the British were fair, faced as they were with such an astonishing Franco-French contest.

In any case, the French dissidents should have refused to join in the attack. Admiral Muselier and General Leclerc plainly advised against the employment of French troops against the French in Syria. De Gaulle had agreed that Frenchmen should never fight against Frenchmen. He had already made a mistake about Dakar, believing that Dakar (where there were no Germans and no trace of Germans) would welcome him. General Dentz, who was in command, could not honorably yield up Syria to the English and the French dissidents. He was bound to make an attempt to repel the invader. Had the Hindus and Australians come alone, he would doubtless have put up a mere show of resistance, for he was outnumbered and outmatched. That French should fight French was a greater tragedy, and the contingents of the dissident General Gentilhomme added bitterness to the short struggle. In France, the news that De Gaulle had engaged his followers in fratricidal combat was received with great indignation. I am convinced that the cause of De Gaulle was injured by this misconceived action. It was bad enough that, as the French thought, the British wanted to drive them from the Near East; it was intolerable that Frenchmen should help in this enterprise.

An armistice was signed at St. Jean d'Acre, between the British and the Vichy army, and the honors of war were accorded to General Dentz, who had done no more than his duty demanded. It was stipulated that Dentz and his men should not afterward be prosecuted. The British did not regard them as traitors. Those who cared to join the dissident French forces might do so, under no compulsion. The response was poor. Most of the soldiers preferred to return to France. As for General Dentz, in spite of the conditions of the armistice, he was arrested at the Liberation, condemned to death and, although he was not executed, he spent many months with irons on his legs and died under the most miserable conditions in prison.

General Catroux had promised independence to the Levant, and the Syrians demanded the fulfillment of the pledge. So Syria was lost to the French, not to the Gaullists, not to the Pétainists—to the French. It is one of the saddest stories of the war.

10

Occupation

WHEN Palmyra (Syria) fell, I was with a little group of residents of Monaco, when someone proposed that we should call for champagne to celebrate the occasion. I always wished to conceal my thoughts from the curious crowd of cosmopolitans living in relative safety in the sunny principality. The idea of drinking to the most distressing event since the downfall of France—the clash of French with French, the war (however minor) of France and England—shocked me inexpressibly. I rose in silence to take my departure.

"What's the matter? Aren't you glad?"—someone asked.

I could not refrain from replying that I was sad, sad to think that two friendly countries, which had started the war together, should have come to blows, sad to think that Frenchmen had fired on Frenchmen; whoever was right and whoever wrong, I could not find it in my heart to rejoice.

And I added, on a sudden impulse: "I shall accept no more invitations to cocktail or any other parties while men are fighting and dying."

I thus gave great offense to people whose chief fault was a total lack of both realism and imagination. They were no different from the majority of our fellows who look on war from a secure corner, heedless of the suffering, the moral anguish of those who, less fortunate, cannot look on lightheartedly, as at some exciting game which does not concern them personally. In that declaration, without meaning to pose as a moralist or to teach a lesson to the indifferent, I made, as one was bound to make in the war, a number of enemies.

In some respects, life was more difficult in the south of France than in the north. There was no food—or so little—produced in the region: we depended almost entirely on outside supplies. The restrictions were, I think, more severe than elsewhere. And yet, side by side with semistarvation, there was an atmosphere of junketing. The black market quickly organized itself; Italian soldiers smuggled in rice from Italy; meat of a doubtful quality was carried in suitcases by voyagers from Central France; bread tickets were peddled by hotel porters and even by schoolgirls from the Lycée; fishermen sometimes earned more in a week than they had earned in a year before the war; the growers of olive trees managed to abstract a percentage of their harvest from the common pool, and the sequestered oil went to privileged persons; long after fresh milk had become a memory for most of us, I saw huge cans openly displayed at certain doors; and I was given the addresses of several restaurants where one could eat well for what were then prodigious sums.

My sense of civic duty forbade me to have any dealings on the black market until the beginning of 1943, when I realized that it was quixotic to starve while others feasted. How it was that many of my acquaintances managed I did not know. Their means were apparently limited but, somehow, many of them contrived to live in the expensive hotels and to "entertain" with a fair show of opulence. It is true that money was offered on loan (at a high rate of interest), to be repaid after the war, to persons who were known to be well off. Even the poor found ways of increasing their resources by keeping rabbits in their bedrooms and fowls on their balcony. They could also sell their ration of tobacco or cigarettes at several times the price it had cost them. Sometimes they deprived their children of necessary nourishment to make money. I once saw a poor woman enter a grocer's shop with coupons for ten cans of condensed milk—allotted to her for her family—and, having obtained the tins for something like 12 francs a can, coolly ask the grocer to buy them back at 300 francs per can.

Before the Casino, just before the hour of opening, the inveterate gamblers, whom an earthquake would not disturb, lined up to rush to their tables far more eagerly and more punctually than they would have gone to work. We strolled in the well-kept gardens, unchanged except for scores of abandoned cats that had made their home there. We sat on the sun-filled terrace by the Tir Aux Pigeons, overlooking the blue Mediterranean Sea. We met each other on the principal avenue, exchanging comments, or wandered on the quay where the oleanders bloomed. Music was still playing in the space behind the opera house on which the chairs and tables of the Café de Paris were scattered. At night, a few cabarets were open and, in one of them, the eternal strains of a gramophone disc, then newly brought from America, could be heard:

> "Oh, Mister Paganini
> Now don't you be a ninny . . ."

There were occasional incursions of the Gestapo, but more frequently of men masquerading as members of the Gestapo, false policemen, sometimes French, who ransomed the richer inhabitants.

The Italian residents were the most disturbing element. They could not refrain from expressing their political opinions, with the result that, before the armistice with Italy, Fascists were rounded up and, after the armistice, anti-Fascists were similarly treated.

Our life was filled with the darkest shadows. Restrictions of all kinds pressed heavily upon us. We were cut off from all communication with those we had left behind in the occupied area. I have before me a number of printed post-cards of the most formal type, which were all we were allowed to send from one zone to another. They were returned to me because I had written innocuous messages, which were not covered by the regulations: such as "Love from all," "Hope to see you soon," and similar suspicious phrases. The trouble was that, however harmless might be these unauthorized additions, one was never sure that a terrifying visitor would not demand an explanation.

After a time, we learned to cheat the Germans. I knew a man who made a profession of crossing the line of demarcation, dodging the German police. He carried letters. He was caught only once, and spent a few days in prison.

I am reasonably sure that the game of crossing the line clandestinely was the beginning of the Resistance that developed later. One of the mistakes of the Germans was to suppose that they could separate Frenchmen from Frenchmen without awakening the spirit of ingenuity that is peculiarly French. Once the French learned that it was not so difficult, after all, to trick the Germans, that they could cross the most carefully guarded line, they thought of other much more dangerous methods of cheating the occupant. The Maquis, as it was called, began as a simple sport of traversing forbidden frontiers. . . .

The little restaurant in which we ate, where, mingling with the workers, I listened to their stories of privations, of their relatives who were captive in Germany, and where I felt my heart go out toward these humble folk, was soon closed to us. The "patron" could not obtain provisions.

There were no longer gay piles of multicolored vegetables in the picturesque little market. But, in the surrounding country, greenstuffs could be obtained at high prices. It was necessary to go on foraging expeditions, which were out of the question for us.

A neighbor, *croupier* at the Casino, undertook to bring back whatever he could find. He and many others went on foot or on bicycle with big handbags, and for a time they were content with the results. But, presently, I know not by whose decree, all private purchases in the countryside were banned, the foragers, returning tired in the evening, were stopped by the police and the *gendarmerie,* and their foodstuffs confiscated.

The coupons we were officially given—ostensibly to ensure a fair distribution—did not represent the wherewithal to keep body and soul together. There were, on the other hand, the most abominable *ersatz,* so-called Colonial honey, sweetmeats made of crushed and rotting dates, coffee made out of burnt barley, cleansing substances in whose composition not an ounce of fat entered, and a variety of noxious compounds on which we eagerly seized, until they in their turn vanished from the shops. For months my wife and I lived on "rutabagas," Swedish turnips fit only for cattle, and "topinambours," Jerusalem artichokes, almost uneatable, indigestible, and with little nutritive value. I wondered why farmers had suddenly taken to growing unwholesome products on a large scale, and why all other production had apparently been stopped. France is in many parts a rich and fertile country and, although the Germans were living on French food, there were more Frenchmen in Germany than Germans in France, and the drastic shortage was inexplicable.

We could not help feeling that there was dreadful mismanagement. It extended long after the war years, well after the Liberation, and not until 1950 were rationing and governmental control virtually ended. The moral for me is clear: rationing and governmental control in France, while they may be necessary in exceptional periods, are so inefficient that they become positively harmful. The system may work better in more highly disciplined countries, but its effects on public morality and on social well-being tend to be nefarious.

The restrictions were mental and moral as well as material. One felt that one could not talk freely, except to a few chosen companions, that to express oneself in public was to endanger one's liberty. More than once, in spite of my resolution to maintain silence, I found myself drawn into discussions that I would have done well to avoid. There is always a vast majority of stupid folk to misunderstand and distort one's remarks; but, in normal days, they have fewer opportunities of exercising their malice. Social intercourse becomes impossible if one cannot converse freely, make even foolish remarks as they rise to the lips, go somewhat beyond one's thought in the heat of argument, without fearing the consequences of misinterpretation.

During the occupation, one was always at the mercy of informers, who did not hesitate to carry tales to the Germans or the Italians, or to treasure up their gossip for a later revenge. The passions roused by the war were private as well as public. We were bidden to hate the enemy, but the enemy, by a simple mental process, was identified with our neighbor, or our wife, or our husband, or our employer. To make the identification more complete, we watched each other to ferret out symptoms of sympathy with the Germans, or the Russians, or the Americans, or the English, or whoever else could be fitted into our conception of the enemy, who varied according to our ways of political thinking. In France, there opened up the prospect of unlimited revenge for the Gaullists upon the Pétainists, for the Communists upon the "Fascists," for the Anglophiles upon the Anglophobes. The pretext for such revenge would be a word, spoken or invented, at any moment during the long strife in which most people in France changed their opinions four or five times, which justifies, in our eyes, our dislike of our relatives, our acquaintances, or our "boss." That is what civil war means, and France, knocked out of the real war, presently fell into a civil war, at first smothered but in the end to burst into flames.

Hence, the worst restriction placed upon us was the ever-increasing restriction on love for our fellows. Beware! That man or woman whom you greet every day in the street, or in the restaurant, whom you receive in your home, whom you encounter in your business, does not think precisely as you think and, therefore, he hates you, and he will cherish up every imprudent utterance for the day of reckoning!

Pascal has defined man as a mixture of angel and beast. Now, it was good form to boast of the beast. Those who would have shuddered a few years before at the spilling of blood were now elated at the enormous sacrifices to Moloch. Soldiers must slay in order not to be slain, but I found it nauseating that in sumptuous drawing rooms far from the front, men and women living in comfort should complacently exult in apocalyptic horrors and call for more, without a thought for human suffering, without a vestige of pity. . . . Restrictions on our culture, on our intelligence, on our ideals, on our unselfish imagination . . . Restrictions on the angel, finally overthrown by the beast . . .

I must place here, where it belongs in point of time, though it was later that I learned of it, an incident that lends some color to the belief, still prevalent in some French circles, that there was an understanding between Pétain and De Gaulle. It had this justification: in June 1941 Colonel Groussard, who had served under the orders of Vichy, went to London to see Churchill and, as he hoped, De Gaulle, in full accord with the marshal and with General Huntziger (soon afterward to be killed in an air accident). His mission was to ask the British not to treat France as a potential enemy and, while continuing to support the Committee of De Gaulle at London, to regard the government of Vichy as the friend and future ally of England.

Churchill, whom he saw, is said to have recognized the "superhuman task of your chiefs, in protecting France and the French. I will ask them to remember that England is still in the war, and to have faith in the future. . . . If I governed France, I would not tell the Germans that I detested them. The worst must be warded off. I would try to gain time. Tell Vichy that I have a profound respect for the person of the marshal. I have never thought that he wanted the Germans to win."

These are wise and statesmanlike utterances. I trust they were indeed made by Churchill.

It was better for England, goes on the report of Churchill's statement, that Pétain rather than Doriot should govern. The prime minister admitted that Pétain could serve France as much as De Gaulle could do "if he used the resources that remained to France to the advantage of our two nations."

I find in Churchill's appreciation of the marshal an acute observation. Groussard excused shortcomings of the marshal because of his great age. No, it was not a question of age, it was a question of his capacity, replied Churchill. He had been a soldier all his life, obeying orders. Now, he was asked to solve problems of which he knew nothing, with the classic ideas and training of a military chief. That is exactly the view which I had formed.

Churchill was comprehending enough to declare that he did not mind attacks in the French press, which were calculated to deceive Germany. It was a matter of measure and of design. When, for example, British bombs fell on French towns, apparently without adequate military reason, I could not blame the authors of dignified protests. What was reprehensible were newspaper campaigns systematically exalting German action and systematically denouncing everything that was British. French subserviency to England was not to be expected: French praise of England for Mers-el-Kebir, to take a single instance, would have been contemptibly anti-French. In their defeat, the French could not be refused the right to judge British or Russian or American policy that appeared detrimental to French interests. It was in agreement with the traditions of fair play and of democracy that the victim of blunders should try to make his voice heard; it was actually in the real interests of the Allies that the spontaneous reactions of the French should find expression.

It remains true that an artificial hostility between England and France was not utterly undesirable: it might be an excellent piece of strategy, an effective *ruse de guerre,* if rightly used, and Churchill showed his good sense in agreeing to it. An open entente with England would have immediately destroyed the armistice and its acknowledged benefits both to England and France.

Nor was Churchill wrong in declaring that there were traitors even among the ministers of Vichy. They could only be neutralized by the sounder elements, the patriots who were resolved to yield nothing except under compulsion and who prized English and American friendship as a means of ultimate salvation.

These negotiations with Churchill were taking place behind the back of Darlan, and Groussard appealed to the secret agents of the Gaullists to hide his visit from the Dauphin.

I relate this episode because it throws light on the complicated character of the relations of Vichy with London. Groussard, the former chief of staff of Dentz, was not a traitor. Huntziger, the minister of war at Vichy, was not a traitor, and Pétain who gave these talks his blessing was not a traitor. They would have been happy to reach an accord with De Gaulle, to work in harmony with him. Unfortunately, De Gaulle, himself, was absent from London, but

Huntziger authorized Groussard, on his return, to organize a liaison between the war ministry and the Gaullists in France. Groussard was soon afterward arrested by Darlan; and, unable to work usefully in France, he escaped to Switzerland, where he directed an information bureau. How different would have been the history of France had he succeeded in framing a secret Pétain-De Gaulle pact!

As for me, I could not be idle. I wrote a book which was a cry of admiration for the France I had known and loved so long, a book (*Le Livre de Saint Pierre*) which brought me hundreds of letters, touching in the extreme, from academicians, ministers, distinguished Frenchmen of all professions, whose patriotism burned more brightly than ever. And I began to compose, to be published in the free zone, without German censorship, a book which would sum up the correspondence I had with European thinkers, containing my political and social philosophy, and including the scheme of an Atlantic Union and of international cooperation after the war, of which we hear much discussion today.

11

Hitler Strikes at Russia

On June 21, 1941, we had apparently settled down to a long period of relative stagnation. France could only watch and wait. She could do nothing to change the course of events. She could only hope. The word *collaborationist,* which has been heard so much since the Liberation, was not often used in France. The word there was *attentiste,* that is to say, marking time. For those who were impatient, the Gaullists, it was a term of reproach, as though any other policy was possible to France. England too was waiting, like Micawber, expecting something to turn up. Russia was waiting, though not neglecting to grab the spoils. America was waiting—wondering whether and when she would intervene in Europe, about which matter there were divided opinions. Germany was waiting, because the moves after the downfall of France, though not without importance in the general disposition of forces, were not decisive. The favorable moment for the invasion of England had passed forever. The battles in Africa, though stirring enough, did not deeply engage

Germany, and it seemed to France that the advances and the retreats in the desert had mainly a propagandist value. Rommel, who was a picturesque figure, capturing the imagination of the masses, had then, after all, a mere handful of men. The successes of Germany in the Balkans could lead to no decisive result, and the real struggle, if it was to come, had not yet begun. Unless and until something bigger happened, the war was moving toward a stalemate.

My belief that Hitler had originally intended to circumscribe the conflict, just as the original plan of Churchill was to extend the war, to fight on the periphery, to throw as many nations as possible into the combat and so lengthen and weaken the German lines, had received confirmation, though the folly of Germany's Italian partner had aided the Churchillian strategy by forcing Hitler to shift somewhat from his central position. The strength of Hitler lay in his central position, but he could not win the war by staying there. The strength of Churchill lay in larger facilities of communication. Paradoxically, every battle won by Germany far from her centre was a disadvantage to her. I thought of two boxers, the weaker making full use of the ring and, by clever footwork, draining the strength of his opponent. But if Germany could not win the war by fighting out of effective range, neither could England. It followed that something must happen. It did. Someone must take the initiative in earnest. Hitler did.

Until that day in June 1941 the vast majority of Frenchmen were mere onlookers.

On the 22nd of June the storm burst. Germany was at war with Russia! It was incredible. Had not Russia signed a pact with Germany which was profitable to them both? Profitable to Russia, because she had won, without a blow, territory after territory she had coveted. Profitable to Germany, because she received immense quantities of material of which she stood in need. The blockade by England was quite ineffective so long as Germany could draw from the vast lands to the east much that she required for her consumption and for the prosecution of the war.

The question is often asked as to when and why Hitler decided to make war on Russia and as to the responsibility for the German attack—was it Hitler's or Stalin's? Puzzling as it seemed in 1941, we can now answer this question with some assurance. It was once believed that Stalin was surprised and aghast over the attack, and that the responsibility was wholly that of Hitler. This view can hardly be maintained today. The critical episode was the interview of Molotov with Hitler in Berlin, on November 13, 1940. It dealt with the division of the Old World between Germany and Russia. Hitler, although believing himself already victorious, made almost incredible concessions to Russia, which had not at the time suffered at all seriously in war—having gobbled up Poland without resistance and lost few men in the war with Finland. Russia was to be allowed to hold eastern Poland and the Baltic provinces, to have unrestricted right to use the straits leading out of the Black Sea for her warships—the Russian aspiration which was the most prominent cause of the First World War—and full right to occupy the vast territory south of the USSR, all the way to the Indian Ocean, including a warm-water port on the Persian Gulf. In addition, Hitler agreed to mediate with Japan to promote Russian designs in the Far East.

Despite these almost apocalyptic concessions, Molotov countered by additional and outrageous demands in Central Europe and the Balkans, and insisted on an immediate answer. Both the demands and the manner of their delivery threw Hitler into wild rage. James Byrnes, in his *Speaking Frankly* (pp. 289–290), correctly estimates that this date was "the decisive moment" that Hitler decided to attack Russia. If this be true, and it most probably is, then the immediate cause of the Nazi attack on June 22, 1941, was

Molotov's behavior in Berlin on that fateful day in the preceding November. It is, of course, true that Hitler had been toying with the possibility of attacking Russia before this time, but there can be little doubt that Molotov's demands induced him to set his timetable ahead by months if not years.

The next question is what lay behind this. Was it merely lack of diplomatic finesse and good sense on the part of Molotov and Stalin, who did not intend to provoke Hitler to war and were surprised when it came? This would appear to be the opinion of Mr. Byrnes and of some historians of Russo-Nazi relations, but this interpretation hardly accords with many other facts that we know. Stalin was offered more spoil than he should have expected in his wildest dreams. If he wished more, he could have afforded to wait until an advantageous moment in the future.

The real explanation would appear to reside in the uncanny shrewdness and foresight of the ruler of the Kremlin, who foresaw ultimate war with the Führer and realized that it was far better to fight this war when he could be almost completely sure of British aid and reasonably certain of American intervention, rather than at some future date when he might have to reckon single-handed with a vastly stronger Germany. It would seem most reasonable to suppose that Stalin deliberately instructed Molotov to make exaggerated demands on Hitler, and in such a manner that the only probable reaction of Hitler would be a decision to make war on Russia. There is little doubt that Stalin may have been surprised and alarmed by the speed with which Hitler decided to go to war, and many writers have mistaken his possible chagrin over this for a desire to avoid war altogether.

Further evidence against the thesis of a naïve Stalin, rudely shocked and surprised in June 1941, is afforded by the great Russian troop concentrations on the eastern border of Germany and the fact that there were vast movements of

German troops and materials eastward in the winter and spring of 1941. Russian intelligence service, later credited with superhuman cleverness and efficiency, could hardly have been dumb enough in 1941, when they had special facilities for operating in the land of an ally, not to have been fully aware of these German troop movements.

At any rate, whether Stalin deliberately provoked war or was surprised and dismayed, there can be no doubt that what led Hitler to undertake the desperate gamble of the two-front war, which he had so vigorously condemned in *Mein Kampf*, were the greed and bad manners of Molotov in November 1940. Hitler's concessions to Russia at that time, in the light of the trivial Russian aid to Hitler, bordered on the fantastic in extent and generosity. If Stalin did not wish to provoke Hitler to make war on Russia before England was knocked out of the war, then the idea of Stalin's ruthless sagacity must be ruled out. However annoying, exasperating and threatening to Hitler Molotov's demands may have been, they were, from the standpoint of Russia's interests and logical greed, utterly trivial compared to what Hitler offered Stalin in the East—the great Eurasian land mass, the Near East with its boundless riches in oil and minerals, the long-coveted warm-water port, and even the good possibility of seizing India. But these might mean little, if Stalin later had to battle Hitler alone. Better to gamble on war when help was assured, and then gain more of the Old World when Hitler had been disposed of. That it was a desperate gamble to goad Hitler to war may readily be admitted, but Stalin won. Hitler was destroyed, Stalin became master of more than half of Europe and much of Asia, and the end is not yet.

On the other hand, Hitler's attack on Russia was the sheerest idiocy, opposed by Goering and all the able military leaders of Germany. However exasperating Molotov's demands may have been, there was no likelihood that Stalin would attack Hitler. German generals have now admitted that there was little probability that Hitler could have decisively defeated Russia and put her out of the war, even if he had been able to start his attack on May 15, as originally planned. But there were good prospects that a German drive on Spain, the Mediterranean, and the Middle East might have forced Britain to make peace.

Hitler may well have believed that his war with Russia would not long involve him in a two-front war, even if it took some time to overcome Soviet power. England, his only remaining enemy in Western Europe, had earlier encouraged Hitler as a safeguard against Russian expansion and ambitions, and there was some ground for expecting that an attack on Russia might lead England to abandon the war and thus also prevent American intervention.

It is possible that Hitler relied on the mission of Hess to influence England; it is possible that he counted, in any case, on the anti-Communist feeling in England and in America to change the character of the war. Would Hitler be hailed as the champion of the West? Would Stalin be regarded as the veritable enemy? Russia had flouted the principles for which England had entered the war, had mocked the Allies at Moscow, had proved to be a peril to the *status quo* in Europe. Would not England encourage, if she would not help, Germany to finish with the Bolshevik danger that Churchill had so consistently and vigorously denounced?

If such was the hope of Hitler it was soon shown to be baseless. Without hesitation, despite his earlier description of the Soviet leaders as "foul baboons," Churchill declared that Germany was the first (and, for the moment, the only) enemy of England, and that any country which fought against Germany would be welcomed into the Allied camp.

In retrospect, it has been the custom of critics of President Roosevelt in America and of supporters of Churchill in England to denounce Roosevelt for his concessions to Stalin at Teheran and Yalta, often made over Churchill's protests.

Nevertheless, there is little doubt that Roosevelt's mistakes, even at Yalta, were not as serious, so far as promoting the rise of Russia to domination of the Old World is concerned, as Churchill's adamant refusal to withdraw from effective participation in the war after June 22, 1941, and to permit Hitler and Stalin to reduce each other to impotence and remove totalitarianism and its imperialisms as an imminent danger to Europe. The liquidation of the British Empire, which Churchill so deplored in his rhetoric, began in practical fact on June 22, 1941 (the Empire was never threatened by its servile admirer, Hitler), and the process is still continuing.

I can best analyze the effect of the decision of Hitler in France by recalling a conversation I had, after the war, with a Frenchman whom I take to be typical of a considerable section of the population. He was unquestionably patriotic, as he understood patriotism, but his hatred of Russia and of Communism entirely eclipsed his hatred of Germany and of Nazism, just as with others the detestation of Germany and of Nazism obliterated the abhorrence of Russia and of Bolshevism. He had joined some association or other which professed anti-Communist views; and he was fortunate, at the Liberation, in escaping with the penalty of *indignité nationale,* a punishment hitherto unknown, and sufficiently severe since it prevented him from managing the business he had established, as well as depriving him of civic rights.

"Until June 21, 1941," he told me, "I was, like most Frenchmen, bitterly anti-German. Fear and hatred of Germany is born in us. My father had told me of 1870. I had myself fought from 1914 to 1918. I had been called up again in 1939. How could we forgive the relentless foe? I had never listened to the blandishments of Briand. I did not believe a genuine reconciliation of our two nations possible. I could not forgive Germany for our defeat. The propaganda of Goebbels could not affect me. I was for the marshal, but against any form of collaboration. In short, I was the average Frenchman in my sentiments.

"But on June 22," he continued, "we regarded the war with Germany as ended; a new war had begun. It was no longer a Franco-German war. It was a Russo-German war. I had seen the ravages of Communism in France—our defeat was due in some measure to Communism in our midst. For me, the chief menace to our country, to our civilization, was Communism. That, of course, did not change my attitude toward Germany. On the contrary, Germany was doubly the enemy because she was the accomplice of Russia. Nothing would have made me change, except the new war, not against France—that was over and done with—but against Communism. I regarded it as a Crusade, in which we could temporarily forget our differences."

This was not a war like other wars, country against country, in which the sentiment of patriotism is simple and the duty of defending one's nation is clear. "It was," he argued, "a war of ideologies, in which our thoughts are confused, our loyalties complicated. Look at the French Communists themselves: unhesitatingly against their own country when Russia called for a war against what she called Imperialism; and patriotic, if the term is not misused, only when Russia happened to be opposed to Germany. My choice was between Germany and Russia, Nazism and Bolshevism, with France a helpless but not impartial onlooker."

I could not better state the attitude—as my interlocutor said, a purely mental attitude—of a great many Frenchmen, who did not renounce their opposition to Germany as the invader, who were not hostile to England or America, than in the language of this man who was betrayed by his "ideology." Just as most of the English and the Americans could close certain compartments of their minds during the war, so did these Frenchmen contrive to close certain compartments of their minds. The average man, to arrive at any conclusions at all, is bound to think in blinkers.

On the other hand, June 22, 1941, was the date on which the Communists, or sympathizers with Communism, found themselves released from an equivocal position. They were free to serve Russia while incidentally serving France. For the most part, they were ordinary Frenchmen, who may have suffered in their conscience when they were obliged by their "ideology" to fulminate against French and other "Imperialisms" and to support Germany, the ally of Russia, against their own country. From now onward, they could boast of their "patriotism" all the louder because it had been dimmed for nearly two years. They went over to De Gaulle, who received them in the name of the union of French resistants to the oppressor, and at the Liberation they could claim that they were the only true resistants, the party which could count more of their members shot by the Germans (*le parti des fusillés*) than any other.

Thus did politics enter into the Resistance, as well as into Vichy. Thus was the whole meaning of the union of Frenchmen against the invader bedeviled, and as was to be anticipated, Communists and anti-Communists began a sort of civil war which, after the Liberation, consisted in abusing the adversaries of Communism by opprobrious names—Vichyists, Pétainists, collaborationists, and traitors—and in proceeding to "liquidate" them accordingly.

There arose, then, these two contradictory movements in France as a result of the "new war": a movement of sympathy with Germany because she was fighting Bolshevism, and a movement of hostility to Germany for the same reason. In both cases, the change of attitude was opportunist, affecting neither the fundamental patriotism of one group nor the fundamental a-patriotism of the other.

As for the majority of Frenchmen, they remained exactly

what they had been, observers, on the whole rather thankful that France was out of the war and had no choice to make.

No doubt, Hitler was confident that, with England neutral or neutralized, he could win his new war in ten weeks. His armies were immense; they were equipped as no armies had ever been before; they had sustained insignificant losses in the earlier campaigns; and as nothing succeeds like success, they went forth in high fettle to conquer. It is possible, though not likely, that they would have done so, had not their entry into Russia been delayed by mopping up operations in such countries as Yugoslavia and had Hitler listened to his best generals. They came within a stone's throw of Moscow, and they besieged Leningrad. They broke irresistibly through the Russian armies with their tanks, penetrating deep behind the Russian lines, and then returning to take the Russians between two fires. The bewildered Russians were encircled, and they surrendered by hundreds of thousands. Meanwhile, the German aviation bombed armies and towns. Thousands on thousands of Russian cannon and tanks were taken in the first few weeks. It was officially announced that Germany was victorious once more. And what a victory! A victory far greater than the victory in France!

The cry of victory was a colossal error. Hard as the Germans had pushed, swiftly as they had advanced, neither their ardor nor their speed was sufficient. The winter surprised Hitler, as Hitler had surprised Stalin. In my library are some bound copies of *Punch,* and I turned up the famous cartoon of the Crimean war, in which General Winter, implacable and ruthless, lays his icy hands on the armies. Napoleon had done better than Hitler: he had got inside Moscow. It was easy to penetrate into Russia; it was not so easy to retreat from Russia. Penetrate? How far? Where to stop? Russia was sucking in Germany, draining her of her manpower and matériel. Unless there was a veritable counterrevolution in Russia, Germany's efforts would be in vain. Of course, we were treated to all kinds of scientific arguments as to the elimination of the factor of distance in modern warfare, the development of motorization, the marvels of engineering skill which could make roads as quickly as you could race upon them, efficiency in the organization of supplies, and so on. In all these matters, Hitler was incomparably better off than Napoleon, but the elemental forces were on the side of Russia.

Russia possessed space—for all practical purposes endless space. She could also employ, as she had employed before, the barbaric weapon of *la terre brûlée*—"scorched earth"—burning the ground as her armies fell back. I will not discuss the value of the tactics of the scorched countryside from a military viewpoint; it may be that systematic self-destruction saved Russia, as it had saved Russia over a century before when Moscow was fired. It may be that Russia can afford to lay herself waste. But the weapon is, nevertheless, barbaric, and its introduction into the lands of the West, in France in particular, the wide-spread resort to sabotage on political as well as military occasions, and all forms of national suicide are the negation of civilization.

The failure of the Germans in Russia facing the winter of 1941 convinced me that they had lost the war—unless they withdrew from their advanced positions and made peace with Russia, as they might well have done. Certainly, Germany did miracles in improvisation: furs were lavished on the soldiers; the military machine worked marvelously. But of sound and comprehensive planning, of far-reaching foresight, there was no trace hereafter: there were only fumblings, hesitations, doubts, which destroyed the confidence of the officers of the German army in the infallibility of their chief. A strong man would have cut his losses: Hitler could only flounder on and on. . . .

A lath painted to look like iron! Neither the negative audacity which withdraws, nor the positive audacity which stops at nothing! Half-measures, remorse, vacillations, bluster instead of courage, hysterics instead of fortitude, obstinacy instead of perseverance, incapacity to make war and incapacity to make peace! Hitler was at last judged, judged by Stalin, judged by his officers, although the myth of Hitler lingered longer in the mind of the masses.

As for the reaction in France, the idea was germinating in many minds that even the successes of Hitler would eventually weaken the Germans, to the advantage of France, and that, by merely waiting, France would become relatively stronger. In all my conversations which reflected the views of Vichy, I noted a new hope that France might yet be the arbiter of the European situation, a hope apparently far-fetched and unjustified and based on the realization that all the cards had not been played, that unexpected tricks might still be turned. Germany, while desirous of sparing France, distrusted her intensely. Hitler and Goebbels were particularly suspicious of France's ultimate aims and opposed the arguments of more optimistic Germans who saw in the wave of anti-Communism a pledge of future French assistance. Assistance? To Germany? Hitler scoffed at the notion. What assistance could France offer anybody? And if, indeed, Germany had ever supposed that France could safely be armed, what guarantee could there now be that she would use her arms for Germany?

12

Italy Makes War

Living so close to the Italian frontier—the Italians had annexed Menton, only a few miles away—we heard much gossip about Rome. Italian officers, dressed too showily, strutting too proudly, were conspicuous. They were friendly, and asked nothing better than to enter into genial relations with the population. We avoided them, but I had two friends who had spent many years in Rome, or rather in the City of the Vatican, recording the history of the Popes; they were, therefore, well known to the Italian authorities, and seemed to have no scruples about talking with the officers. We obtained amazing glimpses of the mentality of the temporary masters of southern France.

It was surprising that officers, some of them of high rank, should be ready to express themselves without the smallest reserve to foreigners. The nature of their confidences was still more startling.

We learned then, at an early stage in the Italian occupation, the true sentiments of the Italians. The epithets which they applied to the Germans were crude. The French dislike of the Germans was as nothing compared with the Italian disdain. Italian pride was hurt by what was considered to be a German occupation of Italy almost as real as the German occupation of France. It was not long before I was convinced that, if ever the tide turned against the Germans, the Italians would abandon them. The Italians, descendants of the Romans though they may be, are among the poorest fighters in the world: I do not blame them for preferring the pleasanter arts of peace, but it was strange to find high-ranking officers, as well as the common soldiers, speaking in terms of utter detestation of their allies to casual acquaintances in an occupied country.

It was easy to foresee that some day the Italians would confirm the reputation they had of never ending a war on the same side as they began it—unless the war lasted long enough for them to change sides twice!

It was not the corrupting influence of Fascism that caused a military "degeneration" of the Italians: their unwillingness to fight for anything save self-preservation existed long before Fascism, and the greatest mistake of Mussolini was his assumption that he had changed the Italian character.

The military success in the Ethiopian campaign against ill-equipped, untrained, and quasi-barbarous opponents may have given him a mistaken impression that the Italians had returned to the militant virility and impetus of the days of Garibaldi. If so, he was to be fatally disappointed. There has been no more ignominious spectacle in modern warfare than the Italian military record in Southern France and North Africa during the Second World War. The Italians had a special reason for fighting enthusiastically in the Ethiopian war, for it was a war of revenge—a war to avenge a blot on national honor and the brutal treatment of Italian soldiers. In March 1896 King Menelik of Ethiopia had disastrously defeated the Italian army at Adowa and had tortured with incredible and humiliating barbarism the Italian soldiers whom he had captured. There was no such emotional basis for war against France and Britain in 1940 and thereafter.

Italy was a liability and not an asset to the Germans. I love the Italian people, perhaps the most charming people in Europe. One loves people, whatever their faults, for their kindly qualities, and the kindly qualities of the Italians need no eulogy. It became clear that there would be, sooner or later, an Italian defection, and with more judicious diplomacy the defection might have occurred much earlier.

Mussolini himself expressed the harshest criticisms of Hitler. When, for example, the Führer awakened the Duce in the middle of the night to tell him of the invasion of Russia (about which he had not consulted his partner), the private comments of Mussolini were illuminating. "I hope he loses his feathers in Russia," he said. "Let us hope for a British victory. I am glad to hear that the English are bombing Germany night and day. . . ." And much more in the same strain, which duly filtered from Rome and was repeated with great gusto by the Italian officers in France. I wonder that it never reached ears at Berlin. It certainly reached mine.

The blabbing officers, apparently unconscious that the war was going on, dressed themselves well, discussed affairs freely, had no secrets, and were obviously well content to be outside the battle area.

There were in the South of France, where the Italians or inhabitants of Italian origin were numerous, Italian clubs, where Italians could go to obtain supplies of cigarettes. Most of them, oblivious of the war, or perhaps because of the war, went to collect their cigarettes, a fairly innocent motive for frequenting the Casa. After the Liberation, the lists of those who obtained cigarettes from the Casa were found, and the cigarette seekers, who probably cared nothing for politics and had no strong patriotic feelings, were regarded as traitors to France, with dire results for themselves and their families.

Let me here neglect chronological order to remark that the later attitude of the Italians, as I judged it from my window in Monaco, was identical with that described by my Rome friends. When the Germans took over the control of southern France, trainload after trainload of Italian soldiers went back to their country, shouting joyously and singing gleefully. The railway ran between the port and my house, high perched on a street stairway. The soldiers were returning as they imagined to a defeated country. In fact, the war was to drag on in Italy, but they did not know that. For them, the war was ended. It had ended in disaster.

I could not but recall how sorrowfully the French had accepted the débâcle. They demanded the armistice, insistently, almost unanimously, and they were relieved when at last it was concluded. But they had heavy hearts. They looked on it as a sad necessity. It was as though someone very dear to us had, after terrible sufferings, died; and we were at once glad that the sufferings were over, and afflicted by the passing of the dear one. Nobody in France would have laughed or sung. We all wore faces of woe. The tragedy of the defeat crushed us to the earth, and we thought we should never smile again. In the due course of nature—for we have, happily, a marvelous capacity of forgetfulness and of adaptation—we regained in some measure our spirits and, according to our different temperaments, we resumed our living, some of us with resignation, others with indifference, others again with stern vows to avenge the defeat. However we subsequently reacted, no Frenchman rejoiced in the calamity that had overtaken his country.

The Italian soldiers, on the other hand, returned to a land which, for all they knew, was in ruins, like schoolboys going home for the holidays. The railway carriages into which they were crowded were decorated with branches of trees, were bright with flowers. The soldiers sat on the steps or stood in the doorways, cheering, exulting, waving their arms; and instruments of music, mouth organs and accordions, played the liveliest airs. There was no sign of downheartedness. There was only jubilation. For them, as they imagined, the war belonged to the past, and they were already virtually demobilized. What did it matter whether they had won or lost? They would soon be out of their uniform, they would be free men once more. So they were merry.

I will not say that the Italians would not have comported themselves somewhat differently in a war that was indubitably their own war. This war was not their war, and never had been. They had been forced into it by the ambitions of the Duce, who himself had been animated by resentment against the French and English, and at the same time by disdain for the rival dictator in Germany, whom he regarded as an upstart without political talent. And they had been forced into it by the war-minded elements in the court, the Fascist political circles, and not a few of the general public, none of whom really expected much fighting would take place, it being assumed in June 1940 that Hitler had virtually won the war. The Italians had been, many of them, under arms for many years. They had gone through the Ethiopian campaign. They had been kept on the alert or had fought during the Spanish struggle. They had not been released while Europe was manoeuvring and counter manoeuvring, marching and countermarching. They were tired, and they never had any stomach for a fight that concerned them only indirectly.

My friends, improperly as I think, used to talk with Italian soldiers, and when Sicily was occupied they had this conversation with an Italian soldier:

"Aren't you distressed to think of the fate of Italy?"

"Why should I be? I am not an Italian."

"Not an Italian? What are you then?"

"I am an American. Haven't you heard that Sicily is American now?"

He was not at all sorry that Sicily was "American." On the

contrary he was glad to suppose that his nationality had changed overnight.

It was not out of any new political conviction that the Italians changed sides in 1943. Badoglio was charged by the king to capitulate, not because of any serious alteration of popular feeling—except that of increasing weariness with the war.

Field Marshal Lord Alexander tells us that Badoglio and the king miscalculated just as badly in 1943 as they and Mussolini had in 1940. Mussolini had thought the war practically ended when he struck France. Badoglio and the king thought the Allied armies were strong enough to sweep away the Germans from Italy without real fighting. But, before the Allies could reach them, they were obliged to flee from Rome. As for the Italian "resistance"—in the sense in which the word is used in France—that is to say, the irregular forces operating against the Germans, it was ineffective until the Allies had all but overcome the Germans in Italy. Then, also under Communist leadership, it carried on the same program of terrorization and assassination that we shall describe when we deal with the Liberation and Revolution in France in 1944–1945.

I would not, in thus reviewing the conduct of Italy in the war, gratuitously place her in an unfavorable light. We must take countries for what they are, and not criticize them for what they are not. There are observers who pretend that the nations resemble each other, that their special characteristics are imaginary, or merely the result of political conditions and education, perhaps of religion, and who, in their zeal for a vague sort of internationalism, would reduce us all to a uniform pattern, a uniform greyness. They are wrong. Instead of standardizing the nations or obliterating their distinctive marks, we should cultivate the salient features of each nationality and, in aiming at unity, jealously preserve variety. We would not have a single kind of flower in our garden: we can enjoy them all in their rich diversity; and they may make a charming and fragrant whole.

At St. Florentine in December 1941 Pétain met Goering and exhorted the Germans not to press too hard on France. If there were not perfect equality, there could be no collaboration. This was a legitimate argument to use against the oppressor. The marshal made the attitude of France conditional on treatment that Germany was not likely to give. In reality, he was, while not bluntly refusing, cleverly evading collaboration. He produced a long list of German promises which had not been kept. He protested against the exorbitant requisition in France—one third of the provisions, he said, going to feed 500,000 German soldiers, while the forty million French had only two thirds of the provisions. He continued for some time in this strain until, at last, Goering cut him short with the exclamation: "Say, Monsieur le Maréchal, did you win the war, or did we?"

In his New Year's message, in 1942, Pétain infuriated Darlan and the Germans by referring publicly to his "partial exile" and to his "half liberty." The words had a deep significance, which we in France understood. They were a definite disavowal of measures to which he had not freely consented. Darlan demanded that they should be scraped off the disc. The marshal stood firm, and the warning that there was no collaboration but only a German *Diktat* went over the air.

Otto Abetz, the smooth-tongued German ambassador, persuaded Benoist-Méchin that a good approach to Franco-German collaboration might lie in the defense of the French colonies. France was bound by the armistice to keep them for herself and not allow them to be taken by the Gaullists or England. If she surrendered them, if they were seriously menaced, Germany would be entitled to denounce the armistice and act as she pleased in a conquered country. Would it not be better, Abetz insidiously asked, for Germany to lend her assistance to France against possible aggression?

It was reported that a council of ministers sat and decided that there could be no question of war with England, with or without German help. Still, if certain conditions were first fulfilled, such as the release of the French war prisoners, the evacuation of Alsace-Lorraine by the Germans, and a guarantee that Rommel would respect the integrity of Tunisia—then France would see! That is the version which Abetz would have accredited. At the worst, it strikes me, after a long experience with diplomacy, as quite excellent diplomacy, committing France to nothing and posing impossible conditions. But even this version is denied. It is denied that there was such a council meeting, that the problem was ever officially considered.

The marshal had decided that, in no circumstances, would he accept German military help. General Juin, the successor of Weygand in Africa, went to Berlin to discuss the problems raised, and Benoist-Méchin asked for the liberation of General Giraud, then in captivity, for the defense of Tunisia—whether to keep out the British or the Germans, or both, is not clear. We knew that Goering wanted to use Bizerte to supply Rommel; and we knew that, at the same time, orders were given by the French to General Nogues in Morocco, to General Koeltz in Algeria, and to General Barré in Tunisia to oppose the entry of Rommel into their territories. We knew, also, that Goebbels at this time was denouncing Pétain as the veritable inspirer of *attentisme*, in other words of manoeuvring and tricking the Germans by delaying tactics. His view was that the marshal, while not wanting a victory of the Russians, did not want a German victory either, and hoped that the two enemies would exhaust each other. Goebbels discerned better than most persons the policy of Pétain, and that policy was unquestionably the only sound policy for France.

Nor was Hitler eager to cooperate with the French. In

March 1942—the negotiations were dragging—Goebbels asked whether Germany should offer an acceptable peace to France, in order to induce her to abandon her "neutrality" and take an active part in the war again—an active part which could only be envisaged by the Germans as co-operation with them. And he disclosed that Hitler would not hear of it. "France will always be our adversary," he concluded, "and we must eliminate her as a military and political power." In April, Goebbels remarked that, though France might oscillate, there was no hope of a real evolution of sentiment.

Goebbels was a shrewd judge and, with exceptional opportunity for forming my own opinion, I think his reading of the French attitude was one hundred per cent correct. I had never any doubts. It was unthinkable that France—the France of Pétain, or any other France—would ever cast in her lot with the Germans, especially as the policy of waiting had borne fruits. America was in the war, Rommel was in difficulties, and the German advance in Russia was clearly leading Germany to perdition.

There was only one black spot in the picture: the British bombing of the Renault works near Paris excited a storm of indignation against England. Pétain protested, as he could not help doing, but he ordered the immediate and almost secret burial of the victims, without public ceremony, in order to remove any cause of agitation or of prolonged propaganda. For my part, I considered British bombings in France at that stage highly injudicious, quite apart from humanitarian reasons, and I did my best to tell my friends in England that inconsiderate bombing, without military necessity, was a mistaken policy that rendered the task of Pétain more onerous and jeopardized the delicate equilibrium that he was endeavoring to establish while awaiting the moment for action.

13

America Enters

On the 9th of December, 1941, Admiral Leahy announced at Vichy the entry of the United States of America in the war.

The news was startling, but not for me. I remembered the stages by which America had come into the First World War, after many declarations by President Wilson that she would keep out of European quarrels. I have watched history in the making long enough to know that it often does repeat itself—or rather that men repeat the actions of their predecessors. From the beginning, I was certain that, however many times President Roosevelt assured the American people that they would not be drawn into the war, the upshot of it all was inevitable and therefore predictable.

President Roosevelt's "New Deal" administration seemed to be going on the rocks after the summer of 1937. Armament and possible war appeared to be the most likely way to retain tenure and promote the New Deal—a provocative program carefully analyzed by the scholarly American international lawyer and publicist Frederic R. Sanborn in his *Design for War*.

Human wisdom cannot see far ahead: nevertheless, there were not wanting voices on both sides of the Atlantic which were raised in warning against the results of a fight to the finish. The finish of what? Of our civilization? By chance, I came upon the statement of the great English military expert Captain Liddell Hart in June 1940 that a long war must lead to a bad peace: "You may call me a defeatist, but I insist that victory has less to offer than an indecisive war which leads to an agreed peace. The idea of complete and overwhelming victory is the greatest folly on earth: such victories only mean bankruptcy, moral as well as economic." And Wilfred Wellcock, the pacifist writer, said: "It lies in our power to draw the German people from Hitler, should he desire to continue the war in spite of our offer of a satisfactory peace." William Gallacher, in his presidential address to the Co-operative Congress in Glasgow, at Whitsuntide, 1940, stated: "Of one thing I am profoundly convinced—that the Allies should immediately and without equivocation declare their peace aims. Let the world know, let the neutrals and the German people know, that we seek no punitive peace . . . that there is room and a place in the new postwar Europe for 80,000,000 Germans to live in peace and harmony with their fellow Europeans." In other words, he advocated what I, and many others, had advocated for twenty years before the war began, namely, a comprehensive peace conference which would endeavor to settle the more vital matters in dispute in Europe without hostilities.

Particularly did I advocate a comprehensive conference in my little book *War Unless*. . . . In another book, which fell still-born from the press in the fatal month of May 1940, entitled *Peace Through Federation*, I quoted a number of political leaders, some of them now conspicuously in power, who preached the same solution, alas, too late! I will only cite Clement Attlee, later prime minister of England, who said in March 1940: "The biggest fear in the minds of the German people today is that if they desert Hitler they will experience what they experienced after the last war." The objections to any compromise, once the war had begun, were that Hitler would obtain a new lease of life, and another war would occur in a few years. To this, the distinguished member of Parliament, Alfred Salter, replied: "I am sure that if the war continues for two years, and finishes by the economic exhaustion and starvation of Germany, another war is certain within the lifetime of the next generation."

I have recalled these expressions of opinion in England because they had echoes in America. When Sumner Welles made his tour of Europe on a mission of investigation, the American people doubtless hoped to remain aloof from the war or, rather, to exercise their enormous influence and economic strength in the direction of a European agreement. His findings were negative, but for a time they aroused hopes in France that, somehow, Europe would still be spared from a trial of strength. The opportunity of America as arbitrator was unparalleled in history.

Both the peace lovers in Europe and those who felt that nothing should be allowed to stop a conflict which they deemed necessary looked to the United States: the former for an intervention in favor of peace, the latter for the wherewithal to pursue the strife. Strange as it sounds, Europe, or at any rate the Allies, despite Mr. Churchill's boasts, did not possess the wherewithal to pursue the strife. This was possible only with American aid. Nor could Europe make peace without America. The alternatives were clearly placed before Roosevelt: he apparently believed that he could not be neutral.

I had met Roosevelt only once, in the White House, and on this inadequate knowledge (supplemented though it was by conversations with certain leaders of the Democratic Party), I had formed an estimate of his character. I regarded him as a friendly statesman with broad though vacillating views on social justice. It was evident to which side he leaned. He was opposed to any brand of Fascism or Nazism, though his hatred of these chains on the elementary liberties of mankind rather blinded him to the existence of another extreme form of totalitarianism in Russia. At least after June 1941 he appeared to think that Russia had struck out a new path which would eventually lead to greater liberty.

When Churchill, forgetting his own bitter diatribes against Bolshevism, plumped wholeheartedly for Russia as against Germany, dubbing Germany Enemy No. 1, to be smashed at all costs, even at the cost of extending the domain of Bolshevism, he found in Roosevelt his *alter ego*. The two men, one representing the British Empire, which covered the four corners of the world but was now in danger of disintegrating, the other representing a great expanse of compact territory, far more advanced in the practical application of material science than any other nation, understood each other on this point from the outset, although their backgrounds and motives were quite different. One stood for the traditional might of a past in peril; the other, remembering the European origins of America and opposed to European colonialism, stood, at least in his rhetoric, for the triumphant future. I judged Roosevelt to be a unique mixture of emotionalism and political astuteness, a born politician who knew how to manage the masses.

On this, then, Churchill and Roosevelt were agreed, though they were agreed on few others: the immediate aim of smashing Germany. They were willing to set aside everything else in the pursuit of that objective and to let tomorrow take care of itself. How well the morrow took care of itself is clearly seen: the British Empire has crumbled, the continent is politically chaotic outside of Russia, Russia is dominant in the Old World, and we face daily the menace of a third world war.

In France we looked to America to rescue us from Germany's clutches. But how? By force of arms, by economic pressure, or by authoritative mastership imposing a new conception of a united world on the belligerent nations?

After the German attack on Russia, it was argued that America could not defend democracy by fighting for and with Russia, for, if Russia won, the Bolshevisation of Europe would follow. Much as Germany, that is to say Nazism, was detested, it was thought in some American quarters illogical to support Russia, that is to say Bolshevism, which was equally or more detested. The confusion was hardly clarified by those Americans who declared that two totalitarian systems were at war; the unique enemy was totalitarianism, not Nazism, not Bolshevism as such, but totalitarianism in any form. To help Germany against Russia or Russia against Germany was to help totalitarianism. The dilemma compelled many Americans to cry: A plague on both your houses! let them destroy each other! This point of view Senator (later President) Truman set forth with great vigor at the time of Hitler's attack on Russia. Subsequent events have amply proved that this was a far more statesmanlike and farsighted policy than that of Churchill and Roosevelt.

While it is now well known, and General Marshall confirmed it in his final report on the War, that Hitler had not even the most remote plan of attacking the United States, the war party in that country circulated wild stories about German plans to occupy the United States as soon as Western Europe had fallen. President Roosevelt actually talked dimly about Hitler's timetable to invade the Middle West of America via Dakar and South America, even though the distance from Brazil to Iowa is greater than that from Berlin to Iowa. After the fall of the Low Countries and France in 1940, the interventionists gathered added strength in the United States and, from then onward, it was only a matter of time when the United States would enter the conflict. President Roosevelt sent Harry Hopkins to London to assure Churchill of American support in the War. On January 11, 1941, Hopkins told Churchill: "The President is determined that we shall win the war together. Make no mistake about it." Secret Anglo-American staff conferences began in that month and lasted through March. At their end, the American naval commander, Admiral Stark, wrote to his fleet commanders: "The question of our entry into the war now seems to be *when* and not *whether*."

Many of the President's advisers wished to make war on Germany right after France fell; but the noninterventionist sentiment in the United States was overwhelming right down to the day of Pearl Harbor. Further, despite a long list of belligerent acts toward Germany and Italy: shipment of a vast volume of small arms to Britain right after Dunkirk; the stripping of American air defenses to be sent to Britain, Russia and China (which led to the resignation of Secretary of War Woodring); the destroyer-base deal of September 1940; extensive material aid to Britain "short of war" after lend-lease; convoying American and British vessels carrying war materials to Britain (and later Russia); and the order to "shoot on sight" German submarines seeking to sink such vessels, Germany and Italy declined to take up the gage of battle, as Roosevelt and Churchill hoped they would. Hence, the latter had to seek a way into the war through the back door of Japan and the Pacific. It was for this purpose that Churchill and Roosevelt met off the coast of Newfoundland in August 1941. The decision made here led straight to Pearl Harbor; indeed, the road to Pearl Harbor had been decided the month previous by the drastic embargo imposed on Japan.

Four events, especially, heralded the entry of America into the war. The first was the determination, even if it meant war, to aid England to the limit, running through the shipment of arms and airplanes to Britain, the destroyer-base arrangement, lend-lease, and, finally, the decision to escort cargoes across the Atlantic and place the supply of material to England under American protection. The American policy reminded me of a boxer holding out his chin. Sooner or later it would be hit—unless Germany abandoned her attacks on shipping and left the Atlantic free. The second was the signing of the Atlantic Charter, ostensibly setting forth their common aims for a better postwar world by Churchill and Roosevelt on the 14th of August, 1941. The third was the virtual blockade of Japan. The fourth premonitory sign was the intensive preparation of North Africa by the government of Vichy to receive American troops.

No one who followed events intelligently could be mistaken as to the meaning of these preliminaries. The Churchill-Roosevelt interview on board a battleship "somewhere in the Atlantic" was a curious meeting between the prime minister of a belligerent country and the president of a country as yet nonbelligerent. Judging it from the French viewpoint, in spite of its theatrical setting, it fell singularly flat. The Charter did not produce the impression in Europe that it might have done had it been couched in more vigorous terms. It struck one as a perfunctory piece of work. It had not the power of Wilson's Fourteen Points which so largely contributed to Germany's collapse in 1918.

The Charter, which it is cynically and dolorously interesting to read today, expressed hope for a better future for the world by the conjunction of the national policies of England and America. It did not favor any territorial changes unless they were in accord with the will of the interested peoples freely expressed.

This pious hope has not been achieved, since a large part of Germany has been taken by Poland, and a large part of Poland has been taken by Russia, and all the Baltic states have become Russian, and considerable tracts in the Balkans have gone to Russia, and the whole of the new Poland, and half of Germany, and the whole of the Balkans are under

Russian control, without any consultation of the interested peoples, not to mention the Near East where new states have been created and old ones extended, or the Far East where the expansion of Bolshevism has become formidable, if not overwhelming.

The right of peoples to choose their own form of government was proclaimed—and on the nonfulfillment of this desideratum since 1944 it would be superfluous for me to comment.

As for the participation of all states, large and small, victor or vanquished, on a basis of equality, in the pool of raw materials which they need for their economic prosperity, it remains to be conceded. The same remark applies to the promise of international collaboration, in order to assure for all better conditions of work, of economic progress, and of social security.

After the "final destruction of Nazi tyranny," peace was to be established, and all nations were to live in safety, freed at last from want and fear. Alas, nine years after the defeat of Nazism, freedom from fear or want has not yet come to a world in which peace has never been so precarious, fear so prevalent, and want so widespread, and in which imprisonment, deportation, slavery, and death are the penalties for deviation from official opinion.

There is, of course, a clause about the freedom of the seas. And, finally, the employment of force is deprecated, and the general disarmament of nations is advocated. The crushing burden of armaments, said the Charter, is to be lifted from the shoulders of the peace-loving nations. Unhappily the burden of armaments is now vastly heavier than ever, and weapons whose destructive power exceeds anything we imagined in the wildest nightmare before 1941 are being prepared in feverish haste.

Far be it from me to repudiate these amiable sentiments: the Charter, destined to furnish a moral basis for the war, is unexceptionable, but it furnishes a striking example of the vanity of human wishes and of the hypocrisy of official propaganda.

As for the negotiations with Japan, conducted mainly by Secretary Cordell Hull until July 1941, it was plainly to be seen that they would fail. I have often reflected regretfully that Japan had been a valued ally in the First World War and that, with her demolition, the last barrier to Bolshevism disappeared in the East. England had long preserved friendship with Japan, realizing that she was the only efficient country of the Orient; but Japan was tempted to expand at the expense of China, and certain factions in America were incensed at her war of conquest in a disrupted country. Secretary of State Henry L. Stimson wished to impose sanctions and, perhaps, war on Japan in 1932, but he was sternly restrained by President Hoover, a firm friend of peace. President Roosevelt was a romantic but ardent partisan of China because, as he frankly admitted, his ancestors had enriched themselves through trade with the Chinese a generation earlier. The League of Nations was powerless, and I saw Japan walk out of the League rather than be censured.

Now, in 1941, the United States demanded the withdrawal of Japan from China; Japanese ships were seized; the Panama Canal was closed to Japan; petrol and war materials were refused. American diplomacy was in an impasse; Japan could not retreat without loss of prestige. Japan's efforts to reach a diplomatic settlement, including extensive concessions in the Far East and a meeting between Premier Konoye and President Roosevelt, were rejected by Secretary Hull, with Roosevelt's approval. The peril loomed darkly but, nevertheless, the American ships in Pearl Harbor were surprised by an attack from the air on December 7, 1941.

It is not my business here to inquire where the blame lies for the disaster of Pearl Harbor, where six of the largest American warships were sunk or disabled, besides a number of cruisers and destroyers. The matter has been handled most completely and accurately by the American writer, George Morgenstern, in his *Pearl Harbor: The Story of the Secret War,* the conclusions of which were later confirmed by the greatest American historian of the time, Charles Austin Beard, in his *President Roosevelt and the Coming of the War, 1941.* All America was aroused. It was now a fight to the finish. England, in her turn, immediately declared war on Japan. Germany and Italy declared war on the United States. The European war had become, almost overnight, a world war.

We in France were intensely interested spectators. We could be no more; but we were vividly conscious that, at last, there was some real prospect for the deliverance of France. We had maintained our faith, we had entertained hopes, but these had hitherto not been based on realities. When England stood alone against Germany, even though America sent arms, there was no solid reason to expect a German defeat. It is foolish to suggest that De Gaulle and his adherents, few in number and totally dependent on England, changed the odds in the slightest degree. The resistance of Russia, after the first huge defeats, was gradually stiffening but, as yet, no sensible gambler, looking on with a cool eye, would have risked his money on a Russian victory over Germany. Now, however, with America committed to the fight, the balance was tipped against Germany. The whole outlook changed.

The position before Pearl Harbor was: on one side England, with insufficient troops, material, and money, with shipping that was barely able to maintain a regular supply of necessities, and Russia with inexhaustible man power but in retreat; on the other side an apparently invincible Germany, armed as no other nation was armed, her prestige unshaken, though she had not won either in the steppes of Russia or on the sands of Africa, supported by a feeble Italy, a handicap but not an enemy. Had the position been stabilized on those lines, the prospect would not have been encouraging.

The new line-up of forces completely transformed the situation. America might take years to develop her full strength, but it was certain that, in the end, she would be more than a match for Germany, on account of her greater population and her incomparably greater industrial potential. Japan, in some measure, counterbalanced the American effort, but still the margin in favor of the Allies was considerable and would rapidly grow larger. If the year 1942 continued to show the immense might of Germany, from the hour of Japan's fatal move the final result could hardly be in doubt. The war might be long, but its issue was now all but certain.

So thought all Frenchmen whose passions did not warp their judgment. Until 1942, they might well be excused for their scepticism; but after that year those who could not or would not read the writing on the wall were men who were blinded by their political convictions or commitments.

There were some who were so blinded. The principal fault of the French is their love of politics. It has always been so, since the Romans noted their incorrigible lack of discipline, their tendency to wrangling, their hopeless divisions. The recent history of France is the history of a nation in which the sense of national unity has only at rare intervals prevailed over partisanship. Often France has been saved from total ruin only by a last-minute rally round a Providential Man. The great Revolution, in which, with Europe menacing them, the French were busily engaged in cutting off one another's heads until Napoleon came along to impose his authority on the rival clans, is the outstanding illustration of the French temperament, and the whole of the nineteenth century, with its repeated overthrow of monarchs, its oscillations from right to left, its record of violent revolutions and counterrevolutions, emphasizes the salient trait of French restlessness. In 1870, the débâcle culminated in civil war under the sardonic eyes of the Prussians. Only a minority of the presidents of the Third Republic retired unscathed at the end of their term of office. Ministers come and go with lightning speed. Governments rarely last for more than six months. The number of parties or splinters of parties I have seen in my time is almost incalculable. Outside Parliament, there was always a challenge to the existing régime, from Boulangists or followers of De La Roque, or Doriotists, or Monarchists, or Communists; and De Gaulle has been denounced by the Fourth Republic as the leader of a faction.

Whether the aged Pétain was the right man to choose in the hour of anguish in 1940 may be questioned but he did offer some promise of union—*Union Sacrée,* as we said in 1914. By 1942, the union was broken. Apart from the diversion fostered by the *émigrés,* there were in Vichy a score of organizations, living on the secret funds which are a bad feature of French public life, each pursuing its own end; anti-Semitic, anti-Masonic, anti-this and anti-that, organizations for one thing or another, all of them sectarian, none of them frankly and comprehensively French. At Paris, the numerous cliques and clans could hardly be counted. Some of them were for collaboration, others against, but there was always a struggle inside each association, and often it was impossible to tell on which side they were, or whether they were on both sides at the same time. As in all countries where parties pullulate, there were a number of police groups which competed with each other and opposed each other. What was true of France under the occupation was true, both in respect of parties and police, of France before the war, as it is true of France after the Liberation.

It becomes increasingly difficult for me, from 1942 onward, to speak of French opinion as though it were a bloc. Therefore, when I state that the assurance of American intervention was received with joy in France, and that the end of the Hitlerian domination of Europe was foreseen, it must be understood with the important reservation that a variety of groups did not share the general joy. Both on the extreme left and on the extreme right, the prospect of an American domination of Europe was regarded as a misfortune.

For the Communists, the distrust of America is sufficiently explained by their fanatical support of Russian imperialism, menaced by American participation in the war. Already, looking beyond the American war with Germany, they sensed the coming struggle between America and Russia, and while accepting American aid, since it was necessary, they minimized America and represented Russia as the sole effective fighter in the field against Nazism.

The reluctance of the ultra-conservatives to see America triumphant in Europe was based on a fear lest American civilization which is, after all, very different from the traditional culture of Europe, should completely change the European mentality. It may be thought odd that, even before the protagonists had taken their respective stands, before the issue was joined, Frenchmen should discuss a future which was yet undefined. That is, however, in keeping with the French liking for abstract debate. France was, at one and the same time, both inside and outside the war. By a peculiar psychological twist, she employed her leisure, forgetting her immediate plight, to indulge in ardent polemics. Assuming that, eventually, Germany would succumb, there would be left, face to face, two great powers, and two only—the United States and Russia. Could two great powers live in the same world without engaging in a struggle for the supreme mastery?

Long before Marshal Smuts delivered his amazing speech to the British Parliament (at the end of the following year), I listened to much talk on its main thesis. The speech was prophetic, and it crystallized what was passing in many

French minds. But what may be properly said in private is not always fit for publication, and that Smuts should have forecast the future as he saw it to the British—and to the world, for his discourse was given the widest publicity in France and in most European countries—was extraordinary. He announced that the defeat of Germany would leave America and Russia confronting each other. Besides these two *colossi*, other nations would pale into insignificance. England would be permanently enfeebled. France would be extinguished as a great power. Italy would not exist as an international force. Germany would never recover. A gloomy picture for Europe! What was the purpose of the South African prime minister—who had become a minister of the British Empire—in speaking so frankly? Did he not mean to issue a solemn warning against pushing the war to an inexorable conclusion?

The death sentence passed on France was bitterly resented by the Pétainists. The Gaullists were equally perturbed. The pro-Germans were hostile. Pétainists, Gaullists, and Hitlerites were equally touched. What was the use of striving, if France, if Europe, were doomed? England, who had won the admiration of most of the French, was condemned to be a little island in the North Sea, with an empire which would detach itself or treat the mother country as a minor member of the Commonwealth. Europe was a small peninsula of the immense Asiatic continent, without independent life. No wonder that many of the French shrank with horror from the prophecy of a world in which only the two giants of America and Russia would count. No wonder that they rejected either the American solution or the Russian solution. No wonder that, today, when the alarming vision of Smuts is far too completely realized, the alternative solutions are viewed with misgiving.

And yet, Smuts was merely saying what Frenchmen were saying more than a year before he made his ominous and disturbing address. We were witnessing the virtual disappearance of small nations, for which we had pleaded since 1914; we were told that material success was in practice more important than spiritual influence. Such realism, however justified by the facts, ran counter to all our ideals.

The twentieth century has been a profound and tragic deception, richer in promises than its predecessors, poorer in performance outside of scientific and mechanical marvels. No other century has seen such sufferings, has heaped up such mountains of dead. Poverty and famine reign in the midst of potential abundance. Hatred of war has produced the most devastating of wars. We are entering a period of "perpetual war for perpetual peace!"

A tremendous world revolution is in progress, wrote Henry R. Luce, announcing that America's Century was opening, in an article in *Life,* which was given great publicity in France, and if it is to bring good and not evil, said he, we must remember that the two billion and more human beings who people the globe are indivisible. Are they? They seem to be splitting up into irreconcilable enemies. Modern wars will be fatal to the species, he declared, and must, therefore, cease. But will they? There's the rub. For the first time, all the material needs of the entire human family can be satisfied. Possibly, but never have so many people lived in utter misery. If the world is to be saved, Mr. Luce continued, America must make it her business to introduce a new order. America alone can cure the divisions of an indivisible world, can transform the horrors of war into a horror of war, can organize the nourishment of the human family.

Unhappily, Russia claims the right and professes the ability, to fulfill the same purpose.

I was perturbed by Mr. Luce's omission of the growth and the ambitions of Russia. I doubted whether the American pattern of life could be applied to Europe. England was content to yield the lead to America: Churchill spoke of himself modestly as the lieutenant of Roosevelt. Later, the Marshall Plan supplemented America's leadership. But it seemed to me, as to my friends who knew both Europe and America, that each country of Europe not only could but should be encouraged to keep its specific character, its individual genius. European civilization was old, it was too traditionalist; it required a transfusion of blood. There should be the fullest collaboration between two continents which I once described as the two wings of the world. Nevertheless, just as Europe would not willingly accept the German or the Russian pattern of life, so it seemed to me that Europe would not accept the American pattern, which was excellent in America but not as suitable in other conditions.

For thousands of years there have been inconclusive discussions and alternating experiences in the matter of government, and it is improbable that the true, final, and universal solution of the problem of ruling men has been found by the United States. From Aristotle to Emerson, from Shakespeare to Carlyle, there have always been political thinkers who believe that all human progress is inspired, not by the masses but by Great Men-Heroes, as Carlyle called them; and, in practice, America, like England, owes her position to her renowned leaders in all branches of activity. It was not in consonance with the teachings of history and of our own observations to seek to standardize nations or to dogmatize about ideas which have only a provisional and conditional value.

So, in the absence of other than intellectual occupations, did I and my friends talk—and write, for I maintained a correspondence with some of the leading thinkers of Europe—when it was evident that the entry of America into the war meant that Europe would be rid of Nazism. We considered that, after many centuries of vain strife, of dismal oppression, of immemorial wrongs, of the misuse of riches, of unspeakable poverty, of governmental tyranny, the hope of the world was that the century should be neither America's

Marshal Pétain during his trial (July-August, 1945). *(Keystone.)*

Marshal Pétain shaking hands with Admiral Leahy. *(Keystone.)*

Marshal Pétain at Nancy, May 26, 1944. *(Courtesy Commandant Tracon.)*

Marshal Pétain's fortress cell. It was destroyed after his death. *(Rendering by André Bonne.)*

The island fortress. *(Véritable.)*

Marshal Pétain, 94, conversing with a guardian
in the courtyard of the fortress.

Seat of government: Hotel du Parc, Vichy. *(France-Reportage.)*

Liberation at Montereau, August 25, 1944. Women who consorted with the Germans had their heads shaved. *(Keystone.)*

Liberation at Bordeaux, August 27, 1944. Some friends of the Germans were marched naked through the streets. *(Rivarol.)*

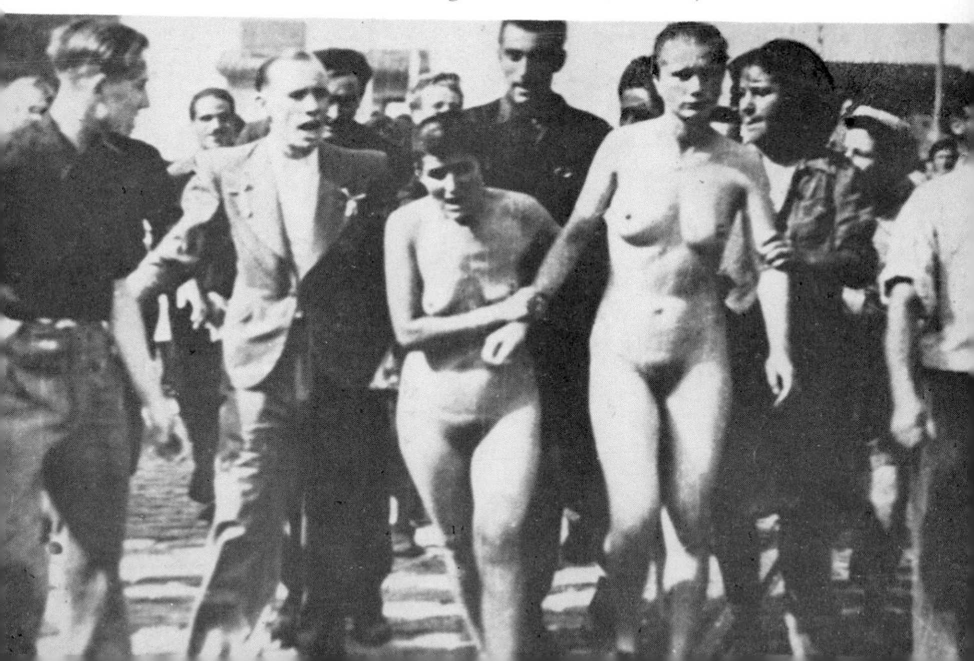

Marshal Pétain alighting from prison car. *(Keystone.)*

Century, nor Russia's Century, but Mankind's Century.

Two giant sovereignties—Russian and American—might not be able to exist side by side, without another war. Two vast sovereignties were, perhaps, more dangerous than twenty or forty. It was not only after the war, but in the midst of the war, that the peril of a new rivalry, after the defeat of Germany, was apparent to anyone who reflected. Not America's, not Russia's, but Mankind's Century, if a third world war was to be averted.

14

Tragedy of Errors—North Africa

The story of the landing of the Americans in North Africa and the subsequent events has been told by many of the participants, French and American. My function is to record the impression it produced in France. I was particularly well informed of the reactions of Vichy, for a friend who maintained close personal contacts with the marshal himself visited me in the thick of the operations. As sometimes happens in the course of my narrative, I am obliged to designate him by an initial, M. Although I know his sentiments, bitterly anti-German, and although he was never compromised in what is loosely called "collaboration," he has deemed it prudent, since the Liberation, not to advertise his relations with the marshal. He would not deny them, but in the atmosphere of terror that later descended on France, he, like many others, some of them occupying high posts today, prefers to remain silent.

The landing in North Africa (November 8, 1942) was a tragedy of errors. It succeeded because everybody, Germans,

French, English, Gaullists, Giraudists, Pétainists, were at one moment or another duped but, on the whole, the Germans were the principal dupes of the "Torch" operations. Had Vichy been let into the secret of the exact date and the precise importance of the operation, misunderstandings would have been avoided, and regrettable incidents which had later repercussions would not have occurred.

Yet the conversations of Admiral Leahy with Pétain, the Weygand-Murphy pact, the multiplication of American vice-consuls in North Africa, and the timely escape of Giraud, the French general who had been designated by the Americans as the leader of the French troops in Africa, were facts publicly known, and a little more confidence in the discretion of Vichy would have averted days of confusion, of contradictory orders and counterorders.

Doubtless the return of Laval to Vichy aroused the legitimate suspicions of Eisenhower. Yet the truth about his return is simple. Pétain had threatened to resign rather than take him back. He described Laval as a "dunghill." Goering, who seems to have been sympathetic to Laval and highly resentful of the "duplicity" of the marshal, counseled the Auvergnat to refuse to return.

Laval's motives were complex. He cast himself in the rôle of lightning conductor. He was a sort of halfway house between a *Gauleiter* or a Quisling and the marshal. The Germans, in general, were well disposed toward him, and he believed that by *finesse* he could render service to France. As for Pétain, disappointed in Darlan, realizing that he was *persona non grata,* feeling that Laval might ward off the worst, he finally yielded to the pressure put upon him and, persuaded that expediency called for the cooperation of the man he had sacked unceremoniously eighteen months before, admitted Laval once more into his cabinet. He retained Darlan as Dauphin, and gave him the post of commander-in-chief.

The chief concern of the American authorities was to exclude De Gaulle from the African scene. They realized that the feeling in North Africa was anti-German, but equally anti-English. The memory of Mers-el-Kebir still rankled. De Gaulle was regarded as a British agent, who had led the British into Syria and had pitted Frenchmen against Frenchmen. The military men in North Africa were especially anti-Gaullist. As disciplined soldiers, they had obeyed the orders of Pétain at the armistice. If De Gaulle was right, then they were wrong. In short, North Africa, which asked nothing better than the opportunity to revenge itself on the Germans, was essentially Pétainist, and the association of De Gaulle with the American enterprise might have fatal results. Churchill acquiesced in this reasoning, and considered it prudent to leave matters in the hands of the Americans.

General Giraud was the man for the Americans, not De Gaulle. Giraud was a brave soldier, though of limited intelligence. He was surrounded by a halo of glory. A few months before, he had, thanks to the connivance of certain elements at Vichy, broken through his prison bars in the fortress of Königstein. Making his way through Switzerland, he had reached Vichy, where the marshal received him and expressed his pleasure. The Germans demanded his instant surrender, alleging that he had violated his word of honor. Giraud replied that he had declined to give his word, and was, therefore, free to escape. The marshal supported him, and Giraud was installed in the Midi of France, out of the reach of the occupying troops. Having listened to the marshal, who explained his policy, Giraud wrote a letter which was published, affirming that he was fully in accord with Pétain. He was, therefore, a marshalite and, as such, would be welcomed in North African circles. Later tergiversations, concealments, lapses of memory, cannot alter the fact that it was in the capacity of the marshal's man that Giraud was chosen, in opposition to De Gaulle, to represent France in North Africa. He, too, was a dupe. He expected to be nominated commander-in-chief, pointing out that, if the Americans came under his orders, they would be guests of the French in North Africa, whereas, if they came under an American commander, they would be invaders. The Americans did not see it in the same light. The position of Giraud was that of a subordinate.

I received the news that he had left the little coast town of Bandol, at night, in a submarine, from a man who, by accident, witnessed his secret departure. It was good tactics, to say the least, for Vichy to express surprise and indignation. Giraud was even now not completely informed of American plans. He thought that the operation was timed for the spring of the following year, and he lost valuable days in discussing his own status.

In the meantime, Darlan unexpectedly came on the scene. He was, it must be remembered, the commander-in-chief of the French forces. He was the Dauphin. He directly, and without dispute, represented the marshal. He had precedence over Giraud and, whatever his reputation might be as an opportunist, it was with him, when his presence in North Africa was known, that the Americans had to negotiate the conditions of the landing. Was his appearance in Algiers purely fortuitous? Did he go in expectation of the American move? It is certain that his son was lying in Algiers gravely ill, and that his visit was represented as purely personal. It could not, however, have been better timed, and everyone to whom I spoke refused to admit that the long arm of coincidence could stretch so far, and affirmed that Darlan and the marshal must have had some inkling of what was to happen. On the other hand, the theory that Darlan was sent expressly by the marshal, availing himself of his son's illness to lend an unofficial color to his journey, is rather discounted by the obvious confusion that prevailed for several days at Vichy, which was not sure whether the American landing was imminent.

There was some excuse for the perplexity of Vichy. The policy of the marshal, made clear on many occasions, was to stay in his post as long as it was possible to avoid a break with the Germans. The denunciation of the armistice, either by the French or the Germans, would provoke reprisals and would create fresh difficulties for the French. To renounce the advantages France enjoyed over other defeated countries without a government, unless for a substantial cause, would be folly.

In August of the same year (1942) the English had made a feint at Dieppe. They came in insufficient strength to effect a landing, and were quickly driven away. Now there were many Frenchmen who, in their enthusiasm, believing that at last the hour of liberation had struck, were ready to cast everything to the winds and rise in revolt. Vichy, better informed, warned them against premature action. Had the marshal light-heartedly welcomed the abortive attempt, he would indeed have been blameworthy. He would have thrown away the substance for the shadow. He would have exposed himself and the nation without the smallest profit. His policy would have been shattered on a mere impulse. He was, in my opinion, wiser. Now, I have always considered the Dieppe feint as unfortunate, in that it induced Pétain to exercise excessive caution. Was the North African landing a repetition of Dieppe? If so, it would be fatuous for France to show her hand. If it was serious, if the Americans came in numbers, then (as Weygand had said) they should be afforded every facility, if possible without openly breaking the armistice. In any case, Vichy could not publicly issue definite orders in contradiction to those which formed part of the bargain with the Germans—i.e., to defend French overseas territories against all comers by their own forces, without which the Germans would take their place—and in contradiction to the agreement reached with the Anglo-Saxons, unless France was prepared to take the consequences.

After the calm reflection which the subject deserves, I hold that the policy of Vichy was perfectly sound, though whether it was well executed is another matter. There was a period of uncertainty, in which Vichy publicly cabled to Darlan to defend North Africa and secretly ordered him to exercise his judgment as the man on the spot. In the meantime, the generals in Africa were at loggerheads. Juin raised objections to Darlan. One general gave the order to resist, another to greet the Americans, and the muddle was worsened by a hitch in the American plans which delayed the arrival of the army.

The "double game" of Vichy—I mean of that part of Vichy which was favorable to the Anglo-Americans—could be justified, had it been conducted with skill. Unfortunately, it was far from skillful. It made confusion worse confounded. Darlan made use of his secret code to tell Admiral Auphan that the American convoys were on their way to Malta, and the Germans were again deceived. Not for long. They soon called on France to defend herself, on pain of their own intervention. Laval was for yielding to the German demands for air bases in Tunisia. Admiral Esteva, Admiral Darrien, and General Barré were opposed to the German invasion in different degrees, but were unable to make up their minds, divided as they were on the true meaning of contradictory orders from Algiers, where Darlan finally launched the order to cease fire on all fronts, and from Vichy. Darlan, himself, was hesitant, and hardly knew which way to turn. At one minute, heaven knows under what pressure, Pétain disavowed Darlan, and the next disavowed his disavowal. Weygand was by far the most energetic of the marshal's advisers; he would have torn up the armistice, sent the remnants of the French army to the mountains, and ordered the fleet to set sail from Toulon. His influence was altogether good, but the influence of Laval was detestable. Laval flew to Berchtesgaden and threatened to resign if Pétain did not comply with a German ultimatum. The old man appeared to yield to the threat, but sent another message to Darlan, supporting him in his agreement with the Americans.

I had the impression that, in this critical moment, the marshal was little more than a puppet in the hands of two men who represented two sides of his policy—Weygand and Laval. When General von Rundstedt announced at Vichy the occupation of the whole of France, Pétain, at the suggestion of Weygand, issued a note of protest against the violation of the armistice. Laval stopped its transmission by radio. Weygand was arrested and deported by the Germans.

Judging from the accounts of what happened at Vichy, I cannot but conclude that the marshal, too old to cope with a situation of which he was inadequately informed, fearing that a false move would have fatal results for France, lost his assurance, and was tossed first in one direction and then in another by his entourage. The more I think that his general policy was justified, the more I believe it was dreadfully bungled in those crucial hours of November 1942. A younger man than he would have been perplexed. Much of his perplexity might have been avoided had he been fully aware of the American plans, and it was a pity that he was not completely in the confidence of the American authorities. He was taken by surprise (as were the Germans), but Darlan was the custodian of his "intimate thoughts," and his "intimate thoughts" were unquestionably favorable to any intervention which promised liberation from the German yoke. How could they have any other sense?

Having established the main points of the North African story, with my friend M., I said: "In your opinion when, in the multiplicity of messages, was the marshal sincere?"

"There is no question," he answered. "When he delegated his powers to Darlan to negotiate with the Americans and to cease fire. All the rest was flummery, meant to deceive the Germans."

"Naturally. When there are public statements and private instructions, where must you look for the real orders but in the private instructions? No sensible officer could hesitate for a moment."

"Unfortunately, there were officers who preferred the public pronouncements, or who doubted, or who acted on old standing orders. Could not more pains have been taken to enlighten them?"

"I am sorry for those who did not understand. At Vichy, there were divided counsels, inaccurate reports, threats, ultimatums. Laval certainly was opposed to the surrender of Morocco and Algeria to the Anglo-Americans, fearing the anger of the Germans. Weygand was all for defiance. The marshal was not personally responsible for some of the misleading messages. Remember that, although he is sound in body and in mind, he has spells of weariness, of lethargy, natural at his age. But the chief points are that his sympathy for the Americans was well known, that Darlan, whether by accident or design, was on the spot, and that he was acquainted with the policy to be followed in case of a landing —to repel it if it was only a commando gesture, to welcome it if it was made in force. Darlan did not know at the beginning: when he had ascertained the facts, he acted as might have been expected, he ordered the cessation of fire in the name of the marshal. He had the marshal's approval in secret messages. The marshal, in semi-liberty, had still a rôle to play. But only the name of the marshal, who was venerated in North Africa, could help the Americans."

"Why did not the Americans consult Pétain privately? All the confusion sprang from that omission."

"Such is my view. But Vichy was a nest of espionage. The Americans distrusted Darlan as they distrusted Laval."

"Yet, Eisenhower personally accepted Darlan as the deputy of the marshal, armed with full powers?"

"The Americans could not do otherwise. They had not expected to find Darlan. They had reckoned on Giraud. Giraud wasted time in pourparlers as to his exact rank and arrived to find Darlan already installed in Algiers."

"I believe that in France there is an overwhelming majority for the marshal, that he is supported by public opinion, as in North Africa. But now men wonder why he did not leave Vichy and fly to Algiers to take command himself."

"That is a fair estimate of public opinion. If the marshal had considered his own reputation, as did nearly everybody else, he would have gained glory by placing himself at the disposal of the Americans. That was the easiest and most spectacular course. But the marshal does not choose the easy way. Nothing could have served him personally half as well as flight. De Gaulle, Giraud, Darlan would hardly have existed without the marshal. But, whether he is right or wrong, the marshal has—shall I say?—old-fashioned ideas of Duty, of Self-Sacrifice, of Service; and he believed that he could still offer some protection to the people by staying in Vichy, by interposing his person between the Germans and the French. He knew that he could crown his career, become a world hero, by deserting the French people. He thought only of the dreadful reprisals that the Germans would take if he went and if the French, in the exaltation of a rash and futile heroism, tried to fight the Germans without arms and without organization. An airplane was at his disposal. He had only to give the word, and his person and his prestige were assured, but the French people would have been butchered or deported. Surely, he has never done anything nobler than to stay."

I record this conversation with my friend M., in my room in Monaco overlooking the Mediterranean, with Africa somewhere in the distance across the blue expanse of peaceful waters. I was satisfied that, whatever mistakes had been made by most of the participants in the drama of North Africa, the marshal had kept his promise to the English "to place the empire in the war" when the time was ripe. My admiration for him was not lessened: on the contrary, his decision to rest with the French in France, so worldly-foolish, raised him to greater heights in my esteem.

Perhaps he was wrong: the question can be discussed from many sides; but of the purity of his purpose there can be no doubt in the mind of anyone who is capable of appreciating the generosity of a fine nature.

Although I wish to confine myself to personal observations, I ought to quote at this point Martin du Gard (*La Chronique de Vichy*) to whom the marshal explained in more detail the reasons for his refusal to leave France: "It would have been cowardly to go. An aviator was ready to take me up. Weygand implored me to escape. What would have befallen you all if I had gone? Look what the Germans have already done to the Maquis. And what of the prisoners' camps in Germany? The reprisals would have been atrocious. In remaining, I stopped them from doing certain things. I prevented the application of measures against the refugees from Alsace-Lorraine, against the Jews, against the Communists. The Jews would all have been massacred, all, as in Poland. I said, once for all, when the roof fell on our heads, that I would not quit the metropolitan country. I thought that all that I am, all that I represent, all that I stand for in the eyes of the enemy, should serve to protect our poor people. I have given my word to the French and I stick to it."

At the outset of the war I had written in a review that it would be won or lost in Africa. Now to the long campaign in Libya, Cyrenaica, Egypt, from Tunisia to the Nile, across the endless wastes of desert, was added the American occupation of Morocco and Algeria. In a few words let me trace the broad lines of the to-and-fro conflict which the Italians could not sustain and the Germans considered secondary in importance. Marshal Graziani quickly discovered that the question of supplies was one which the Italian navy, afraid to expose itself to combat and beaten when it was forced to fight, did not help him to solve. When Wavell, with few troops, had chased the Italians, he encountered the same difficulties. In February 1941 Rommel with his picked Afrika Korps came on the scene and pushed back the British to the gates of Alexandria. The British, under the command of Cunningham, drove back Rommel. The German general returned to the attack and reached El Alamein. Rommel promised to take Alexandria, and Hitler believed that the objective would be attained. The gallant defense of Auchinleck held firm. Then the Germans found their greatest adversary—Montgomery—who, with a thousand tanks, counterattacked. Rommel, who had been temporarily absent, returned to a desperate situation. Inadequately supplied by Hitler, he tried to disengage himself, to effect a rapid retreat, but he could not stem the tide and, by the end of November 1942, when the Americans were disembarking in the French African ports, the Germans were on the borders of Tunisia, 1,400 miles from El Alamein. The French General, Leclerc, moving swiftly from Tchad, joined his forces with the British, declaring that he would stop only at the Rhine.

The Germans then had urgent need of a foothold in Tunisia. It would have been better, much misunderstanding might have been saved for the French in Tunisia, had the American army entered Tunisia without delay. But they were still wrestling in Algeria with the rivalries of French generals. Giraud, finding himself supplanted by Darlan, was discontented. Darlan, with Juin and Noguès, looked on Giraud as usurping their authority. Everybody was freely using the name of the marshal, and the marshal was repudiating them more or less openly, no doubt bewildered by the rival claims. Governor Boisson, of Dakar, who had driven off De Gaulle in 1940, rallied to Darlan. It is impossible for me to exaggerate the loyalty of the African countries to Pétain, and when the Americans reconciled Darlan and Giraud by giving one political and the other military command, Giraud in his proclamation called for the liberation of the marshal, the prisoner of the Germans, together with the liberation of France. The Gaullists in North Africa were certainly inconspicuous at this stage.

In France, most of us cherished the illusion that, with the landing in Africa (not its liberation, for it was never occupied or controlled by the Germans), France herself would soon be freed. One of my most vivid memories is the joy that was depicted on every countenance. It was not an acceptance of Gaullism. Had the African expedition been a Gaullist expedition, it would not have provoked jubilation. We were puzzled by the variations in the statements of Vichy, but most of us did not care to analyze our conviction that, somehow, Pétain had rendered possible the landing and the liberation that was to follow immediately. We should have preferred to hear that the marshal had abandoned all disguise, that he had gone to Algiers. Still, we trusted him and looked for huge stocks of white bread and cigarettes brought by the Americans. One of the French generals, since promoted to the highest rank, the late De Lattre de Tassigny, was as badly misinformed as the public. He too was convinced that, from Africa, the troops would leap into southern France and, with about fifty men and two cannons, he took to the field. His exploit ended when he saw, instead of American troops, the first incursion of German troops in the southern zone. There was nothing for De Lattre de Tassigny to do but surrender. He was nominally condemned by a French court and was comfortably lodged by Vichy until his escape could be arranged.

The occupation of southern France by the Germans brought changes. The problem of eating grew steadily worse and could only be solved by having recourse to the black market. In one important respect the occupation of the free zone—where Marshal Pétain, from July 1940 to December 1942, had taken vigorous action against German spies, at least a hundred being condemned to death by the French Military Tribunals—was unfortunate. It has not been sufficiently brought to light that, long before the Maquis, long before the Resistance (in the special sense in which the word is now used) came into being, there was a clandestine resistance organized with the approval and help of the marshal in the southern zone.

It is incomprehensible to me that a secret which I shared and was known to many thousands of men in a greater or lesser degree (for naturally each section was, as far as possible, kept in ignorance of what was happening in other sections) was not cried from the housetops when the Allies arrived in France, and the consent and encouragement of the marshal in the formation of the fighting forces of France openly proclaimed. I can only suppose that others who could shout louder were resolved on taking all the credit of a movement which was begun by Pétain and that, in the face of intensive propaganda, and at last of terrorism, the truth was hidden.

Yet it can now be revealed that, as early as September 1940, a confidential note by General Colson, then war minister, called for the development of armed forces in France, of which a nucleus had been left by the convention of the armistice. All Frenchmen in the southern zone over twenty years of age were to be organized as far as was compatible with secrecy. For this movement no public propaganda could be used. It was condemned to silence. I venture to affirm that a good deal of useful work was then quietly performed.

The Legion, it is true, turned out badly: it was too numerous, and it degenerated, on the one hand, into ineffective friendly associations and, on the other hand, into the Militia, whose purpose was to put down the disorder engendered by exceptional conditions which enabled criminal groups to identify themselves with genuine Resistants. The Militia, though in part composed of misguided patriots, could not, in the nature of things, make the distinction between criminal activities and real resistance—sometimes inextricably entwined—and soon took the color of an anti-resistance organization.

The *Chantiers de Jeunesse* (Labor Camps) were of a different character. They were intended to enroll and train the youth of the country for military purposes. I had some contacts with the young men, who were aware of their rôle and were full of zeal. In the end, many of them went into the Maquis, but the original impulse came from Vichy.

The secret army, properly so called, was different from either of these movements. It could not operate in daylight; the essential condition of its existence was clandestinity. The word was afterward employed as though it belonged exclusively to anti-Pétain groups but, in reality, it applies far more particularly to the secret army of Vichy. The first task was to discover the reservists, form them into new groups, and enable them to meet without arousing the suspicions of the enemy. From eight divisions it grew, toward the end of 1941, into 24, lightly armed. The chief aims were to maintain the framework of an army, to collect and hide arms and munitions, and to keep up a fighting spirit. General Huntziger, especially, aided the mobilization which had to be effected without publicity. Credits were freely accorded. General Lacaille has testified that the armistice was systematically violated by the collecting of weapons. Under General Picquedon, considerable war material was recovered, repaired, placed in hiding, and distributed, in spite of the vigilance of the German Armistice Commission. It is estimated that arms and munitions to the value of 18 billions of francs, a large sum in those days, were safely camouflaged. There were, besides, large quantities of provisions, raw materials, supplies for sanitary services stowed away. The police, the gendarmerie, transport services, financial departments, with the assurance that the marshal was informed and gave his blessing, helped in the preparations. Heavy artillery was lacking, but *mitrailleuses*, hand grenades, and antitank weapons were made and, in underground factories, armored cars were in process of manufacture. Such an army could only be used as an auxiliary: to engage in unsupported combat with the powerful German forces would be suicide and the repression would be terrible. Officers of the former air force were acting as agents of liaison: they had their secret radio posts and they transmitted a good deal of news to England. All this was being done, be it remembered, before the Gaullist Resistance had attained significant proportions, and some of those who were engaged regret bitterly that the Anglo-Americans did not land in France until eighteen to twenty months after the organization was ready. It would, had the invasion come earlier, have given great help, which would have been (as it had been in Africa) in the name of the marshal.

I have shown summarily the effort; unhappily, it was destroyed in large measure when the Germans occupied southern France. The spies and denouncers, who had been rigorously suppressed by the Vichy government, now had a free hand. The army of the armistice was dispersed. The stocks of arms fell into German possession. Officers were compelled to go into hiding. Yet the effort was not entirely futile. Some of the arms were carried off into the ranks of the less organized Resistance.

Meanwhile, another grave consequence of the occupation of southern France was the attempt of the Germans to seize the French fleet in the port of Toulon.

When the capture of the fleet was imminent, Admiral de Laborde, in accordance with the instructions he had received in July 1940, when the Germans left the ships to the French on condition that they were not utilized against them, and when the English obtained the solemn promise of the marshal that they would not be placed at the disposal of the Germans, promptly scuttled the *Strasbourg*, seven cruisers, an airplane carrier, and other vessels. A few submarines escaped under enemy fire. I was surely not dreaming when I listened to the explosion of joy at the fulfillment of the marshal's pledge. I was surely not dreaming when I heard the exclamations of disappointment and of anger of the Germans, who had imagined themselves possessors of an important naval force. Naturally, the joy of the French was mitigated by their regret at losing the principal part of the navy, but they realized that they were acting under necessity, in defense of their honor, and that they were inflicting a serious blow on German hopes. We considered that there was something sublime in the sacrifice. Churchill was, apparently, delighted at the voluntary deed which spared the British grave embarrassment. American comment was unmistakably favorable. The Communists in France glorified a decision which saved the fleet from falling into German hands.

Moreover, once more the charge of "collaboration" with Germany was dealt a shattering blow. If France was "collaborating," she had only to place her ships at the disposal of Germany—or to allow them to be captured. Nothing would have been easier than to wash French hands of complicity by pleading that the German forces sent to Toulon had overpowered the defenders of the Arsenal. The Germans had sent not only soldiers but sailors, fully expecting to man the fleet. "Collaborators" do not snatch a weapon from their accomplices. When the navy was sunk, the last vestiges of official collaboration were sunk with it.

So I had thought. So thought everybody. It was a memorable day, that on which the admirals, in spite of the enemy's strength, in spite of his occupation of the whole of France—save a little space around the seat of the government of Vichy—in spite of the menace of a ruthless revenge that it was in his power to wreak, scuttled at one and the same time the ships, the hopes and expectations of Germany, and all possibility of a Franco-German alliance.

But it is marvelous how magically facts which seem irrefutable at one moment can be distorted at a later date. To my astonishment, I learned at the Liberation that the sinking of the French fleet was a deliberate act of treachery, a final proof of the connivance of Pétain and Hitler! The admirals, it now appeared, were traitors! They had not even gone down with their ships, as the superior code of the Resistance would have demanded! They were condemned—De Laborde, the blunt bluff seaman with a splendid record of seamanship, to death—though, in view of the sham and illogical contentions of his accusers, he was, after a period in irons, permitted to pass the remainder of his life in prison.

Of course, there were arguments to be found by the accusers. There are always arguments to be found. The admirals were, it was said, not well disposed toward the English, they were still smarting under the wounds of Mers-el-Kebir (that unhappy blunder!) and, if they had chosen, they might have got safely away from Toulon. On the latter point, I can pronounce no opinion: it is one for experts: although it seems improbable that, after being laid up so long, the ships were in a condition to put to sea, with German airplanes hovering overhead. If, however, we assume that the admirals were not quick-witted enough to avail themselves of the few days of respite they enjoyed, it must not be forgotten that they had lived for more than two years under the obsession of standing orders which had been accepted by the Germans and approved by the English and had come to represent in their minds the truest patriotism and loyalty. Darlan, himself, had told them that, if ever he rescinded the standing orders, they were to pay no heed to him, for the annulment of the command would merely mean that he was a prisoner. It must be confessed that others, notably the British and the Gaullists, were not quicker-witted. Of all the strange reversals of judgment, after several years of reflection, that of the judgment passed on the events of Toulon is the strangest.

In Algiers, Darlan, though accepted as the acting French chief, was under a cloud. No one trusted him. The Americans who dealt with him despised him. They seemed inclined, for a short time, to play the Monarchist card, and the pretender to the French throne, the Comte de Paris, living in exile in Spanish Morocco, visited Algiers to discuss the situation with them. He was convinced that his return to France in the wagons of the Americans would be a blunder of the first magnitude, and he went back to Spanish Morocco. The French military chiefs, especially Giraud, could hardly look on Darlan with respect. He was the opportunist in person, a quick-change artist ready to adopt almost any attitude. As for the Gaullists, few in numbers, they were naturally opposed both to Darlan and Giraud. Giraud considered them undesirables. The Americans had no love for them, and looked on rather disdainfully at the quarrels of Frenchmen who should have been united in a common cause.

Darlan lived in fear of assassination. His fears were well founded. A young man, Catholic, with an Italian mother, believed to have Monarchist leanings (though the Monarchists disclaim all responsibility for his fanatical resolution), who had spent some time in a youth camp, a young man named Bonnier de la Chapelle, obtained access to Darlan's rooms and on the 20th of December, 1942, shot him. The wounds were fatal. With extraordinary haste, the young man was tried and executed. He had been persuaded that he would find protectors. Who were these mysterious protectors? They did not intervene, and we cannot now know whether he acted on his own initiative or whether he was armed and inspired by one of the several groups claiming to represent the real France.

Who would succeed Darlan? Noguès, the popular resident-general of Morocco, General Juin, the ablest of the French military men, or Giraud? Giraud was chosen. His power was ephemeral. He was not endowed with political intelligence, and when later the Gaullists came over in force from London, he was soon outmanoeuvred by General De Gaulle.

15

Bird's-eye View of Vichy

It is time to set down my own impressions of Vichy as the French provisional capital. Hitherto, I had relied on second-hand reports, full and fairly accurate. But by this time the friendly consul-general had obtained for me—after long inquiries—a French identity card, and I could travel as freely as any Frenchman.

There was a wholesale fabrication of false cards, as the French police well knew, of which the Germans could not be ignorant. One bishop, who was proud to have served as an officer under Pétain at Verdun, showed me the secret room in which he had cards fabricated for the Jews. Strangely enough, the Germans usually accepted papers, genuine or false, without demur. They were, unless they had good cause for suspicion, easily satisfied. As for my surname, which has no French consonance, it was concealed under the first name of Sisley, the name of the French Impressionist painter with whom I had family connections. Henceforth, I was usually addressed as Monsieur Sisley, which sounds fairly French. A sort of legend grew around me to the effect that I was a member of the British Intelligence Service—though this was absolutely without foundation and, fortunately, did not come to the ears of the Germans until nearly the end, when my arrest was ordered by them.

I went then to Vichy, primarily in order to obtain the release of paper long promised to my publisher at Lyons for a book on political philosophy, *Le Mythe de la Liberté*, for which trip the French official visa had been given. (In the South no German visa was required.) When my publishers tried to get delivery the trouble started. Had they applied to the Germans they could have had supplies, but they would have lost their independence. Nor would they have recourse to the black market. But I also wished to judge for myself of the sentiments of Vichy.

I called on the head of the *Production Industrielle*, lodged in a big hotel. Complete assurances were repeated of an early delivery. Knowing how valueless they were, I asked for the name of the responsible official. I went to see him. He told me that his function was to pass on the command. To whom? He politely told me. I then called on the third person, who informed me that the matter had duly passed through his hands, and he had forwarded instructions. Once more, I followed the course of the instructions. I learned that the execution of the order depended on yet another functionary. I could not abandon my quest at this point, and at last my persistence was rewarded. So many tons of paper were definitely awarded—though I was informed that the local administrator at Lyons could only act within the limits of the practical possibilities. It was for the publishers to press the local administrator, who eventually delivered about half the required quantity.

Incidentally, it may be well to point out here that critics of my views of government and political philosophy have seized upon the title of this book as a means of labeling me an opponent of liberalism and a supporter of autocracy. No person who has read the book could honestly make any such charge. What I tried to show in this book is that the conception of an abstract and universal Liberty, spelled with a capital L, *is* a dangerous myth. There are only specific liberties, but these are very precious and must be achieved and protected. By blindly seeking the mythical abstraction of Liberty, mankind has all too often lost the particular liberties which are essential to assure us a society and government suited to the human personality and an economic régime adapted to the real needs of human beings. Hence, far from attacking liberty and demanding authoritarianism, I sought to suggest ways in which those true liberties necessary for the good life can best be provided and continued.

In all my *démarches* I met only with courtesy. I had numerous talks with officials, who were glad to discuss affairs generally. My views were eagerly sought.

Among the things I learned was that there was an astonishing diversity of views on the best policy for France. I also learned that, if there were countless restrictions in most domains, there was one domain in which there were few—at Vichy. Everybody talked, gave his opinion, declared his likes and dislikes. I had hardly expected such outspokenness. I had thought that the strictest prudence would be observed. It was not so. Discretion was thrown to the winds. Those who were favorable to active resistance did not hesitate to tell me so. Those who recommended relative passivity, proclaimed their conviction. Men worked side by side in the friendliest manner although their politics were entirely opposed.

I had not been a day in Vichy before I knew that the director of the cabinet of one of the most important ministers was arranging meetings of Resistance chiefs with highly placed personages. The chiefs came and went, although they were certainly known to the government which, far from restraining their activities, seemed to smile on them. In short, anyone who thinks that Vichy was one bloc, and the

Resistance another, knows nothing of the strange mixture of men of all political colors in the overcrowded capital.

I record one conversation with the secretary of a minister. I had never seen her before; she knew nothing of me; but she began by asking—"How long will it be, Monsieur Sisley, before the Anglo-Saxons land in France?"

I replied noncommittally.

"Let's hope it will be soon," she said. "We have had enough of the Boche."

"Where do you come from?" I asked.

"Oh, I'm an Alsatian. The government has been very kind to us. Lots of us have been given jobs in the ministries."

Still, she had many compatriots who could find no niche. They were of all classes. They had been driven from their homes, leaving their belongings behind, at a moment's notice—unless they chose to accept German nationality. She told me heartbreaking stories of the poor refugees.

"Does everybody talk like you? Aren't you afraid of losing your job?" I inquired.

"There's no danger," she said. "We are still in France. We are free here. Everybody hopes that the Germans will go, though some would act one way, and others another way."

Vichy was a cross-section of the French nation. All tendencies were represented there, among the ministers as among the humblest employees. There was an extraordinary tolerance of conflicting activities. The Resistance, at that time, owed no allegiance to De Gaulle; it was an interior movement, and would have existed without the *émigrés* at London. It was autonomous and had not yet persuaded itself that the existence of a government in France was treason. Would that the Resistance had always remained so! Would that the tacit understanding had continued to the end! Although the Resistance was in touch with England, sending useful information, it did not feel itself subordinate to England, and there were not a few who were disdainful of De Gaulle and the Gaullists as being in the pay of a foreign, if friendly, country.

There were newcomers to the ranks of the functionaries; but the majority of those who were carrying on under the Vichy government had worked under the Paris governments and hoped to work again under Paris governments. They represented the continuity of functionarism. Is it not of the essence of functionarism to carry on? Should they be reproached for fulfilling their *raison d'être?* What would have happened to France if they had refused to serve? They were *attentiste,* they were waiting and seeing and, in the meantime, serving.

Should the diplomatic service have resigned in a body? Should the police have thrown up their jobs? Should the magistrates have declined to sit? It is not, perhaps, generally known that the magistrates and others connected with the law had voluntarily taken oaths of fidelity to Pétain. I do not blame them. The business of the country had to be done. But I have never understood how the same magistrates could reconcile their conscience to the function they were afterward called on to perform of judging and condemning to death or to prison many thousands of their compatriots who had practiced fidelity to Pétain.

I quickly observed that, at Vichy at any rate, the relations of the officials who were necessarily brought into contact with German officials were correct if not cordial. There was, in general, precisely the degree of courtesy that one would expect between civilized men, each of them endeavoring to do his duty. In this connection, I may be allowed to recall a conversation I had with a British consul just after the Liberation. He told me that, in the first war, he was a young official in Turkey, where he was placed in *résidence surveillée.* He and his colleagues played hockey to while away the time as agreeably as possible. German officers of liaison, equally idle, suggested that they might be allowed to join in the games. The British agreed, and so English and Germans in Turkey played together while the war raged around them. "We did not feel that it was our duty to exchange blows," said the consul. "We behaved like civilized men. Alas, today, I am afraid we should have been shot, if we had been Frenchmen, for 'intelligence with the enemy.' "

The functionaries and the ministers, old and new, had little incentive to work with energy. They realized that they were simply carrying on, that what they did could not endure, that the future was uncertain. They were housed in the most deplorable conditions, in small hotel rooms, with a screen, when it could be had, concealing the washbasin filled with cigarette ends. The furniture of the bedrooms, converted into offices, consisted of commonplace wardrobes containing dossiers, and of hotel tables and chairs. The secretary of Beaux Arts, for example, was to be found in an attic, before a plain whitewood desk, carpetless and curtainless. The radio was directed from the dingiest offices. There were a few elegant hotels; for the rest, highly distinguished men were huddled with their families into one or, at most, two rooms that no ordinary bourgeois family would have accepted on a brief holiday.

"The cure at Vichy lasts three weeks," one of them said to me: "but we have passed three years in these conditions."

The town of Vichy is spaciously planned, with its gritty esplanade in the center and its parks on the outskirts, but its interest is soon exhausted. Two or three overcrowded restaurants, where I met newspapermen (who also were doing their job as honestly as they could—should they have renounced their only means of livelihood for four years?) and ministers and functionaires dining in higgledy-piggledy confusion; a bar where we exchanged gossip and invented stories and caught up rumors; a tea room, where we ate *ersatz* pastry; a casino-theater, a few cinemas; there were no other distractions. At Geneva, which I frequented for twenty years before the war, I had discovered how dreary even the most beautiful city becomes when one is compelled to meet the same sort of people from morning to night. The atmosphere becomes parochial, even though the company is cosmopolitan. Here, in Vichy, it was infinitely worse. France seemed to be narrowed to a tiny space. The most enthusiastic advocates of a renovated France were discouraged. They lacked air and space. They were visibly flagging. The only purpose of Vichy now seemed to be to maintain the fiction of French sovereignty. I think it was worth maintaining, but it was a feeble flame—a feeble flame which we hoped would blaze forth brilliantly again.

I recorded a conversation with the editor of an intellectual review. "I have no material reason for abandoning my Paris home," he said. "I should have a larger public for my review, and I do not suppose the German censorship would prevent me from publishing the sort of articles I print. But I should feel at Paris that I had accepted the overlordship of Germany. Here, I try to tell myself that I am in a free France. It is a form of protest. It is a sort of resistance. Oh, I know that our freedom is relative, that we are perpetually watched, menaced, vetoed. Nevertheless, the Vichy government is a French government. It is the only government we have. I wish it were better, but it is all we have."

"But the French in London," I objected, "consider that all who are associated with Vichy are associated with the Germans."

"I know," he replied sadly. "You have seen for yourself that it is not so. The Gaullists abroad do not appreciate the position. Perhaps, they do not want to appreciate it. If the choice were between De Gaulle and Germany, can you doubt that I should choose De Gaulle? But we have no such choice. Forty million Frenchmen cannot emigrate. Nor can we desert the forty millions who must stay."

He argued that, much as Vichy ministers might be criticized—as ministers everywhere may be criticized—it was an abominable distortion of the truth to identify Vichy with Germany. Vichy was, on the contrary, the only buckler against Germany. Everybody must play his part. Those who took up arms (or the microphone) might or might not be acting foolishly, but they were to be commended, in so far as their intentions were pure. Those who, by temperament, intellectual affinities, or physical condition, could do no more than keep alive the spirit of France, were serving the French cause. Vichy represented for him, as for many others, no foreign cause, but the French cause.

I must record a contrary opinion, that of a friend of mine who was in an important post. "I am disillusioned," he said. "I hoped to be of service and I keep on, although my hope has nearly gone. What purpose does it serve to pretend? Of course the Germans allow us latitude. They do not often interfere directly. They like us to think we are free. But we are a screen for them. In Paris, they impose their will. Here, they want us to believe that our will prevails. But the result is the same—or rather it is worse, since the more we proclaim our independence the more we accuse ourselves of voluntary surrender. Better to obey because we cannot do otherwise than acquiesce because we think it is advisable. We submit unwillingly, for fear or worse, and our submission is interpreted in London as willing collaboration."

"Are you then thinking of going to London?" I asked.

"No, knowing that Vichy is doing its best, I will be no party to the attacks of London. I should like to get away from Vichy, but not to denounce it, not to treat the men of Vichy as traitors. The difficulty lies in doing one's duty and at the same time keeping the unity of France. Anyone can pose as a superpatriot by dividing the French. The problem is to act as a patriot while uniting the French."

Thus were the consciences of Frenchmen troubled. Each had to decide for himself. I sympathized with those in France who were preparing the revolt against Germany, I sympathized with those who could stay no longer in France and who went away—aided very often by the services of Vichy—and I sympathized with those who stayed. What I deprecated then, as I deprecate now, was the attempt, which unfortunately succeeded, to range Frenchmen in two hostile camps. Apart from a handful of miscreants, everybody was eager to see the departure of the Germans. The question was one of method.

Is it not odd that one section of the Resistance should boldly adopt the name of "partisans?" Partisans? Either words have lost their meaning, or partisanship implies a sectional conception utterly alien to love of France as a whole. It is true that there were "partisans" on both sides, but the term was flourished as a banner by one side only.

I tried, as is my wont, to be impartial, and I recognized the defects and the faults of Vichy. But I affirm that there were in Vichy many men who were genuinely moved by the miseries of their country, who were animated by no mean personal motives, who strove sincerely for the restoration of France. I came into contact with young men who were idealists with but one thought, that of remolding the shattered nation nearer to their heart's desire. They were ardently bent on re-creating a France in which the errors of the Third Republic should not be repeated, in which social justice should prevail, in which the spiritual genius of France should be revived to lead the world to a happier future. Their aspirations were pure, their confidence unshaken. Where are they today? Are they, like ministers and functionaries, in prison, in exile, in hiding? I do not know, but their undoubted talents, their sincere enthusiasm, their love of their country and of humanity, are assuredly not being adequately utilized. There was in them no trace of pro-German sentiment; they were not opportunists; they made no concessions to Hitlerism; amid the discouragements, the oppressions, the misunderstandings, the abuse, the propaganda, they were good soldiers not only of France but of mankind.

It is when I think of them that I am most moved by the calumnies of "partisans," by the misguided zeal of patriots who could not or would not discriminate between the vilest recreant and the purest idealist.

Moreover, in the very citadel of Vichy were men—and women too—who actively helped the Resistance. Some of them have profited by their devotion. Others, probably the more numerous, have claimed no reward. It was well known that in the dingy hotels were concealed munitions.

As for the mere talkers, who argued now in this sense, now in that, were they not to be forgiven? Were they not an epitome of France? Is it not in the French character to talk abundantly?

Everything about Vichy reflected uncertainty and temporizing. Even when France is at peace, when no great questions face her, she cannot keep a government in office for long. How, then, could she keep Pétain for four years without growing restive, without seeking something new? De Gaulle, coming to Paris after the Liberation, with his own government, his own police, his own army, with all the opportunities of dictatorship, could not survive for more than eighteen months. Had the war lasted only two years after the defeat, Pétain would today be France's most honored citizen. Unhappily, it lasted four years before the Germans were driven out.

Vichy could not last. It had no dynamic essence. Its function was negative, not positive. It was tolerated. It lived on sufferance. The marshal was too old, too much the prey of contending forces, to continue to give the necessary impulsion; he was overborne by his own ministers.

The Germans had left Vichy unoccupied. Here was a corner of France where the French flag could still be flown. I went with M. to witness the trooping of the colors. It was a

Sunday morning; before the Hôtel du Parc was a crowd of Vichy residents. The guard, with white gauntlets, in leather tunics, took up its post. Military music rang out in the clear air. At a signal, we all uncovered, and as we stood at attention, the flag of France was hauled slowly up the mast. The marshal came out on the balcony to salute the Tricolor. It was, for me, an unforgettable moment. France was invaded, not only in the North but in the South. But there remained one little corner where the French flag flew, and while it flew all was not lost. Purely symbolic? But certain symbols are woven into our lives. In that flag, now flapping and streaming in the wind, was a promise of deliverance. The rite had a religious significance. Conscious as I was of the unhappy condition of the land I loved, I saw in the flag a pledge and a token of the imperishable France. The flag sent out its message of freedom. France was not wholly submerged, was not without hope. France lived, since the flag, bright in the morning sunshine, triumphant in the wind of springtime, waved like a living thing. . . .

Should we have hauled down the flag of Vichy? Should we have deserted France? I do not think so. Were the men who still saluted the flag in France traitors to their country? I am sure they were not.

An exceedingly well-informed and sympathetic American who read the unrevised manuscript of this book offered the following critical comment: "Huddleston does not seem to mind dictatorship at all, and I think his book would be taken more seriously if he displayed as much detestation of dictatorship as he does of a number of other detestable things."

Now, this gentleman, in a long report on my book, showed a most intelligent and sympathetic understanding of its intent and content, but in the above comment he surely failed to comprehend my attitude toward dictatorship as a system of government.

In this book, I am not indulging in any formal discussion of political theory or setting forth my conceptions of the ideal form of government. I have merely sought to assemble, as well as I could, the more important facts about the only form of government—and the head of that government—which could serve France well and with relative stability under the specific conditions that existed from May 1940 until the Liberation.

I have been a lifelong liberal—even a libertarian—and an ardent supporter of parliamentary institutions. Not even the grievous shortcomings of democracy and parliamentarianism in the last quarter of a century have undermined my conviction that democracy, however much it needs to be purified and streamlined, must be the form of government under which mankind will move ahead, if it does at all, to security, well-being and peace. In some of my earlier books, which touch more fully and specifically on political theory and practice, I have developed this idea at greater length. I abhor all dictatorships as a system of government and society. Throughout the book I have expressed my abhorrence of the dictatorships of Mussolini, Hitler, Franco and Stalin, while being honest enough to concede certain important achievements made by each of them. I even abhor the dictatorship set up at Vichy, if envisaged as a permanent form of government for France. Nobody knows better than I do that Vichy did not present a pretty picture as a running governmental machine, however superior it may have been in most respects to the organization maintained by General De Gaulle. I do not even believe that Marshal Pétain was an ideal dictator, even in an emergency. But he was the only dictator who could have served France well, if at all, during the time that he was chief of state.

But all this is not the issue here. France had to have a government which could operate and also survive, providing as much protection as possible against the occupant. Even in peacetime, French parliamentary government, as it existed between the two wars, could not guide the ship of state safely and competently. If it had been able to do so, there would have been no defeat, armistice or Vichy régime. It is obvious to all informed persons that Vichy could not have operated under a parliamentary system. In the first place, if any such attempt had been made, the Germans would have quickly suppressed it; and, in the second place, if they had not done so, only anarchy could have resulted, with all the disasters which would have inevitably followed in its wake.

Most of those who have criticized the Vichy régime as a dictatorship have, at the same time, expressed approval of the rival government of General De Gaulle. But this organization was surely as dictatorial as that of the marshal, and it lacked utterly the virtue of being a constitutional government, as that of Vichy surely was.

It may be well at this point also to dispose of the charge that Marshal Pétain was a Fascist—a charge often leveled against him while at Vichy. The charge has even been made by men who should know better, such as the eminent American historian, Professor William L. Langer, in his able, if semiofficial, study of American relations with Vichy, *Our Vichy Gamble* (p. 383).

Any charge that Pétain was a conscious Fascist is sheer nonsense. He did not even know what Fascism was, in any reasoned or theoretical sense. There is no evidence that he had even ever read the books of Pareto, Mosca, Gentile and others, which expound the philosophy of Fascism, or that he was acquainted at all with Dietrich Eckart and Gottfried Feder, who formulated the "Twenty-five Points" of the National Socialist program.

While the marshal was a wide and thoughtful reader, for a military man, he never developed any well-integrated political philosophy. His thoughts in this field were fragmentary. He had never envisaged himself as a politician or as the political head of a state. From his speeches and policies while at Vichy we can get some comprehension of such political and social philosophy as he had. First and foremost, he was an ardent and sentimental French patriot. He never ceased to invoke the name of Jeanne d'Arc during the dark days at Vichy as a symbol of French recovery from bitter defeat. He had read the political writing of Bishop Bossuet and, from these he had derived a sympathetic appreciation of benevolent paternalism in a political ruler. His spirit of tolerance and humility he had obtained in part from his enthusiastic reading of the *Essays* of Montaigne. It is obvious that he was acquainted with the regionalism of Frédéric Le Play and with Le Play's stress on the importance of the family and the land within each region. Finally, the marshal, himself a good Catholic, was favorably inclined toward the Catholic socialism of Count Albert de Mun.

While all the political and social reforms proposed by the marshal, when in office at Vichy, existed mainly on paper, they reflected in varying degrees the ideas he derived from the sources above mentioned. There was nothing Fascist about any of them.

If Pétain was not an admirer of the French parliamentary system, which had brought so much weakness and vacillation to France, he was, despite all this, a Republican. This fact has been attested by the talented American journalist, Stanton B. Leeds. In his book, *These Men Rule France,* he has written (p. 322): "Pétain, the most influential of them all [the French generals], was a Republican who, more than anybody else, saved the [Republican] régime at the time of the Stavisky troubles."

16

Conversation With Pétain

As I have explained earlier, I had come to Vichy at the beginning of 1943, on the request of my French publisher, to obtain paper for one of my books. Learning that I was in Vichy, Pétain invited me to see him, and I spent the greater part of a day in conversation with him. I must suppose that he wished to confide in an Anglo-American writer, whom he had known at various epochs of his career ever since the First World War. I did not hesitate to respond to his invitation. Apart from my high opinion of him, I should have replied, had I been challenged, that, having seen most of the outstanding men of my time, it was my duty as a veteran journalist to see Pétain. Churchill, when reproached in 1941 for proclaiming Anglo-Russian solidarity, said that if hell made war on Hitler, he would pronounce a eulogy of the devil.

When I called upon the marshal in the middle of the morning, I found him little changed since those days when I used to see him in a little restaurant near Villeneuve

Loubet, the village in the South to which he had retired, charged with honors and with years.

He was approaching his 90th year—87 to be exact—and he was exceedingly well preserved, erect, robust, broad-shouldered. His clean-shaven cheeks were pink with health. His well-trimmed mustache was cut away from full red lips. There were no wrinkles on his ivory forehead. His hands were plump and carefully groomed. There were no gnarled veins or yellow patches which betray old age.

His steady blue eyes were the most striking feature of his face. Astonishing eyes, calm with intelligence, surveyed me penetratingly. Everybody who has seen the marshal has remarked the frank imperturbable gaze of his extraordinary blue eyes. He took my hand warmly and began: "Let us consider ourselves as two Frenchmen, let us talk together as Frenchmen, frankly and in full confidence."

I do not know how that simple remark strikes the reader, who is deprived of the inflections of the voice, deep and rich and warm, though slightly quavering, but to me it seemed the right thing to say if our conversation was, indeed, to be confidential. The marshal was noted for such appropriate formulas. They removed all restraint, as between us, and at the same time enclosed us in a private world remote from indiscreet ears.

His room was small though elegant. The desk was neatly arranged, and few papers were in evidence. On it was a vase filled with flowers. A score or so of books in a polished piece of furniture caught my attention, and I noticed *Le Soulier de Satin,* the play by Paul Claudel of which everybody was talking and which was produced at the *Comédie Francaise* about that time. The sun shone through the third-floor window overlooking the esplanade. There was no antechamber: the silver-chained usher stood outside in the corridor. I thought of the magnificence I had known before the war: the imposing rooms of the Élysée, the splendid apartments of the Quai d' Orsay with their ornamental mantelpieces, their high, painted ceilings, their priceless tapestry, their choice *meubles.* The contrast of all this with the surroundings of the marshal, relegated to a hotel room, with similar rooms all about him filled with functionaries, dispelled any suggestion that the new chief of state loved ostentation. Although I stayed much longer with him than is usual in such meetings, I observed that we were not interrupted. It seemed to me that he was rather solitary, that he was left alone, and was not kept acquainted with the details of his charge.

We exchanged our views about the future of France—views more or less banal but redeemed by an undoubted fervor. Said the marshal:

> France is sick. She will perhaps take a long time to recover. It may be that the worst days lie ahead. But I have no doubt of her survival. She has passed through many tribulations. Long before we were born, and long after we are dead, France pursued and will pursue her mission. Every nation has known defeat, but what is important is the spirit in which defeat is faced. If we maintain our unity, if we maintain our faith, France will emerge victorious after all.

He said this, and much more in the same strain, not in the ranting conventional tones of an orator, but with a quiet conviction, a complete sincerity, that persuaded me (though I needed no such persuasion) that his policy was not one of drift, and that the *attentisme* of which he was accused was animated by an active principle. There was no acquiescence in fate; but only the wary watchfulness and the infinite patience of an old soldier.

For my part, I ventured to express the view that the closest union with England and America was necessary to raise France from her present humiliating position. The marshal nodded:

Of course the salvation of France must primarily reside in herself. But cooperation with America and England is indispensable. There have been divergences which have shocked me, but no profound breach. They are due to misunderstanding, perhaps to national egotism. I do not think there has been an adequate appreciation of our position. We are under duress, we cannot act as we please, we cannot express ourselves freely. But we have behaved with honor and have done nothing to jeopardize the position of our friends. I must think of France first, but in doing so I think also of the allies of France.

Certainly, if one of the marshal's German "custodians," as he called them, had listened in to our conversation, he would have sent an alarming report on the state of the marshal's sentiments. Such reports were, in fact, sent and, as Goebbels's diary shows, there was nothing but distrust of Pétain in the German mind. The fanatical or mercenary pro-German Frenchmen in Paris were even more hostile to the marshal than were the Germans, and intrigued to have him swept aside. Pétain was the chief barrier to the men who would have ranged France with Germany. The marshal continued:

My task would have been easier had I not been assailed from all sides. Or perhaps not—it may be that, if I had not been assailed, the Germans would have taken more drastic action. I have been saddened by the lack of comprehension, but recriminations will not mend matters, and my personal feelings are of no importance. There must be a wholehearted reconciliation, for it is not on resentment that we can rebuild the world.

And then he became reminiscent, and we spoke of the first war: "They were good comrades, the American and English generals. We must never forget that in joining hands we won the war, and if we are now temporarily *hors de combat* the future will depend on the preservation of the bonds that bind us."

I will confess that I was greatly relieved at the turn the conversation had taken. I had not been altogether without misgivings. If I had been compelled to listen to violent reproaches, bitter criticisms, I should hardly have known how to reply. For, from the French viewpoint, or at least from the marshal's viewpoint, there was much cause for complaint. He went on:

> Monsieur Churchill promised that, if we were obliged to make an armistice, he would do nothing to render our plight more painful. I personally have no responsibility for the débâcle. We have tried to fulfil all our promises faithfully. We have not, for example, ever thought for a moment of surrendering the fleet, though that would have been a powerful counter in our dealings with Germany. Rather than allow our ships to be used against America and England, we scuttled them in the end. . . . I do not see what greater proof of our loyalty we could have offered. . . . In point of fact, we rendered great service in concluding an armistice. It checked the *élan* of Germany, it kept her from the Mediterranean which she might well have reached in the first year of the war. And if the Germans had bolted the Mediterranean, the war would have been lost.

All this seemed to me, as now, crystal clear, irrefutable, the plainest commonsense. Given the utter discomfiture of France—and it is sheer nonsense to pretend that France could, in 1940, have continued to fight—the highest patriotism was to save whatever could be saved by negotiation. The armistice gave France a government which, however handicapped, was not altogether without the means of resisting German exigencies, bargaining step by step, awaiting a favorable moment to reenter the struggle. It was unquestionably a piece of superior strategy on the part of Pétain, and a colossal blunder on the part of Hitler who had the ball at his feet and could easily have forced his way through Spain to Gibraltar. The marshal was not at all inclined to elude the question of the armistice:

> Both Weygand and I were called in when it was too late. The situation was hopeless. I did not act in a military capacity, I consulted the generals in the field. They were the men to decide. The

judgment of Weygand was conclusive. The armies were no longer coordinated. In spite of their courage, they were broken and in disorderly flight. Our effectives were outnumbered. The contribution of our allies [i.e., England] was insufficient, and indeed the British acknowledged defeat by escaping from Dunkirk. Belgium and Holland had collapsed. America could do nothing in time—many months elapsed before she entered the field—and, as for Russia, she was then leagued with Germany. The inferiority of our matériel was manifest. Our outdated aviation was virtually nonexistent by this time. The politicians were so persuaded that all was lost that they resigned.

As for the civil population, they were flying before the enemy advance, encumbering the roads, making it impossible to bring up fresh regiments. I need not remind you of what you saw for yourself. Nor need I remind you that there was a unanimous demand for a truce, and that I was reproached for not making a speedier decision. The war had become a mere massacre. Nearly two million soldiers were prisoners. It was high time to stop a useless slaughter and the capture of still more soldiers. To succumb to superior forces is not disgraceful. Every nation has had reverses, and it is sometimes in such moments that a nation can rise to the height of its grandeur. But it must remain a coherent whole, morally intact, and so dominate its defeat. . . .

I seldom interrupted the marshal, who was thus stating his case, but at this point I cited the words of the historian Guizot which were then ringing in my head: "France has known the vicissitudes of fortune, now high, now low; but when she is lowest she always retains the will, and always finds the means, to overcome adversity."

The marshal nodded his head gravely. "That is true of the past, it will be true of the future."

I did not doubt that he had the will, and was seeking the means, to overcome adversity. That he was more prudent and, apparently, more passive than those who were not charged with his responsibilities and could afford at a distance to devise rash methods and premature revolt, at the risk of shattering the national unity which seemed to the marshal to be a paramount necessity, was due to his position. There was a difference in perspective between London and Washington and Vichy.

Whatever may have been his estimate of the relative strength of the opposing camps at an earlier stage—and such estimates varied in London and in Washington as the tide of fortune ebbed and flowed—he made it plain to me that, after the American landing in North Africa, no doubt remained in his mind: *"Je vous dirai aujourd'hui—peut-être je ne l'aurais pas dit hier—que les Allemands ont du plomb dans l'aile."*

I give the literal translation of a pronouncement that startled me: "I will tell you today—perhaps I would not have said so yesterday—that the Germans have lead in their wings"—the bird has been hit, it must fall.

Although the signs of German weakness were multiplying, there was no general belief, as yet, that Germany would inevitably be beaten, and this conviction of the marshal thrilled me. In a flash I saw it disposed of the charges of "collaboration," since no sensible man who foresaw the downfall of Germany in the near or distant future would willingly lend assistance to a doomed foe. In fact, until this time, "collaboration" had been a vague word, used on both sides without definite meaning. It had, perhaps, served to prevent an open rupture of the armistice, but in practice there was only German coercion. That is precisely what irritated Hitler, infuriated the pro-German adventurers of Paris, and made the marshal an object of suspicion.

That he, believing as he did in the final destruction of Germany, would yield an inch except under sheer compulsion, was unthinkable.

"May I ask on what you base your opinion, Monsieur le Maréchal?" He answered:

I will tell you. It is perfectly clear that Germany is outclassed in the air. The battle of Tunisia has demonstrated her inferiority.

She will never catch up again. In Russia she is in retreat, but I would not accept that as decisive, for territorial reverses, if good order is maintained, may actually be advantageous when the lines are too extended. What is significant is that Germany cannot hold out (*tenir tête*) against the Anglo-Americans in the air. She started with overwhelming strength—we know something about that in France—but now the tables are turned, she is outmanned and outmachined, and the end is inevitable.

On this point the marshal was emphatic. He repeated his opinion again and again, and it was in the light of his considered judgment of the situation that I watched all the subsequent manoeuvres of the marshal, persuaded that, if he made surrenders under terrific pressure, it was only to gain time.

Although I put few leading questions, I did summon up courage to ask him what he thought of the proposed and long-delayed landing of the Allies in France. His reply astonished me. I immediately made a note of his words, which struck me as enigmatic: *"Je ne vois pas la nécessité d'un débarquement en France si les Allemands s'en vont."* (I see no need for a landing in France if the Germans go away.)

The marshal envisaged a general retreat of the Germans, an abandonment of France as the Russian and Allied pressure increased, in order to shorten their lines. There was talk of an Allied attack through the Balkans, the "soft underbelly of Europe," as Churchill called it, which would have been preferable to a landing in France, because, as the Germans were pushed back, the Russians also would be "contained" in Russia. Looking back, one sees how much better such a plan would have been: it would have saved us from the menace of a third world war. Certainly it would hardly have suited the Russian book, for Russia wished to make secure her hegemony over the Balkans. Since we went to war to prevent a German hegemony, it was logical to suppose that we should do everything to prevent a Russian hegemony. Surely one of the major blunders of the war strategy of the Allies was that they conceded too much to Russian ambitions.

The marshal, it seems to me, was justified in making this calculation. Had the Allies so operated, France would have been spared material destruction and civil strife. Logically, a great offensive in the Balkans would have automatically liberated France without bombings, without further fighting on her soil, without the division of France into Gaullists and Pétainists.

Without fighting on French soil? I remarked: "If only the French were in a position to hasten the German retreat!"

"Who knows?" returned the marshal, looking steadily at me with his clear blue eyes. "The last word has not been spoken."

The marshal's army had been prepared in North Africa (for it was indeed the marshal's army, faithful to him and not to De Gaulle, which was in North Africa) and, as I have indicated earlier, long before the Maquis came into existence there was in France a secret army composed of officers of the regular forces, with instructions to remain quiescent until the time came for action. In the youth camps, under pretext of physical training, Vichy was methodically preparing young men to march at the word of command. There was hidden, with the authorization of the marshal, in various parts of France, a store of munitions and arms, which until nearly the end escaped the vigilance of the Germans.

He continued: "I have asked those who have confidence in me not to go too fast, not to precede me. We must be patient. We must be ready to act in unison."

The *attentisme* of the marshal was part of a plan, and ran in no way counter to other plans, provided these other plans did not break the unity of France at the Liberation. Alas, he reckoned without the fanaticism of "partisans," the political aims of men more concerned with their party or ideology than their country—and he reckoned without the acquiescence of the Allies in Russia's scheme of expansion.

I was particularly eager to learn from the lips of the marshal the truth about the landing of the Americans in North Africa. Was he in connivance with Admiral Darlan, who had gone to North Africa just before the landing, ostensibly to visit his sick son, and who there made a pact with the Americans? His relations with Admiral Leahy suggested that he was engaged in a delicate game—on the one hand, delegating his powers to Darlan and welcoming the Americans; on the other hand, pretending to repudiate Darlan in order to delude the Germans. The truth is that, long before (in the autumn of 1940), he made an agreement with Churchill (the Churchill-Rougier accord and the Halifax-Chevalier accord) to "bring the Empire back into the war" at the appropriate time. Darlan had standing instructions to act in accordance with the marshal's "intimate thoughts," even though official messages seemed to disavow him. If Pétain could continue in his rôle of protector of the French people, if he could prevent the Germans from wreaking vengeance on them, so much the better.

I asked him if he would care to elucidate the matter. He looked long at me. "I must not express my intimate thoughts," he said.

I suppose I seemed disappointed, for, laying his hand on my arm he added: "Be sure that my intimate thoughts are wholly with France, without regard for personal consequences. It is my business while I am here—and I must not leave—to save the French from the worst that might befall them. If they were at the mercy of a *Gauleiter,* with nobody to interpose between them and the occupant . . . To everyone his rôle."

I mentioned that I had heard that an airplane was in readiness in 1942 to take him to North Africa. "It is my duty to stay," he answered. "Of course, I could have left if I had chosen to do so. But my task lies here."

Suddenly changing the subject he asked me point-blank: "Do you think I have said enough about social justice?" I responded that: "It is impossible to say too much, Monsieur le Maréchal, for it is the most important of subjects. The war will indeed be lost if there is not an amelioration of the worker's lot. If the chains are not broken, you may be sure there will be a revolt, and it is surely better that it be conducted peacefully, legally, without violence."

"Precisely what I think," returned the marshal, and we talked about this subject for some time. His views were progressive, though savoring, perhaps, as was natural, of a sort of paternalism. In any case, his sympathy for the workers was evident and sincere.

Another matter on which we talked, I have referred to at greater length elsewhere in this book. I will only say here that I had prepared a memorandum, as it was my custom to do whenever, in the course of my professional duties, I interviewed statesmen. I like to offer something to public men in return for their confidences. My memorandum contained the principles of a just peace. I affirmed that France, being in some sense outside the war, should deliver a message to the world, laying down conditions which would be acceptable to all men of goodwill. I insisted, of course, on territorial integrity, on national independence for all countries in the framework of a European federation, of which France should be the pioneer and the champion. I urged the marshal to deliver a discourse by radio, with or without the permission of the occupant, in order that the world should realize that France, though defeated, was not dead, that she did not look on silently and indifferently.

"You are right," said the marshal, "but it is becoming more and more difficult."

"Whatever practical result may come from such a message," I insisted, "France must speak out, in order to be true to her noblest vocation. And who knows? The lead of France may have an electrifying effect. In any case, France must show that she has not abdicated, that she will never abandon her mission. . . ."

I said much more, and the marshal read the memorandum approvingly. At last he sighed. "If you will work on it I will consult Laval. You know that he must give his consent."

The consent of Laval! It is not my desire to criticize Laval more than may appear necessary for an understanding of French reactions during the war, but it was certain that Laval had a very different sense of values. His bargaining with the Germans was on the purely material plane: it was unlikely that he would be sympathetic toward a universal appeal on the spiritual plane, or that he would be impressed by the need of a resounding moral vindication of France. I realized that, after all, the marshal was no longer free, that not only was he controlled by the Germans but he was obliged to consult Laval before he could address a supreme message to France—and to the world.

17

Algiers

As I was taking the train back to Monaco, I was asked if I would escort a young Jewess to her father, a rich foreign banker, who had taken refuge in the principality. Her Jewish features were unmistakable, and traveling for her was an adventure that might well end badly. As, however, I had the warmest sympathy for the Jews, who were being rounded up and deported by the Germans, I did not hesitate to give my consent.

At Lyons, which we reached in the morning, we discovered that there was no train for the Midi until the evening. It was a Sunday, and the rain fell pitilessly. Lyons on a wet Sunday is to be shunned. Tea rooms were closed. Cinemas were crowded. There was nothing to do except to drink innumerable coffees in the most secluded corners of cafés. The girl was rather pretty, but I confess that I have rarely passed a more unpleasant day. At any moment we might be called upon to show our papers and, if mine were in order, I suspected that hers were not.

At that time, the collapse of Germany had begun, Lyons was swarming with members of the Gestapo (as, perhaps wrongly, we called the German police—in reality there were several distinct organizations) and with members of the Resistance who behaved with a singular lack of discretion, assuming the airs of conspirators, unnecessarily carrying suitcases containing compromising papers, and arranging mysterious rendezvous. They had what they called "letter boxes" in queer houses. Voluntary betrayals were not uncommon, for in the movement were double agents. Involuntary betrayals were also common, for the nerves of suspected persons were not invariably proof against the fear inspired by the Gestapo. Somehow, we got through the day without mishap, and took our places in the evening train.

At once I was aware of a pair of scrutinizing eyes above a pendulous mustache. The man in the corner seat surveyed us continually. I whispered to my *protégée* to cover up her face and feign to be asleep, and I calmly endured the disquieting gaze, lit a cigarette, tried to read, and wondered when the attack would begin and how I should explain the presence of my companion. For an hour or so we remained silent, and at last the man got up, walked out of the compartment, and we saw him no more.

Would he return? Where had he gone? His absence was almost as disturbing as his company. Though the girl and I had become friendly, we had spoken of indifferent matters. I had no desire whatever to be admitted into her confidence. But now, faced with a real though undefinable danger, she began to talk of her projects. She did not intend to join her father. She had a lover, in the Maquis at Digne, and she was on her way to him. She would get off the train at Les Arcs, in the middle of the night. She had documents to deliver. I had no intention of deserting her, but her secret was embarrassing. It placed me in a false situation, compromised me in an affair that was not my own. I expostulated with her, not for her activities, but for her refusal to join her father. I was in some sense her guardian, responsible for her, until I had handed her over. But her mind was made up. At Les Arcs she left me.

Soon after her departure a German policeman entered the compartment and asked me for my papers. I produced them. He examined them carefully, and could find nothing wrong. At last he said: "But where is the lady you were traveling with?"

"Traveling with? There was a girl in the seat opposite. I know nothing of her. She left the train a little while ago. I understand she has parents in the neighborhood."

"And you never met her before?"

"Certainly not. I am a writer, living in Monaco, which is not an occupied part of France. There is nothing which forbids me to travel on my lawful business."

What was my lawful business? I told him frankly: I had gone to Vichy on behalf of my publishers to get paper which had been promised. I had a letter which confirmed my statement. "You know the formalities, the delays of officials, bound by red tape. You have some experience of that in your own country," I said laughing.

He grinned, and I told as humorously as I could how I had been sent from one department to another. The story amused him. "And you know nothing of the girl?" he asked again. "Nothing, she was a pleasant little creature. Why should I not indulge in conversation to pass away the hours of a tedious journey?"

He grunted, saluted, and left me. I was glad to be rid of him so easily. What would have happened had the girl been in the train, I cannot say. Although I had done my best to persuade her to stay, I was now delighted that she had stuck to her resolution. On my arrival I rang up her father, who was living under an assumed name, and told him what had happened. He was displeased, and I did not accept his invitation to meet him to receive his rather grudging thanks.

Back in Monaco, I listened, like everybody else, to the

radio. Few precautions were taken by listeners. In principle, we were not permitted to hear the news from England, but one could hear it issuing from open windows wherever one went.

The year 1943 was the year in which German strength, having reached its high-water level, began to recede. It was in Russia that the first of the big catastrophes, from the German viewpoint, occurred. America had poured tanks and cannon and airplanes into the Soviet Republic, and the Bolsheviks were now manufacturing munitions, locomotives, airplanes, trucks behind the Urals. Cities previously unheard of and still largely unknown sprang up in Siberia. It was impossible for Germany to conquer the tremendous spaces. The plan of Hitler was to reach Astrakhan on the Caspian and Stalingrad on the Volga, and then turn north, encircling Moscow and rolling up the Russian troops. To the south, he would take the oil wells of Maikev, Grosny, Baku and the oil port of Batum. Then the Germans might push through Turkey, through Syria, to the Suez Canal, and through Iran to the port of Bassorah on the Persian Gulf, and link up with Japan.

A grandiose scheme! But it was not difficult to observe that troops were being withdrawn from France, and there were many divisions which were not German on the Russian front: Rumanian, Hungarian, Italian, which were usually a source of weakness to the Germans. With the depletion of the Western Front, Stalin was justified in demanding that the Anglo-Americans land in France but, in the long view, they would have done better to take the road of the Balkans.

There was much skepticism in France as to the plans of the Anglo-Americans. Month after month went by without any sign of an assault. A friend of mine, who visited the Vendean coast, assured me that a landing there would be relatively easy, that the boasted Atlantic Wall was almost nonexistent there. In the Midi there were practically no

German defenses, as I could ascertain for myself. As for the German army, in the South at any rate, it was largely composed of boys and old men, of nondescript races altogether different from the first occupants.

Stalingrad was the pivot of the German plan. The Germans forced their way to this new Verdun—a town which was destined to become, as was Verdun under the command of Pétain in the First World War, the grave of German hopes. The outer defenses fell to Von Paulus. The battle seemed to be over. But Stalin decided to resist at all costs. Street battles of an extraordinary violence were engaged. We followed as well as we could the terrific struggle. We watched, in imagination, the German army, cut off from its supplies, melting. Hitler should have retired, but he was hypnotized, as it seemed, by the name of the town. The Russian counteroffensive fell heavily. We were told that a quarter of a million men on the German side alone fell in the struggle and, at last, the haggard Von Paulus and his staff were taken prisoner in a cellar. This was the first really grave check administered to the Germans.

But we did not neglect the foolish fight in Tunisia, in which Frenchmen fell. It might have been spared had the Allies shown a greater spirit of decision, instead of wrangling with the authorities in Algiers. As it was, the German General Krauss presented an ultimatum to Admiral Dorrien, calling on him to surrender, on pain of annihilation. No prisoners would be taken, since the French army had been "disbanded": the German bombers would wreck everything. Half an hour was accorded Dorrien to decide. He yielded, and afterward died of despair in prison. Admiral Esteva, an excellent officer, with a narrow sense of duty, unable to interpret the contradictory orders he received, though Darlan, Giraud, Juin, Noguès, and Boisson had interpreted them in favor of the Anglo-Americans, opposed the American forces. He, too, paid for his inability to understand, and served a long term in prison. Yet, there is little doubt which way his inclinations lay: he would willingly have fought the Germans. So were good men sacrificed.

We learned, too, of the amazing march of Montgomery across nearly 2,000 miles of desert, to effect his junction with the Americans. These events thrilled us, pointing clearly to the eventual German downfall. What chance had Hitler, alone, against England, America, and Russia, to say nothing of the contribution that the French might now make?

That contribution would have been more decisive had not the French quarreled for precedence, as though the war was only another parliamentary crisis. De Gaulle, isolated in London, saw himself displaced by Noguès, Darlan, Giraud. Had he ventured to come to Algiers in the first stages of the struggle, he would have been opposed by the quasi-unanimity of the North Africans. The English, however, declined to let him down. For them, he was the sole chief of the French Resistance, though, in fact, it was composed of many elements, some of them violently anti-Gaullist. Roosevelt would have nothing to do with him. De Gaulle represented one-man government, surrounded by police, spies, agents of all sorts, supported by Communists and adventurers. Yet Giraud, the American choice, was even worse, feeble in character, inferior in intelligence, without value as an administrator. In retrospect, one sees how much better it would have been had Pétain himself, abandoning his rôle of buckler for the French, flown to Africa to take command! Everybody, except the fanatical Gaullists and the Communists, would have welcomed him.

The story is told, and was told in the early months of 1943, so swiftly does satire wing its shafts, that when at last De Gaulle, who long refused to see Giraud or to hear of a reconciliation, finally, under the threat of having British subsidies cut off, consented to come to Casablanca, Roosevelt remarked that the military situation in France demanded a Napoleon. To which De Gaulle is said to have replied: "I am Napoleon!" Roosevelt then remarked that the financial situation called for a Colbert. De Gaulle answered: "I am Colbert." Roosevelt insisted that the political situation required a Clemenceau. "I am Clemenceau." Whereupon, Roosevelt told his intimates that it was a pity De Gaulle was not also Jeanne d'Arc, with an Inquisition to burn him. *Se non è vero è ben trovato. . . .*

However, at the end of January 1943, Giraud and De Gaulle met, without result.

The prima donna of French resistance returned to London, there to pursue a sort of vendetta against all sections of the French who were not in his movement. I am willing to render homage to De Gaulle for his accomplishments, but it was not in the spirit of an electoral contest that the Resistance should have been conceived. In Africa, the regiments of Leclerc, of De Gaulle, were busily recruiting from the rival Pétainist ranks. By the spring, Giraud had 125,000 votes (or rather soldiers) while De Gaulle had 15,000. General X was dubbing the Giraud men "Fascists." I knew no more lamentable display than the sectarian disputes of North Africa.

Not until June 1943 was the *Comité Français de Libération Nationale* set up at Algiers, and by this time the incapacity of Giraud had been proved. The *émigrés* from London outnumbered the Giraudists. They eliminated Noguès, Peyrouton, Boisson, Admiral Muselier, who were associated with Vichy or were heretics. Giraud shared the presidency with De Gaulle, but not for long. He was soon nominated commander-in-chief, that is to say, "liquidated" as a political chief, and later lost his post as a fighting general. Finally, an attempt to assassinate him sent him into private life. De Gaulle had won in this personal struggle.

Roosevelt continued to refuse support to De Gaulle. He

would not, he said, give him a white horse on which to ride into the French capital. But Russia was only too ready to recognize the general and to introduce into the Committee of Algiers ever-growing Bolshevik elements. While Roosevelt was opposed to any recognition which would automatically, without elections, place De Gaulle in power when the Allies reached Paris, and Churchill withheld recognition from what was, after all, a minority of the French people, Stalin was quite ready to play the De Gaulle card, and De Gaulle was quite ready to be so played. The *Comité Français de Libération Nationale*—a self-appointed body—was declared by Russia to represent France. The Russian Ambassador, Bogomolov, who had, with the ambassadors of most other countries, remained at Vichy, was now transferred to Algiers. All other pretenders than De Gaulle and the C.F.L.N., were completely discarded. It was a triumph which was to cost De Gaulle—and France—dear. One cannot admit the Communists into the antechamber without running the risk of their taking possession of the whole house.

The men who, in good faith, had come over to Algiers but who were anti-Communists, tainted with Vichyism, were arrested. Among them were Pucheu, Peyrouton, Flandin, and Boisson. They had various fates. After long incarceration, Flandin was acquitted, but excluded from active political life. Boisson died. Peyrouton was at last released. Pucheu was shot.

The Communists were, of course, not alone; but they made a pact with Socialists (of the orthodox school, for dissident Socialists were to be punished) and Christian Democrats, otherwise known as the *Mouvement Républicain Populaire,* the M.R.P., who felt that they could go a long way with the Communists and, in any case, decided to share with them political control of France after the Liberation. The older parties, notably the Radical Socialists, were to be crushed by this coalition of political interests. In the sequel, the three parties, bound together, were to govern France for some years. The political bargain, as might have been expected, had dire results for France for, before the Communists left the government in 1947, believing that they could obtain greater advantages in opposition, they took care to place their agents in key posts.

In Algiers, their cold resolve to "liquidate" all antagonism by any and every means openly revealed itself. I listened with growing alarm to the fulminations of the radio, in which the weapon of assassination was recommended. Names and addresses of persons who were guilty of no treason but had taken some action against the Communists, or who for any cause, private or public, were on a blacklist, were publicly announced. Miniature coffins were sent to suspected or potential antagonists. Civil war—in which the weapons would all be on one side—was foreshadowed in scores of broadcasts.

The most curious aspect of the Algerian Committee, or its London branch, was the presence of men who were notorious for their association with big business, with banking, with trusts, and also the presence of members of a party which called itself Christian. Apparently, there was a general fear lest the demagogy of the Communists should have a free run, unless they were controlled by those who could not possibly approve of their vindictive doctrines and their revolutionary decrees, to be applied retroactively, instituting penalties quite unknown to the French code, such as "national indignity," confiscation, disqualification for membership in elected bodies, inability to vote, a gigantic *épuration,* a purge, conducted by the administrations and by special Tribunals of which the juries would be composed of picked "Resistants," in practice largely Communists. The dispossession of newspaper owners was also decreed and, in fact, most of the provincial press was, when the Committee reached France, taken over, with the Communists seizing the lion's share.

These measures, gradually elaborated, contrary to the normal jurisprudence of France, boded ill for the coming Liberation. The Communists were acting according to their kind; they could justify themselves on revolutionary grounds; although they had been on the side of Stalin and, consequently, of Hitler in the first twenty months of the struggle, they now proclaimed themselves the veritable "patriots" and denounced as "traitors" all who were against them. They smeared with suspicion—and doomed to prison and ruin and death—all their enemies, in the name of their new-found patriotism. They were right according to their creed, which called for an intensive "class war" and the establishment, by bloody processes, of Communism. But on what ground the Socialists and, above all, the Christian Democrats, the representatives of capitalism, the antagonists of revolution, could justify their participation, is beyond my understanding. There were mixed motives, intense bitterness, the spirit of vengeance, political ambition, and genuine abhorrence of the Vichy government which had acknowledged an undoubted defeat for which it was not responsible and had in some degree, under the pressure of necessity, "collaborated" with the invader.

I cannot concede that the Christian Democrats showed wisdom in permitting themselves to be dominated by feelings or calculations that brought grist to the Communist mill. Be this as it may, the three party pacts of Algiers, while carrying De Gaulle to temporary power, were in reality anti-Gaullist and saddled France with governments which wrought her much harm and postponed for years any hope of reconciliation of men who had, in different ways, equally suffered under German rule and had reacted according to their opportunities and natures.

The union of Frenchmen should have been the first and

supreme aim of all who pretended to direct the destinies of France after a terrible ordeal. The division of the French into hostile groups was the supreme fault of Algiers. De Gaulle was the standard bearer, but Gaullism was submerged by the rising flood of class and partisan hatred.

In the meantime, our attention was drawn to the events in Italy. For, while the political game was being played in Algeria, the war continued in other theatres. It was a real war, but in Italy, too, it was strangely political. Italy had lost a good third of her effectives; she had been, on land and on sea, badly beaten; she was groaning under the German yoke which was as heavy on her as on France. Pantelleria, which was to have been a new Gibraltar, was tamely surrendered. When Sicily was attacked on July 10, 1943, the 200,000 Italian soldiers, flanked by Germans, put up only a feeble resistance. Many of them fled and exchanged their uniforms for civilian clothes. On July 26 the king (accused by Mussolini of having insisted on entering the war in 1940), the somewhat treacherous Marshal Badoglio, and Dino Grandi decided that Mussolini—"the last of the Romans," as Hitler called him—was a spent force.

The threatened bombing of Rome, for nothing was to be spared in the merciless struggle, created a panic. There was a conspiracy against the Fascist leader by men who had profited for many years by his régime. Ciano, his son-in-law, who, in all justice it must be admitted, had disliked some of Mussolini's foreign policy, preferring a Latin bloc of France, Italy, and Spain in the Mediterranean to the Franco-German-Spanish bloc against Italy that he believed was taking shape, was among the adversaries of the Duce. In the Grand Council, after a dramatic debate, Mussolini was put in a minority. Why Mussolini attempted no resistance while he possessed his own troops, remains a mystery. He called on the king, was arrested, and was carried from island to island until he was at last confined under a guard with orders to shoot him if he attempted to escape, in the fortress of Gran Sassa, 6,000 feet high in the Appenines. We heard that he was to be delivered to the Allies. Cinema companies were prepared to pay large sums to exhibit him. A triumphal procession was planned for New York, with Mussolini led captive, like the defeated generals in ancient Rome. And then, one day in September, came the stupendous exploit of Major Skorzeny and his band, who descended on the narrow ledge of the mountain in small airplanes—Storks—and rescued Mussolini.

It was a changed Mussolini, sick and weary, who met Hitler. He was filled with rancor, vowing vengeance, without either the mental faculties of other days or the means of resuming his old authority. The Italian Social Republic which he set up had a brief and shadowy existence. It did little beyond helping the evacuation of Italians from Germany and some other countries. Mussolini ordered a trial which resulted in the execution of deserters who were in his clutches, some of his earliest companions and his son-in-law, Ciano, but the feeble forces then at his disposal could neither save him nor afford effective aid to the Germans, now their taskmasters. In the end, he was ignominiously butchered by Communist partisans, together with the mistress who was with him in his last painful days. It is sad to think of the humiliating and violent end of a man who had rendered immense services to his country, but finally left it weaker than it had been before his advent. Churchill, who had once paid Mussolini the greatest tributes of which even his rhetoric was capable, rather ungallantly announced Il Duce's death by rushing in to guests assembled at his dinner table, shouting: "Ah! the bloody beast is dead."

A good deal has been written about the "double game" of Marshal Pétain. But the marshal never betrayed anybody. He concluded an armistice with the Germans, after the defeat of France, because he could not do otherwise. He tried to keep contact with the British: he did keep close contact with the Americans. It was perfectly proper that he should deceive, if he could, the Germans, who were not the allies of France.

But the case of the Italians was entirely different. Germany was the ally of Italy. While Badoglio was protesting that the change of government in Italy did not mean any change of attitude of Italy toward Germany, while the king himself was giving the same assurances, a secret armistice was negotiated with the Anglo-Americans, and it was concluded five days before it was announced (September 8). The Germans were in an enemy country, with all the danger that the situation comported. The comparison with the French armistice or with the French Resistance does not hold good. Both the French armistice and the French Resistance, however much they may be criticized on other grounds, involved no act of treachery toward an ally. The French did not surrender their fleet to Germany; the Italians did surrender their fleet to the Allies.

There was still much fighting in Italy, for the Germans, ably led by General Kesselring, in spite of the Italian defection, fell back slowly step by step; and the Allies did not throw in sufficient forces to sweep through the Balkans.

As we listened to the radio, we concluded that the battle for Italy was as good as won by the Allied forces in the eventful year of 1943. What would follow next? Would France be evacuated, as the marshal in his conversation with me seemed to think? Would the second front be opened, as Stalin insisted, on French soil? Or would the Allies decide to continue their thrust, thus forcing the Germans back into Germany and, at the same time, barring the route of the Russians in the Balkans? The second alternative was by far the most sensible. Churchill favored it. He was right. The Allied advance through the Balkans might have spared us the menace of a third world war.

18

Resistance—Real and False

BEFORE dealing with the vital problem of what is known as the Resistance—that is, the active, more or less organized Resistance, quite distinct from the resistance of Vichy—before endeavoring to strike the balance between its good and evil results, I must explain the position of the marshal. He had referred me to Laval and had suggested that he himself was not free. At that time I hardly realized how fettered he was. Only when I met by accident, in the streets of Vichy, a former acquaintance of my journalistic days in Paris, was I fully informed of his position.

Paul Marion, whom I thus encountered, was an ex-Communist who had edited an anti-Communist newspaper. Laval had made him minister of information. His functions were, in fact, shared by Paul Creyssel and René Bonnefoy—the former in charge of propaganda, the latter in charge of the press. Neither of them was an extremist, both of them carried out their duties with a certain objectivity. This is what Marion told me to explain his own silence.

After the landing in Africa, it was decided in a council of ministers that, in the future, the signature of the marshal was not necessary on state documents. A decree bearing the signature of Laval alone would be valid. Thus was real power given to Laval, and withdrawn from the marshal. Clearly, the marshal had become a mere figurehead. The decision might be defended on the ground of Pétain's age, his incapacity for strenuous and continuous scrutiny of the daily problems. It was held to be inadvisable for him to waste his time and his strength on routine business.

Now Marion, in a press conference, had underlined the meaning of the act. He intimated that the marshal had become a nonentity. When the marshal heard of Marion's interpretation, he was very angry. If he could not dismiss Laval, he could refuse to see Marion. At the next council meeting, he looked Marion in the eye and cuttingly remarked: "I did not expect to find you here."

A simple phrase, without importance, you may suppose, if you have never heard the marshal execute an adversary. On Marion it fell like the knife of a guillotine. He fled from the room, and did not venture again into the presence of Pétain. He was virtually in hiding.

Now, at last, a solution had been found. The marshal had agreed to the suppression of Marion's post, or rather its attachment to the presidency, i.e., to Laval. Marion was disposed of. But there was a snag. A new post was created at Paris in the same decree, a post which Laval intended for Marion. Marion told me all this, glad to escape from the wrath of the marshal and the atmosphere of Vichy.

Alas, for Marion! A quarter of an hour later someone told the marshal what the decree implied. He ran down the three flights of stairs which separated his rooms from the office of the prime minister, stalked majestically into the midst of the astonished clerks, and demanded the paper. They gave it to him, he tore it up and, without another word, returned to his apartment.

Although the personal authority of the marshal was considerable, he thus enjoyed little legal status in 1943. A great deal was done of which he was kept in ignorance. Doubtless, I furnish an argument to those who regret that he did not resign, or leave France, after the American landing in Africa. From Algiers he could have directed the Resistance and have prevented the struggle for political power and personal prestige.

How could it be expected that groups of men who were virtually outlaws, drawn from all classes of society, in perpetual peril, whose leaders in some cases were congenital rebels, untrained, unscrupulous, living in primitive conditions, however elevated were their patriotic sentiments, however "pure" their intentions, would behave invariably with due regard to persons and property? They were herded with others glad to throw off the inhibitions of civilization. Among the guerrillas that were formed in France there were, as was inevitable, a considerable number of undesirables, behaving like bandits, turning their hands against their compatriots. Do not suppose that I slander the Resistance in France: I honor it greatly: I count among my friends who were in the Resistance men whom I regard as the most chivalrous I have known. They are the first to regret that their comrades were not all of their pattern. They are the first to regret the unavoidable degeneration of the movement brought about by irregulars who joined the Maquis.

Nor should it be thought that only habitual criminals behave abominably. In the breast of peaceful citizens a demon often slumbers. I remember the confession of a distinguished scientist that he was delighted at the opportunity of "bashing in the face of some of his fellows with a spanner." An astonishingly large number of us, though we may not suspect it, rejoice in the opportunity to revert to savagery. Cruelty, usually repressed, is in our nature. We must not blame the *franc-tireurs* of France if they were associated with a certain number of armed terrorists, who made war on their fellow countrymen rather than on the Germans.

Today, in 1952, I cannot pick up a French newspaper without reading of attacks by armed men on banks or rich persons, of battles with the police, of well-planned robberies, of daring exploits. [In the summer of 1952, a prominent English scientist, Sir John C. Drummond, and his family were brutally murdered and robbed while on an automobile tour of southern France.]

The increase of crime is not of course entirely due to the experience with the Maquis—though often the assailants falsely claim the title of Resistant—but I suggest that the breakdown of the ordinary conventions in 1943–1945, the impunity with which bold acts could be committed—and applauded—created an atmosphere which is antisocial and dangerous to public and private security.

On the other side there was formed, in the later stages of the war, a Militia which fought not against the Germans but against the Maquis and eventually found itself an auxiliary of the German army. In the name and under the cover of restoring order, it was cooperating with the enemy. Yet, distinctions have to be drawn between the "pure" in the Militia and the "impure." Some of the "pure" undoubtedly believed that they were performing an imperative social duty. Nothing has touched me more, in these postwar years, than the tributes paid by the best of their adversaries in the Maquis to the best of the Militia. The fact is that both the Maquis and the Militia, deadly enemies, had to be recruited from the same classes, containing good and bad; and many who, almost by chance, chose the Militia and were shot as traitors might easily have chosen the Maquis and have been celebrated as heroes.

In civil warfare the smallest circumstance may decide a human destiny. The two ideas, of patriotism and of social order, are in themselves respectable, and when they come into opposition how can it be expected that men of limited intelligence, caught by this or that propaganda, will always choose aright? There were unmitigated scoundrels who inflicted tortures which defy description on their adversaries and on innocent nonpartisans, but there were also youths on both sides who wished to serve their country.

Assassinations of isolated German soldiers, though not unknown in the first year of the occupation, may be said to have begun systematically in 1942. The individual German soldier was no more guilty than the individual soldier of any other country. He was sent to occupy France and, on the whole, he was disciplined. Both De Gaulle and Marcel Cachin, the venerable Communist leader, countenanced deeds which, if practiced on our own occupying troops today, would be denounced. The right of an army to defend itself in occupied territory can hardly be disputed. The Germans unhappily took hostages, a practice which apparently is not condemned by military conventions.

In one case with which I was acquainted, a student, a mere boy, had lingered with his companions in the streets after curfew hour. He was arrested by a German patrol. The next morning he would normally have been released, for his offense was not grave. But that night German soldiers were assassinated; and hostages were taken in the prisons. By pure chance my young student was among them, and was shot.

Incidents like these increased the tension between the German authorities and the population. The Communists announced that for every Communist executed ten German soldiers would be killed. The Germans replied in kind—they would execute ten, fifty, a hundred if necessary, for every German soldier killed. The resentment grew. "Incidents" became more and more common.

Otto Abetz, the German ambassador, deprecated violence in France and urged that "collaboration" should be voluntary. He believed that it was more likely to be achieved by the consent of the "left," which favored the idea of a united Europe, than by the "right," traditionally chauvinist. Hitler sometimes inclined to a "white" peace, sometimes to a new Versailles Treaty in reverse. Sometimes he was for military rigor and then for civilian indulgence. When he was persuaded that he was the dupe of the false "collaborationists," he recalled Abetz, rendering him responsible for the failure of "Montoire." Later, Abetz was sent back to Paris. But the gulf between the French and the Germans, at first narrow, widened as the months went by and as the methods of the Germans changed.

It would be tedious to recount the history of the Resistance. Until the end, that is, until just before the landing in Normandy, it was confined to a relatively few persons. There was a growing body of sympathizers, but of active participants only a minority. In one town that I know well, there were a few hundred adherents—until September 1944, when suddenly thousands put on armlets (sold for a few francs) and paraded with the real Resistants. The scorn of the real Resistants for the "Septembrisards" is justified.

In France we were all affected by the shortage of foodstuffs and by various restrictions, hard enough to bear, but life continued placidly for the masses. The railway men did not refuse to run trains for the Germans, the workers did not refuse to make tanks or munitions for the Germans; they went on quietly earning their living, as they were bound to do.

But in narrow circles the excitement of those days was intense. Colonel Passy (many of the Resistants adopted the names of underground railroad stations) was organizing the De Gaulle police at London and trying to establish liaison with the Resistance in France. Colonel Rémy was the chief secret agent in France. The British established sections and networks of Resistants in France, some of which owed no allegiance to the French chief in London. There were other movements which were not linked with London at all. There were little groups of amateur politicians who met in cafés and, talking too loudly, were arrested and deported, though their activities had been exhausted in idle words. There were clandestine bulletins and tracts, dropped into letter boxes or slipped into the pockets of passers-by or scattered in the street, in the hope that they would be picked up by sympathizers. Poets were declaring in literary magazines that "the dawn was breaking"—and thus were able to claim in 1944–1945 that they had been heroic Resistants.

There was far too much coming and going, men and women carrying compromising documents, running the risk of being arrested themselves and of causing their whole network to be arrested. Naturally, there were many false brethren in the movement, ready to sell their comrades to the Germans.

There was no unity, no coordination. Above all, the masses were not engaged. There were a few specialists in sabotage, who wrecked trains (containing French passengers as well as German soldiers) and committed other destructive acts which fell more heavily on the French than on the Germans.

One of the principal organizers in France, who was arrested, deported, and executed, it is suspected through the treachery of his lieutenant, is reported to have said that Gaullism was no part of the movement in France. Gaullism existed in London, and later in Algeria, but in France it was confined to a few of the Resistants. There were at one time far more Giraudists than Gaullists.

The question arose whether the sections could be fused under the leadership of De Gaulle. For him, it was important to obtain their adherence and to demonstrate to the British that he was in effective command. The task was gradually accomplished by a few devoted men and women, who went from group to group.

On the debit side of the movement we must surely place

the extraordinary disregard for human life which was developed. Every time members of a network were caught, their comrades suspected one of their number. Perhaps the suspicion was justified, perhaps it was not. In any case, it was only a suspicion. But, without trial, a death sentence might be passed by two or three "chiefs." It was carried out by the professional "killers." In a recent case a man, who was then minister, acknowledged that he had decided to "suppress" a conspicuous member of his group because he had been arrested by the Germans but had been released. Why had he been released? What information had he given? It was resolved to send him, in the hospital where he lay, a jar of poisoned jam. In this case, another Resistant protested and the project was abandoned. The point is that the project was actually entertained and plans made to carry it out, and that, afterward, it was admitted that the designated victim was probably guiltless. It was thought a perfectly proper thing for a few self-appointed "chiefs" to "liquidate" their companions. I cannot help thinking that conditions which erase all sense of justice, which cheapen human life, must have a lasting evil effect on the community.

As for the liquidation of men and women—and even children—who had nothing to do with the Resistance but who were lightly accused of having pro-German sympathies, they were numerous. It may well be that, in some cases, the executions were, I will not say deserved, but at any rate had some plausible excuse. But in many other cases they were utterly indefensible. Doctors were rung up at night, asked to attend a patient who was dying, and killed at some dark corner. Priests were murdered. And, of course, when lawlessness begins, sadistic crimes, without rhyme or reason, are bound to be committed. Robberies, murders, tortures, perpetrated under cover of the Resistance, were reported from every quarter of the country. The criminals of France, and they are many, had opportunities such as had never been presented to them before. When, years afterward, they were charged with the most atrocious deeds, they claimed to have acted on orders of a superior and to have belonged to the Resistance which they had disgraced. Only recently have people begun to talk and to give evidence against these brigands who professed to be Resistants; and even now their label of "Resistant" often protects them from the appropriate penalties.

The feeling was that the Resistance must be regarded as a block, that it would be condemning itself if it condemned its black sheep, and that the mantle of Noah must be thrown over the foul performances of what a famous French Abbé has called the "Resistentialists."

I exaggerate neither the number nor the nature of the crimes of an army of evildoers who took advantage of the Resistance. Books and articles have been published giving irrefutable facts and figures on this aspect of the movement, so that, today, in France the just are confounded with the unjust and there is an unfair appreciation of an effort which banded together heroes and villains.

"You can't expect the Resistants to be choir boys" was a phrase frequently heard, but at any rate the Resistance should not have knowingly admitted jailbirds into its ranks. The first and most important *épuration* (purge) should have been the *épuration* of the Resistance. Because it failed to accomplish this purification, because, on the contrary, it seemed to exonerate from blame all who were associated with it, whatever the character of their culpability, the Resistance itself is seriously discredited in the eyes of many discerning Frenchmen.

Another criticism which, now that the true story may be told, can be leveled against one branch of the Resistance, a branch which kept its autonomy to the end, is its provocativeness. The Communists are quite right when they claim to be the earliest organized body who opposed the Germans —though they had regarded the Germans as the allies of the

Bolsheviks until 1941. Their aims were political and, to attain their goal, they did not scruple to sacrifice human lives or to inflict damage on their country. It was important for them to become the martyrs of the occupation, to arouse indignation against the enemy, at any cost. They claimed, as members of their party, every hostage who was shot, every terrorist who attacked isolated Germans. They encouraged revolt of every kind and were not displeased when the Germans were stirred to bloody reprisals. They filled their coffers by raids on financial establishments, by ransom levied on private persons, and accumulated a war fund (for the pursuance of the class war) which has been estimated at billions of francs. They wiped out their adversaries, actual or potential, and they had no scruples to check them.

Though the parachuting of arms—and of considerable sums of money—from England began on a small scale in 1942, it was not until the following year that it really reached its height. In 1943 tens of thousands of Sten guns (*mitraillettes*), hand grenades and machine guns were delivered by air in carefully chosen and lonely places and were collected by the Maquis and distributed. A great many arms were hidden at the Liberation and not handed over to the authorities. Every now and again, depots of arms are discovered, and it is doubtful whether they are all in safe hands even today. In the event of the breakdown of the public order and grave disturbances, they might again be used by Communists and the criminal element to murder their fellow Frenchmen.

When, at last, there was a semblance of unity and of organization (always, however, relative), there was an influx of troops. They had to be paid. Questions of money took on an urgent shape. As before, there were the two clans, the "pures" and the mercenaries, and the mercenaries demanded good payment for their services, regarding the Resistance as furnishing profitable opportunities. Some of the Resistants made extra money by selling their information to the Americans. Some of them treated directly with the Intelligence Service. The funds made available to the Resistance were often well administered: others were less strictly accounted for, and a good deal of money went astray, finding its way into private pockets or the coffers of a party.

It was in May 1943 that the *Conseil National de la Résistance* (C.N.R.) was formed at Paris, seventeen persons being present. The Germans, a year earlier, had prepared a scheme by which one French prisoner would be exchanged for three voluntary workers in Germany. The pay offered was high, and French workers were tempted to go. Whether in France or in Germany, they had to work to live, and work usually meant work for the Germans. I held the "relève" to be a swindle. Had the Germans released an equal number of French prisoners, it might have been tolerable, but three workers for one prisoner was a one-sided bargain. Nevertheless, the appeal touched a number of Frenchmen who would have despised the temptation of higher pay. It touched the chord of chivalry, of generosity, of altruism: who could think of the men who had been behind barbed wire for three years without wanting to do something for them? We must not, therefore, condemn indiscriminately the voluntary workers; as in everything under the occupation, there were mixed motives. Young men were often animated by the thought that, having been spared for so long, it was now their duty to replace their unfortunate fellows.

The voluntary scheme was but the prelude to the order of compulsory service. Soon it was found that the number of volunteers was too small, and all young men were nominally drafted into the ranks of workers in Germany and deported. We have seen how the order was applied. The Vichy government did its best to evade it; it placed young men in "indispensable" services, it postponed the drawing up of statistics, it gave instructions to the prefects to hide as many men as possible, and the results of the compulsory drafts in France were comparatively poor.

It was not the government alone, compelled as it was to appear to yield to German demands, but rather the young men themselves who discovered ways of escape. There was one way of escape open—the Maquis!

It may be said, therefore, that Germany, by the decree of compulsory service, really created the Maquis. It had existed before on a small scale. Now it was to grow into a much larger force. It was to supply the troops hitherto lacking to the Resistance.

The escape to the Maquis did not always denote, in its origins, a spirit of anti-Pétainism or even of anti-Vichyism. It was simply and solely a revolt against the idea of being sent to Germany. Nothing had prompted many of these young men to espouse Gaullism, or Resistance in general, until their liberty was menaced, until they were liable to deportation. Deportation!—dreaded word! The recruiting sergeant for the Resistance and, therefore, ultimately for De Gaulle, was Fritz Sauckel, the *Gauleiter* for Thuringia, whom Hitler had put in charge of the problem of forced labor. The Maquis was made by Germany: the Resistance became a reality in 1943 when, by insisting on a form of "collaboration" that was slavery, an end was put to any possibility of genuine "collaboration."

So now we had an increasing body of "Resistants." For the first time! I do not consider the political groups, the conspirators, the train wreckers, or even the French spies acting on behalf of London, as a serious obstruction to the Germans. Nor do I consider bands of armed men who molested French farmers to have been deadly foes of Germany. The sporadic attacks on German soldiers could in no way cripple the enemy; on the contrary, the consequences fell heavily on the French. But the Maquis was capable of causing considerable embarrassment to the occupying troops if it developed. Whether, in fact, it did not unduly injure

France, whether it encouraged a mentality that would ultimately produce antisocial effects, is another matter. In any case, the Maquis existed and had to be reckoned with.

While the Communists were furbishing their arms for a revolutionary *coup* and were prematurely blowing up bridges, cutting telephone lines, and so forth, these recruits to the Maquis were taught how to manipulate arms. They were a higgledy-piggledy collection, young men of good family and education thrown together with others who were lacking in civic virtues. It was not the best of schools for the rising generation. Their life was often hard, they were herded in groups of thirty in the mountains, on the plateaux, in woods and forests. Often they found friendly assistance in the towns and villages.

Yet, again, the undesirable elements, as was inevitable, mingled with the Maquisards. There were Red Spaniards, of whom half a million had escaped to France after the Spanish civil war, anarchistic Italians, and other foreigners of doubtful character in exile. At Nîmes, seventeen men, mostly foreigners, were hung under the arches after being taken in arms; and at Clermont-Ferrand houses were fired by the Germans because someone had shot at the marching troops. Certain villages suffered terribly, men and women were executed, and the churches and houses burned. The whole world has heard of the unspeakable massacres of Oradour and of Tulle. I would not willingly rekindle the hatred that sprang up on both sides, but it is impossible to pass in silence the lesson of a prolonged occupation that began "correctly" but degenerated into an orgy of assassination. We were plunged back into the horrors of the Middle Ages.

The effects are lasting. Europe has undergone a sad decline. Most of the kindlier feelings, the nobler thoughts which used to inspire us are scoffed at by a generation that in its youth lived through the terrors of our epoch, and vulgarity and immorality and materialism reign in a world that has lost its higher hopes and aspirations.

19

Return to Paris

With the insatiable curiosity of my profession—an irrepressible curiosity which retirement had not destroyed—I told myself that, to complete my picture of the occupation, I must again see Paris. To ignore Paris would be like leaving Hamlet out of the play. If it is often said that Paris is not France, just as New York is not America; it is truer to say that France is not France without Paris. Every region of France has its own characteristics, its special population, its accent, its manners, and is an indispensable part of France. But it is a part only, whereas Paris contains all the provinces and adds something of its own. It is more than the capital: it is the compendium of France.

In my years of exile in the South I had many compensations: the blue sea, the sunshine, the mountains, the gay-colored villas, the fields of flowers on terracelike ledges of rock, the gnarled olive trees, the graceful palm trees, and if we did not get enough to eat, it is easier to go hungry in the warm South than in the cold North. Still, I had ventured as far as Montpellier, as Marseilles, as Vichy, and a variety of cities in the South. Why not, before the war was over, have at least one look at Paris?

My wife tried to dissuade me. I had narrowly escaped arrest on many occasions. She foresaw disaster: I might end the war in prison. But I argued that I had been in peril only because I had made public statements that did not please the Germans. My identification card would preserve me from harm.

A Parisian friend of mine had the same urge to return. But when he made inquiries, he found that his apartment had been sealed up because he was suspected of being a Jew. To return, he would have to prove that he was not a Jew, and that his father and mother, his grandfather and grandmother, were of "Aryan" race. The "proof" consisted in the production of baptismal certificates. Now, he hardly knew where his father and mother were born, much less his grandfather and grandmother, belonging as he did to a family of soldiers who had moved from garrison town to garrison town. Even had he known the date and the place of their birth, it did not follow that they had been baptized, for France is a country in which freethinkers abound. Moreover, in the constant bombings of France by the English and the Americans, archives had been lost. The quest for "proof" of his non-Jewishness seemed hopeless—until he found a priest who was prepared to furnish him with all the certificates required.

After he had gone back, my desire to visit Paris became more urgent. I have now known five different types or moods of Paris: the Paris of the frivolous *insouciant* days before 1914, the Paris of the 1914–1918 war days, at once darkened and animated, the Paris of the postwar days, seething with new life, in which literature and art renewed themselves, the Paris of the German occupation, and the Paris which has emerged from the ordeal and which has not yet overcome its sadness. . . .

Nothing could have prevented me from returning in 1943. I hardly knew what to expect. There had been many bombings, but the center of the city was as yet unscathed. For how long? Would anything be respected in the war? In my League of Nations days we had agreed that cities should never be bombed. We had agreed that peaceful inhabitants should be spared. Germany had begun the sky attacks in Poland, bombing Warsaw and the other cities, and the civilian refugees who were clogging the highways, as she also bombed Rotterdam and, soon after, the French refugees; it was not long before we had forgotten the pledge we had taken in the early days of the war, and now we were pitilessly bombing not only German towns but also French towns which were unprotected and helpless. I had seen the bombing of Marseilles (a mistake, an aviator told me later!), a whole quarter in ruins, the dead running into thousands. I had been in bombings at Cannes, at Nice, in the little places about the Var Bridge. I had heard that Rouen, almost my home town, with its hundred spires, a veritable museum of the Renaissance and the pre-Renaissance, had lost many of its priceless architectural jewels. Was it not conceivable that Paris, with its treasures of all the ages, would be wrecked? I must see it again before it disappeared in the universal havoc.

My misgivings were not fulfilled so far as Paris is concerned, but how many other towns have been shattered? When the monuments of our civilization, the glorious heritage of our past, were ruthlessly destroyed in Germany and Italy, when the populations of Cologne and Hamburg were burnt and shriveled up in the heat of phosphorus bombs (why has there never been an outcry against the use of phosphorus bombs?—are they not just as inhuman as the atomic or hydrogen bomb?)—all of us who, doubtless because we were not in the thick of the fighting, had not lost our sensibilities as human beings were horrified. It was, however, the danger in which Paris stood that prompted the

European friends of my little circle to propose—rather futilely, for what can stop the spirit of destruction when it is once let loose?—the creation of what we called a *Conseil de l'Humanité*.

There was little prospect that the proposal would ever emerge from the stage of epistolary communications. Now that the war is over, what purpose would it serve to put forward a plea for the preservation of whatever is dear to us in the memorials of time? Who would listen to a plea for the sparing of civilians? Obliteration bombing, carpets of bombs, indiscriminate destruction, are now a recognized part of war. It is undeniable that we have retrogressed. Before the war, everybody who pretended to enlightenment would have agreed to a self-denying ordinance. Today, in our fear, we cannot agree even to rule out the atomic bomb, and there is nowhere any serious proposal for the abolition of bombers or the restriction of their use to purely military objectives. Where all this is leading us has been underlined with appalling clarity by the English publicist, F. J. P. Veale, in his *Advance to Barbarism*.

We think, indeed, that military objectives include everything and anybody whose extinction would distress the enemy. I have devoted my life to moral causes which today are scarcely regarded as subjects worthy of discussion.

It is not a question of sparing this or that nation: it is a question of sparing ourselves. We are all the poorer for the destruction of a single item of our patrimony. When I think that France, before the war, classed ancient buildings as "national monuments," when I think that Spain passed laws forbidding the exportation of works of art, and when I think that we have smashed innumerable relics of antiquity, heirlooms of the centuries, I realize how far we have set back the clock. To declare that we can replace monasteries, churches, museums, cities by better constructions in concrete is a bitter mockery. Can we also replace men and women in concrete? What is worse than our material loss, is the loss of our sense of values. . . .

I am not digressing. The threat to Paris was real. It was a threat by us and a threat by the Germans, and it was only by a miracle that Paris survived both threats. It was miraculously saved in the war that is said to have ended. Will it be saved next time? We have engaged ourselves on a slippery slope, and there is no stopping halfway. Must we bomb and bomb until:

> The cloud-capp'd towers, the gorgeous palaces,
> The solemn temples, the great globe itself,
> Yea, all which it inherit, shall dissolve;
> And, like this insubstantial pageant faded,
> Leave not a rack behind.

It was not easy to travel in time of war. The trains, reduced in number, were overcrowded. The corridors were chock-a-block. There was no room to stir, and to enter trains was sometimes an acrobatic feat. Often passengers were clustered on the steps. The door of the water closet was open and three or four people were standing inside. Clinging for life to the steel bars was a little crowd on the buffers. We were packed tighter than the troops in the legendary wagon labeled:

Eight Horses or
Forty Men,

for at least the number of troopers was limited. Besides, it was quite possible that a train wrecker had removed the rails. It was more than likely that a bomber would let fall his explosives on us. Sometimes an airman would machine-gun the unfortunate travelers. If we escaped these dangers, we were constantly reminded of them as we passed roofless houses and broken walls hit by a bomb intended for a bridge or a railroad. If we did not escape, it would be little consolation for our relatives to know that a few German officers had shared our fate. . . .

There were no taxicabs at the Paris station. There was no other means of locomotion than the Metro—the Paris underground. Bad enough at the best, the Metro was now as overcrowded as the trains, the air was fetid and, as half the stations were closed for the sake of economizing on power, light and money, one was left far from one's destination. A porter demanded hundreds of francs and his fare to carry my suitcase from the station to the Metro and from the Metro to my hotel.

I had expected to be shocked, but I had not counted on being so depressed as I was at the sight of enormous Swastika flags almost covering some of the buildings in the rue de Rivoli. German soldiers and blonde girls in uniform were in the streets. The hotels were nearly all requisitioned. Here and there were barricades around the entrances to restaurants reserved for the Germans, and one was compelled to walk in the roadway.

The first friends I called on were old ladies whom I had known for thirty-odd years, ladies who once entertained in their spacious salon. Now they talked prices to me. I had thought foodstuffs scarce and dear in the South, but they seemed to be scarcer and dearer in the North. It should be remembered, when I quote a few figures which I noted, that the franc had not yet fallen, that it was nominally worth more than ten times what it is today. Yet butter, which used to be 15 francs a kilo, was than 1,500 francs on the black market, the only market for most things. Cigarettes, which used to be two or three francs a packet, were over 100. A chicken was about 1,000 francs—in francs of the period. A tin of milk ran to 400 francs, and a tin of sardines about the same. A suit of clothes cost 20,000 francs of the period—roughly thirty times as much, quality for quality, as before the war. Household utensils were almost unobtainable.

Men and women clattered in shoes with wooden soles. Soap, real soap, was a luxury which only the richest could afford. When I went to a modest restaurant, my meal cost me ten dollars, or fifty shillings. I could not understand how the ordinary Frenchman lived at all. The insipid and unnutritive vegetables, the small portion of horrible bread, which was about all he could get, reduced him to a skeleton. I shared the poor fare of a number of my friends and came to the conclusion that, bad as things were in the South, they were better than in Paris. Perhaps, in the whole of my travels, Lyons was the best-fed city.

One evening I called on a doctor whom I had known, and there found a fairly satisfactory table. He managed to obtain food from the country. But his wife burst into tears. She told me her story. She was of Jewish birth, though she had married a Christian. Her brother had been deported. She had foolishly, according to her husband, declared her origin. Therefore, she could not walk in the street without displaying on her breast a hideous yellow badge. She could not stir out of doors at all after an early hour in the evening. She was not allowed in public places, such as concert halls and theatres. She had grown neurasthenic, and her husband was afraid she might take her life.

I went to pass another evening in the cafés of Saint-Germain-des-Prés. There were black blinds on the windows. The light was dimmed. There were a few literary folk with whom I was acquainted, drinking and talking wearily. I thought of the animated throngs of former days, our joyous conversations, our excited exchange of ideas, our loud discussions . . . and I left. But in the street there was not a soul to be seen. Where did the Parisians pass their *soirées?* The heart of Paris was as deserted as a country lane. Oh, for the live throngs which used to circulate in the brightly lit thoroughfares!

Everywhere there was gloom. The war had dragged on

until it had squeezed out the last drop of gaiety from the once Gay City.

Then came an air raid. They were now so frequent that the jaded Parisian did not trouble to take refuge in the cellar or in the shelters. What was the use? If a bomb struck, no shelter was secure. Everybody had become fatalistic. The worst of it was that when the sirens shrieked, the Metro came to a standstill and the passengers were immobilized underground for several hours.

What did the Parisians think of the air raids? There were divided opinions. But everybody was saddened. They all thought that Paris should have been spared. It was true that no great damage had been done; the bombs were intended for the factories in the suburbs, but this fact did not mend matters for those who worked in the factories or those who lived in the suburbs, and one never knew when a bomb might fall on a densely populated quarter of Paris. The aim of the airmen was astonishingly poor. I afterward spoke to an airman who had taken part in raids on crowded centres, asking him if his imagination did not picture the scene of death and devastation which he produced. He replied that he deliberately closed his imagination to the consequences of the raid, that he thought only of pulling a lever and of getting away. He told me that he usually closed his eyes as well as his imagination. Have we not all practiced the art of closing our eyes and our imagination to the consequences of our acts? Have not our recent statesmen, above all, practiced the art of closing their eyes and their imagination?

Most of the Parisians were resentful. The bombing definitely did harm to the Allied cause. Paris is proverbially forgetful and, I daresay, the sentiments of 1943 have largely disappeared. But not so in the ruined regions of Normandy. One town that I know had 2,000 inhabitants killed or wounded out of a population of 5,000, and hardly a house was left standing. It is better not to ask the survivors what they think today. Under the official friendship for England and America, there is a smoldering sense of injury and resentment. When I went later to call on the prefect of a Normandy town, the usher, whom I had never seen and who might be expected to observe discretion, began by asking me what I thought of the wrecked town, and he went on to blame, in this particular case, the Americans who flew high and spread out a veritable carpet of bombs. He was a little kinder to the English, who flew lower and took better aim at their objectives, but they too often failed to hit their target. It is probable that nobody has written of French feelings, for there has been a conspiracy of silence; but it seems to me better that we should realize the deep anger that the air raids on France awakened. For my part, I do not pretend to judge of military necessities, but I can judge human feelings.

Propagandists made the most of a minority of Frenchmen who imprudently went out into the streets and waved encouragingly to the Allied bombers. That minority existed. But it did not represent the general French attitude. The French had grown indignant with the occupants; they were ready to revolt if there was the smallest chance of success, but they were pained at the idea that there was no means of separating the Germans from the French, and that they were, in fact if not in intention, lumped together as the enemy to be hurt by bombing.

After a few days, I left Paris more depressed than when I entered the city. I decided, since I was unmolested, to continue my journey to my Normandy village. I found it impossible to enter the train by the door, but by dint of pushing and of being pushed, hauled and tugged by willing arms, I managed to get through the window and to find enough standing room, though it was painful to be jerked backward and forward as the speed of the train slackened or accelerated. Jostled, shoved, prodded by knees and elbows, I arrived at last, more dead than alive, at the market town of my village. The only vehicle in which to pursue my journey was a cart which had carried manure. In this evil-smelling, broken-down cart I rode with a young peasant who had been prisoner in Germany. We went through the market town, and I was grieved to find that the centre from which radiated most of the streets of the town had been completely razed. From the post office to the old church there was a blank. The bridge had been blown up. As we proceeded, the peasant told me of the daily visits of the airplanes and showed me the marks of machine-gunning on the houses. I could see no purpose in the attacks of which he complained bitterly, assuring me that even the workers in the fields were sometimes fired on.

My mill, which had been confiscated by the Germans, was now in ruins. The courtyard was a forest of weeds and a wild flowering bush which is called, in my region, Spanish lilac. My orchard was a tangle of undergrowth. The garden paths could not be discerned in the wilderness. The roof of the house was badly riddled, and let in the rain. The water pipes were broken. The central heating had exploded. As for the rooms, they were in an indescribable state of confusion. My books and my papers, crumpled, torn, dirty, strewed the floor of my study. There was, of course, not a vestige of household linen, the curtains had been stolen from the broken windows, clothes, carpets, furniture had been removed. I spent an hour surveying the wreck, and then went to lunch with my friend the Paris doctor who lived by the twelfth-century church. Then I took the train back to Paris and immediately left for the South. How glad I was to be back again after this glimpse of life in the North!

The depredations of the Germans, the squalor and the misery, the subdued air of the Parisians, the apathy of the peasants, the incomprehension of the Allies who, long before the contemplated landing, bombed, as I thought, quite unnecessarily, even the countryside, furnished subjects for sad reflection. I must assume that there was some plan, some purpose, in these raids. I must assume that they were not purely haphazard and utterly wasteful. But if, occasionally, the effects were terrific, as they came nearer and nearer to us in the South, I was chiefly struck by their lack of accuracy. There must have been hundreds of raids on the Var bridge near my home; but the Var bridge was never hit for months, though most of the villas in the vicinity were destroyed. When, at last, it was blown up, it was by accident: the Italians, when they retired, had mined it, and the Germans appear to have been unaware of the fact until a lucky shot brought down the whole structure. As it turned out, the destruction of the Var bridge neither helped the Allies nor impeded the Germans, who safely withdrew into Italy when there was a landing in the South. The only result was gravely to inconvenience the French and to require an expenditure of money that France could ill afford.

France had suffered in the few months of warfare in 1939–1940 but, nevertheless, remained virtually intact and she would have remained virtually intact had not the war been pursued on her soil more or less aimlessly, inflicting far more damage on the French than on the German occupants. If crops were burnt, the Germans took neither more nor less than they had demanded: it was the French who went short. The sabotage, the bombings and, eventually, the battles on French territory cost France over a million houses, much of her industrial equipment, her ports, her factories, her communications. Though France was virtually out of the war for four years, she lost as heavily as though she had been actively engaged. I cannot help wondering whether it was worth while, from any viewpoint, to wound France so grievously.

It is true that, in a material sense, she has made a marvelous recovery, but in a moral sense recovery is slow. France, despite her defeat, might well have kept her moral and material resources and have been the leader of Europe in the struggle, of vital importance for the future of our race, for the very soul of Europe.

Alas, her unity was broken, and the youth of the nation was corrupted by a hundred ways of earning illicit money without working. A prefect with whom I lunched told me of a banquet given by collegians to celebrate the first million francs made by one of them. An artisan, employed by me, told me that, in a café where he was making repairs, the well-dressed sons of humble artisans like himself were playing dice for stakes of a thousand francs. Youths in their teens boasted of having made in a few months more than their fathers, honest professional men, had been paid in a lifetime. Where did the money come from? Would those boys ever be content with ordinary occupations? One girl I knew, who had won high honors at the age of sixteen, now abandoned her studies to trade in false tickets. Another of the same age stayed away from her classes to carry messages for the Resistance. Lying and cheating and immorality and the making of easy money, contempt for the rules of society, disobedience, lack of discipline, experience in the manipulation of deadly weapons which could be turned on friend or foe, these were the factors which were calculated to produce a country not of heroes but of gangsters. Deeds which have always been regarded with abhorrence were given fine-sounding names, but such training of youth must have deplorable consequences for a nation.

Nor was it only youth that was misled. I saw in my own circle small shopkeepers who suddenly grew rich beyond the dreams of avarice. There was a wine dealer in a humble way of business, who married off his daughter and gave a wedding breakfast that cost him half a million francs. There was a garage owner who amassed a fortune which ran into billions of francs by buying cars and selling them to the Germans. Foodstuffs were "cornered" and fabulous profits were made. There was, inevitably, an exploitation of the occupants, who did not hesitate to pay whatever prices were proposed, since they were paying with French money. The French money did not leave France: it merely went into other French pockets. There was banditry. There were mysterious funds that seemed to fall from heaven. How far the Vichy government, how far the Germans, and how far the civil war that raged in France were to blame for the widespread corruption, I will not try to analyze. The fact is that there was a breakdown of orderly society, a repudiation of morality, a loosening of restraints in the later stages of the occupation, and the victims were the decent members of the community. I murmured the words of the poet:

> Nous sommes l'Empire à la fin de la décadence
> Qui regarde passer les grands barbares blancs. . . .

20

Counterresistance

TOWARD the end of 1943, rumors of peace between Germany and Russia took shape. I had information, well authenticated, that conversations were proceeding at Stockholm and even at Moscow, where the Japanese were acting as intermediaries. (It should be remembered that Russia did not enter the war against Japan until the eleventh hour had long struck.) The German retreat was bringing the Russians nearer and nearer to Berlin. But Russia was tired of sustaining the principal weight of the war, and the Anglo-Americans did not show any eagerness to create the "second front" for which Stalin called in vain.

There were many reasons that Russia and Germany should come to an understanding and mark out their spheres of influence. The chief argument on the Russian side was the desire to win without the Allies, since the others would not share the risks. It is to be noted that the Russians, with more foresight than might have been expected, were careful not to ravage German territory: they left that work to the

Anglo-American air forces. A Russo-German peace, which would unite the two strongest nations on the continent, would offer an irresistible force against "Western capitalism."

The French authorities had some information about the conditions that were put forward. I have every reason to think that the pourparlers were not far from succeeding. But they failed in the end, partly because Stalin grew greedier as his armies advanced, and Hitler became more obstinate. He would not consent to an arrangement by which he would "lose face," and he missed the opportunity that was offered him.

Nothing was more to be dreaded by the Anglo-Americans than peace made behind their backs. The prospect of a fusion of the forces of Russia and Germany rightly alarmed diplomats, who were aware that the idea of a great bloc has haunted the minds of Russian and German statesmen for generations.

I learned, too, that agents not disapproved by Vichy, and Frenchmen in America, were suggesting a cessation of hostilities between the Anglo-Americans and Germany. The victory of Bolshevism began to trouble some of the Westerners. But there were still those who preferred a Russian domination to a German domination—or rather who believed that some way could be found of cajoling Russia after the war. Still, sensible politicians could not close their eyes to the choice: Germany or Russia?

Even if Russia won, would she not be seriously weakened and be obliged to do the bidding of the Anglo-Americans, whose armies had as yet not been seriously engaged? Should not Russia and Germany be left to fight it out? The Anglo-Americans, fresh and fully armed, could determine the sort of peace to be made. So ran diplomatic speculation.

A proposal put forward by some in Allied circles at this time was that the Germans should unreservedly withdraw their troops from all the conquered countries of the West. It particularly interested the French. Marshal Pétain, as I have shown, was not without hope of an evacuation of the German forces from France without the necessity of fighting. That was undoubtedly the best solution from the French national viewpoint. On the German and on the Allied sides there were obvious objections. "A free hand against Russia" would be treachery—and what was worse, it was doubtful, at this stage, whether Germany, even if relieved of the pressure of the West, could put up a decisive performance against Russia. The sequel might well be a Russo-German compromise —which was precisely what had to be averted. As a natural result of the bitterness engendered by years of hostility and unceasing propaganda, there was also, among the highest Anglo-American statesmen, a fanatical determination to defeat and destroy Germany, no matter the consequences.

These debates, which went on in Russian, German, and Anglo-American circles, and of which the echoes reached me, were unreal. The war machine had been launched and could not be stopped. It was no longer a matter of reason, of diplomacy, or even of sentiment. The war machine had got, to mix metaphors, the bit between its teeth. The war machine was autonomous; it was not to be halted by considerations of policy. The war machine cared nothing for the future. The war machine was not an instrument: it was the master.

So, while Stalin was making his sardonic calculations and Hitler was being urged to seek a solution (he had himself, in saner moments, pointed out the impossibility for Germany of fighting on two fronts), and the Anglo-Americans (or at any rate the British, for Roosevelt still had a tender spot for "Uncle Joe") were wondering how both Germany and Russia could be crippled, the war continued, and all attempts to stop it came to naught.

In France, there were preparations for the peace which seemed imminent. These preparations were not to the taste of those who, at Vichy or at Paris, had gambled on a German victory and could not now reverse the engines. The advisers of the marshal informed him that the time was now ripe to abandon altogether the policy of *attentisme* and to play his cards boldly. One of his advisers, who came to the South on an important mission, was by no means a supporter of parliaments, and I was surprised when he called on me to tell me in confidence of the design to convene Parliament in defiance of the Germans. He gave me a draft of the marshal's message, by which he intended to place in the hands of the National Assembly an account of his stewardship, and to leave it to that body to decide what should be done. It would be asked to ratify the measures taken since 1940, when the National Assemby had accorded Pétain full powers. If the National Assembly chose to renew its confidence, the marshal would carry on. It might, in the alternative, nominate a successor to the marshal. There would be full freedom, so far as the marshal was concerned, to criticize, to suggest new measures, to indicate the policy of the future. The public was to be informed by radio of the decision and to learn that democracy was not dead in France.

I thought the plan excellent, and in line with the course I had proposed in my conversation with the marshal earlier in the year. But I had the gravest doubts about carrying it out. Was it possible that the Germans would allow the appeal to a popular assembly? In any event, the only chance of success was to maintain secrecy until the last minute, so that the Germans could not oppose their veto.

If I, an outsider, was informed, how many other persons were informed? If Laval, who could not doubt that the project was directed against him, got wind of it, would he not find means to prevent the message from being delivered and the meeting from being held?

It was rather odd, I thought, that the prospective antagonist of the message and meeting was Laval, a parliamentary man, while some of its keenest supporters were notoriously antiparliamentary. Besides, if it had been impossible to convene Parliament before this date, why was it now considered that the Germans would permit the address to the people and to the institutions of the Republic, without denouncing the armistice and chasing the government from Vichy? And how many parliamentarians, who had taken care to give no sign of life hitherto, would be daring enough to respond to the convocation? My apprehensions were confirmed. It is a thousand pities, for had the National Assembly met, there could have been no further dispute as to whether Pétain or De Gaulle or any other chief was the veritable representative of France.

The secret was let out. The reactions of Germany were immediate. Von Ribbentrop wrote a vehement letter to the marshal, in whom the men about Hitler saw their real enemy, the most stubborn of resistants. Ribbentrop's letter is proof, if proof be needed, of the anti-German attitude of Pétain. It is impossible, after reading it, to doubt that he had consistently opposed, sometimes by inertia, sometimes by ruse, sometimes by plain refusal, the demands of the occupying power in France, and that Germany knew he had, by his delaying tactics, deceived their hopes for a friendly France. If Germany had not broken with the marshal, it was because his renown, his dignity, his representative character had at first impressed Hitler, and afterwards a rupture with the marshal meant a complete rupture with a policy designed to bring France in on the German side. Now Ribbentrop spoke out angrily, and his letter, far from being "humiliating" for the marshal, as it was intended to be and as, illogically, the later judges of the marshal pretended it was (would they have had Ribbentrop flatter and compliment the marshal?) is the best testimonial to his patriotism that could have been written.

At the last moment (November 13), the use of the radio was forcibly forbidden. In the future, all manifestations, all modifications of laws, must be submitted to the approbation of the Reich. The cabinet must be refashioned on lines acceptable to the Reich.

There could be no refusal of the German terms. The armistice was virtually denounced. The Germans, who had allowed considerable latitude to Vichy, who had negotiated with Vichy, now commanded, brutally, without discussion. They would tolerate only the men they trusted in office. But is it not something, is it not much, is it not almost unbelievable, that the marshal should have staved off the inevitable moment for more than three years, and that he should have preserved France until the last few months of the occupation, when Germany was beginning to totter and reel to her fall? I think the success of the marshal, relative as it may be, painful as it was, acquired only by obligatory concessions, is magnificent: as magnificent as his defense of Verdun!

It is curious to reflect that three of the men, including Rochat, the permanent secretary of the French foreign office, particularly denounced by Germany, were afterward condemned to death by the government which came, in the wagons of the Anglo-Americans, from London or from Algiers! Two others were denounced—my friend Lucien Romier, who had wisely counseled the marshal, and Dr. Ménétrel.

Romier died suddenly from heart failure. Ménétrel was killed in an automobile accident. . . .

And now, of course, the men whom the marshal had kept from office came into the government of Vichy, while a German diplomat, Von Renthe-Finck, whom I had seen as an official of Chancellor Bruening at the League of Nations, was appointed as a special ambassador attached to the person of the marshal—his guardian, his jailor. The three men who came in, driving out the *attentistes,* were Philippe Henriot, for propaganda, Darnand, for the maintenance of order, and Déat, the advocate of Germanism in Paris. There was still Doriot, parading in German uniform, one of the leaders of the L.V.F.—the French Legion of Volunteers against Bolshevism, whom even the Germans despised as a renegade. The "Three D's"—Déat, Darnand, and Doriot—they were called.

The protests of the marshal went unheeded. He did not count. How I regretted that, before French liberty, French initiative, had been suppressed, the marshal had not taken the microphone, as I had suggested, and told the world of the ideals for which he and France stood! It would have meant suppression of the last liberties a few months earlier but, since the suppression was unavoidable anyway, it was a pity that France did not first speak out. Now the transmitting station at Vichy was watched: the marshal could only do what the Resistants were doing—distribute as well as he could his mimeographed messages clandestinely.

Henriot I had known well. He had hitherto been extremely patriotic. He was, however, a politician and, somehow, he regarded the war not as a trial of strength between Germany and the Allies on which the destinies of the world turned, but rather as a parliamentary debate, albeit a savage debate, between the government as established and the opposition at Algiers. He had ample matters for criticism in the declarations and doings of Algiers, which harbored Communists and fanatics and breathed the spirit of sanguinary vengeance, and he entered into the verbal strife with a vitality and a virulence that were truly astonishing. Adversaries and advocates of Algiers alike listened to his extraordinary diatribes. They could not refrain from listening to him, so pungent, so vitriolic, so eloquent were his orations, delivered with a fire, a forthrightness, an effectiveness of utterance that his bitterest enemies cannot deny to him. His voice was of a metallic resonance, seizing one in a grip of steel. He was ironic, humorous, pathetic, pertinent, aiming straight at the joints in the armor of politically minded Algiers.

Few men have been listened to with such passionate interest for a few months as was Philippe Henriot. He drove his admirers into ecstasy and his antagonists into frenzy. Whenever I was asked, and I was often asked, by admirers or antagonists, what I thought of him, I could only reply that it was highly regrettable, quite apart from the matter of his discourses, that the gulf between Vichy and Algiers should be widened by verbal violence. That was the fatal mistake. Henriot rendered all *rapprochement* of Vichy and Algiers—or rather of the sincere elements in Vichy and Algiers—impossible. Yet it was precisely such *rapprochement* that was desirable. If it was not effected, then the end of the war would bring fresh disaster on France. There was much to forgive on both sides. Many things had been said and done that had better, in the cause of French union, be forgotten.

I do not mean that crimes, by whomsoever committed, should be condoned, I do not mean that traitors should escape punishment. But I do mean that a mistaken choice of the different ways open to France after the defeat, taken in good faith, a difference of opinion as to method, should be pardoned by the victors in the civil war in the general joy of the Liberation. I do not know whether there would have been sufficient generosity after years of bitterness for mutual forgiveness of errors, had Henriot never spoken, but I do know that, when he reduced the war to a vicious quarrel between Vichy and Algiers, all hope of a reconciliation finally disappeared. That is the mortal fault of Henriot.

He could not place himself on a higher plane than the plane of political debate of an unprecedented acrimony. Yet he must have known that Algiers would come to France, burning with bitter passions. He must have known, when he plunged into the fray, that he was pronouncing his death sentence. He was the Enemy No. 1. of the Resistance and, sooner or later, he was certain to be assassinated—or "executed" to employ the word of the Resistance. He was thin, ravaged by tuberculosis, his boyish face marked by suffering, and it was nothing short of wonderful that, with such a frail and frayed physique, he should himself tap on a little typewriter, twice a day for months, a discourse with a punch in every sentence, that he should hold his audiences spellbound, that, in addition, he should write innumerable articles for the journals, that he should attend to the smallest details of his task. He had evidently decided that it was better to live a few months of intense activity than to live long in obscure inactivity. I think his influence was the most nefarious of all, definitely cutting the French into two clans—but I cannot refuse my admiration for the most prodigious, though short-lived, manifestation of energy and talent of my time. He was, as he expected, killed by indignant Resistants who burst into his bedroom on one of his visits to Paris.

Of Déat I have little to say. He remained in Paris, fulminating aganist Vichy, which he regarded as in connivance with the Anglo-Americans, and at the same time declaring hostility to Doriot, whom he regarded as a vulgar upstart and coarse humbug. Déat was a theorist, the bugbear of the Synarchists, implacably anticapitalist. The marshal refused to see him or to recognize him in the government. In the end, he disappeared, and no one knows what became of him.

As for Doriot, who was not admitted into the cabinet in spite of his allegiance to the Germans, he was killed by an aviator who machine-gunned his automobile. Whether the aviator belonged to the Allied forces or to the German army cannot be stated with any assurance. For my part, I think it more probable that he was "executed" by the Germans, for it is difficult to imagine that an Allied airman could have any knowledge of his movements.

The other outstanding figure in the Counterresistance is that of Joseph Darnand. Darnand was a man who was exceptionally brave but completely unintelligent. He had performed valorous deeds against the Germans in the First World War, and in the second he had become a legend. He was the sort of soldier who would not hesitate to attack single-handed a whole company of the enemy, and by his audacity and courage come off triumphant. In the 1939–1940 war he and Félix Angély effected a raid on the German lines that was extolled to the skies. Angély was killed, but Darnand brought back his body to the French lines. The two men were regarded as heroes. But the heroism of Darnand might be associated with stupidity. He was not the sort of man who would have made a good officer. To promote him to the rank of minister, to give him full charge of the Militia, was sheer folly. I had seen him in public meetings in Nice, his home town, where his reputation was high, dour, determined, strong-willed. He had belonged to the Legion of Former Combatants, a perfectly patriotic organization though afterward condemned by those who would have a monopoly of patriotism. There sprang out of the Legion a *Service d'Ordre* (S.O.L.) which undertook the task of keeping some sort of lawfulness in the country. At the beginning of 1943 the Militia came into existence. Darnand, the hero of two wars, was looked upon as a man who might be depended on to suppress social troubles, and now, in 1944, he was minister, charged to put an end to disorder.

That banditry was rife can hardly today be disputed. The newspapers had been filled with stories of the depredations of bands of undisciplined and irresponsible marauders, who committed the most atrocious misdeeds. A few years ago one would have been regarded as calumniating the Resistance to mention the fact—as though the Resistance was bound to identify itself with gangsterism, as though the Resistance, in its own interest, should not have repudiated any kind of gangsterism! The *réfractaires* in the Maquis, as they proudly designated themselves, were chiefly to be found in the Jura, in the Alps, in the Massif Central. The gendarmes and the Mobile Guards sometimes fraternized with them. Sometimes, when millions of francs were stolen from banks for the men of the Maquis, the managers of the banks were accomplices.

When the representatives of the law were sent on expeditions, they concluded a "gentleman's agreement," by which they took possession of a camp for a few days without fighting, and then retired, leaving the Maquisards free to return.

The Germans argued that it was the business of the French to put down a movement that hurt them more than it hurt the Germans. Now Darnand, without sufficient intelligence to discriminate between the Resistants who were opposed to the Germans, and the Terrorists who were opposed to the French, behaved with the utmost stupidity. Members of the Militia tracked down Resistants, made war on the honest French, rounded up Jews, imprisoned Communists and, under cover of restoring order, made confusion worse confounded. The Militia was a mixed crowd, composed of unscrupulous youths who ransomed the population, who held courts-martial, who executed summarily, as well as of misguided young men who thought they were rendering service to their country. So, in increasing measure, a civil war was produced. Finally, the Militia called on the Germans to help them in their raids, and thus, bit by bit, espoused the cause of the Germans.

I do not see how things could have turned out otherwise. The tragic drama of the occupation was that there were both good and bad intentions on both sides, and that it would have been beyond the wit of man to disentangle the right from the wrong. Whether for the maintenance of order or for resistance to the enemy, efficient performers were needed, and these could only be recruited among fearless men who were necessarily of different degrees of intelligence and morality. In the frightful mix-up of motives, political, personal, patriotic, revolutionary, to give power to even the wisest, to give arms to even the best, was a dangerous enterprise. I am sorry for some of the Militia, but the Militia should never have been formed: the consequences of launching Frenchmen against Frenchmen were far too grave. I am deeply distressed at the fate of many of the Maquis, though I doubt whether it was worth while to form a Maquis that was not made up exclusively of military men under strict discipline.

Of the purely military results of the French contribution after the landing, or just before the landing, I am not competent to speak. But even had they been far more substantial than they were, it may be asked whether the price paid was not too heavy, inasmuch as the effects of the civil war which raged in the latter part of the occupation has had effects which constitute a permanent handicap to France, a moral handicap, in that the mentality of large sections of the community has been changed, a social handicap, in that some of the best of the French have been sacrificed. There are memories that are too painful, and that will long persist. There are ruins that are irreparable. There is bitterness that will not be appeased. . . .

The memory of Glières, in Haute Savoie, where French fought French, the memory of Vercors where the Maquis was thrown prematurely into the struggle through false information of a landing in the South, and where there was a veritable massacre of the besieged before any help could come to them, are among those which rankle. There were tortures which will not be forgotten. There were assassinations of humble folk and of men like Maurice Sarraut, the Radical senator who ably directed the excellent newspaper *La Dépèche de Toulouse,* of Jean Zay, a former minister of education, of Georges Mandel, the associate of Clemenceau, treacherously delivered to the Militia. The countless victims, known and unknown, of the civil war in France have left behind them mourners who are not consoled by the Liberation and its aftermath.

21

How Paris Was Saved

In the month of December 1943, Russia won the war. It was not on the battlefield that the fate of the world was decided. It was at Teheran, where, after many *dé-marches,* many cajoleries, many flatteries, the master of the Kremlin consented to meet Churchill and Roosevelt and was rewarded beyond his wildest hopes by his associates.

Looking back, it is incredible that we should have consented so completely to the demands of Stalin. The consequences of the Teheran surrender were to fructify later, but today we clearly see that the world was made safe for Bolshevism at Teheran. Later conferences merely confirmed the promises there given.

What did we discern, looking down, as it were, from the celestial height of Sirius? We saw that, from 1917 onward, a main danger to our ancient civilization, to our "way of life," was the steady growth of Bolshevism. Not only had Russia fallen a victim to the conception of a purely materialist universe, in which force alone counted, not only had

Russia become a vast prison in which all the liberties of which we were wont to boast were suppressed, in which a group of men, sitting in the Kremlin, had forged a system of terrorism, of totalitarianism, dependent on an army of police and spies, but outside Russia, in almost every country, the missionaries of Bolshevism had made large numbers of converts. In France, especially—and perhaps this was the principal (though not the only) cause of her downfall—Bolshevism had made immense progress. It was not only the underpaid toilers who were dazzled by the mirage of the Russian Paradise, but intellectuals, professors, writers, artists, what is usually called the *élite,* worked for Bolshevism. The great industrialists, hoping to control Communism, as the industrialists in Germany had hoped to control Nazism, staking their money on the Red as well as on the Black, financed the party. The bourgeoisie, timorous and foolish, wondered whether it would not be safer to side with the active minority and help the Revolution along.

In England and in America, Communism made less progress, though in many underground channels it oozed into the political and social body. So-called opponents of Bolshevism adopted many of its principles. Individual liberties were lost. To be sure, there was a relative respect for the human person; but whoever did not live before 1914 can scarcely realize how much freedom we have gradually relinquished to the all-controlling, all-devouring State.

We were warned that the real struggle was between the old Liberalism (no matter what label is put on) and the ever-encroaching Communism which would dictate our movements and standardize our behavior and our sentiments and our thoughts. The bloodier and more ruthless thing named Bolshevism we found abhorrent, but we were approaching Bolshevism by easy stages.

Unhappily, Germany was allowed to become the chief champion of anti-Bolshevism—Germany which had accepted another form of totalitarianism. From the viewpoint of Sirius, it appeared that, whatever were the faults of Germany, that country was the only bulwark and barrier against Russian Bolshevism in Europe.

Could we not, should we not, have strained our energies to correct the defects of Germany, to give her legitimate satisfactions, long before the advent of Hitler? In the East, the only bulwark and barrier to Bolshevism was Japan. Should we not have strained our energies to keep our friendship for Japan, instead of offering all our sympathies to chaotic China, the prey of war lords, ripe for Bolshevism?

From the viewpoint of Sirius, it was at once tragic and comic that Germany, falling under the domination of an extraordinary personage with madness in his brain, should have made war on England and America, his natural allies against Bolshevism. The fatality of history ordained that Japan should range herself against the anti-Bolshevik countries. Thus we had the inconceivable spectacle of Japan and Germany joining hands against the anti-Bolshevik countries, and the anti-Bolshevik countries helping Bolshevism to triumph over its adversaries.

We supplied Bolshevism with unlimited quantities of arms. We taught Bolshevism how to make arms for itself. We insisted on the "unconditional surrender" of Germany and Japan, after inflicting the maximum of damage on them, forgetting that after war there should be peace, after destruction, reconstruction. We disarmed, dismantled, shattered to pieces Japan and Germany, rendering them utterly impotent. We refused to admit anti-Bolshevik countries like Spain into international assemblies. We complacently encouraged Bolshevism to fortify itself—in defiance of our pledges in the Atlantic Charter—in the Baltic states, which were annexed by Russian Bolshevism. We had gone to war to protect Poland, and we abandoned half of Poland to Russian Bolshevism, and permitted the other half to be subjugated by Bolshevism. We had been ready, at one moment, to attack Russia for her action against "brave little Finland," and then we acquiesced in the taking of parts of Finland. We prepared the way for the victory of Bolshevism in China, deserting our questionable *protégé,* Chiang Kai-shek, when he was in danger of being swept aside by the rising Red tide. We gave Bolshevism half of Germany, half of Austria, half of Korea, and much besides. In Europe we were troubled greatly when we saw that all the Balkan states were doomed by our war strategy to fall under the yoke of Bolshevism. In short, hypnotized by the conflict with Germany and Japan (Italy was comparatively negligible), the Allies forgot the permanent menace of Bolshevism, and provided Bolshevism with arms and strategic advantages in the future struggle.

At the same time, in praising Bolshevism as the inspirer of national energy (forgetting that Bolshevism preached and practiced surrender in 1917), the Allies gave a new impulse to the potential enemy in their own countries, where the Bolsheviks were granted full scope for their subversive propaganda and agitation. Vital secrets were betrayed with impunity. We formulated a doctrine of peace which forbade us to check Russian expansion on pain of branding ourselves as "Imperialist" warmongers. We hurriedly disarmed, while leaving Russia as heavily armed as ever, by far the most powerful military nation in the world.

From Sirius one could readily foresee the consequences of the decisions taken at Teheran and extended at Yalta. Roosevelt was convinced that he could convert Stalin, the head of a materialist and atheistic state, the autocrat of the Kremlin, to Christian and democratic views by making concessions that were both anti-Christian and anti-democratic. He thought the hard-boiled Stalin susceptible to his "charms." The Anglo-Americans took a pledge to land in France, and operations in the Balkans were forbidden. This was tantamount to making a present of the Balkan peoples to Stalin.

As for Poland, for whose integrity we had gone to war

against Hitler, boundaries well within German territory were to be accepted, and about fifteen million Germans thrown out of their own country, by way of compensation for the annexation of the eastern part of Poland by Russia. What had become of the Atlantic Charter which expressly forbade the bartering of territories and populations? What were the Allies to receive in return? They were to obtain Russian help against Japan months after the defeat of Germany—help which they did not need, which was never effectively given and was designed simply to enable Russia to participate in the immobilization of Japan in the event of a Russo-American conflict at a later date.

Eight years later, it seems impossible that we should have given up so overwhelmingly much for so preposterously little. The Russians won the war at Casablanca and Teheran. They won Poland, Hungary, Czechoslovakia, Rumania, Bulgaria, Yugoslavia, Manchuria, not to mention the possibility of winning Germany and Austria, not to mention the later winning of China; as for the Baltic states, nobody cared any more about Esthonia, Latvia, Lithuania. . . .

I will, in this place, to show that the Allies were not taken by surprise and that they persisted in their folly, mention the Yalta accords of February 1945, when the war was practically over. The new Polish line in Germany was drawn and the Poles, who had fought valiantly with the Allies, were thrown to the wolves as wicked anti-Communists. Germany was divided into zones, that is to say, the Russians were provided with a platform in Germany from which they might secure the whole country. Berlin itself was placed in the Soviet zone, and the Allies had not even a free corridor by which they could always obtain access to the German capital. By way of reparations, eighty per cent of German industries were to be scrapped, aviation factories confiscated, as well as the factories for the manufacture of synthetic petrol, and exorbitant payments in kind were meant to demolish Germany.

One of the most culpable aspects of the Yalta concessions was the fact that they were entirely unnecessary. No further concessions had to be made to Stalin. His aid was not needed to help conquer Japan—the reason given by Roosevelt's apologists. We now know that Japan was ready for peace on almost any terms before Yalta. Indeed, President Roosevelt had received through General MacArthur before he left for Yalta much the same peace terms that were accepted by President Truman the following August. Walter Trohan published them immediately after V-J Day.

What would be the value of waking up to realities five or ten years too late? If statesmanship is the art of looking ahead, then statesmanship has never in the world's history failed so signally. This statement is elaborately confirmed with extensive documentation in the book by the able American journalist and publicist, William Henry Chamberlin, *America's Second Crusade*. What is most astonishing, and in many ways disheartening, is that many Americans, who wisely and courageously opposed the "second crusade," are now vigorously supporting a third and more horrible crusade in Asia.

In the meantime, the Allied advance in Italy continued slowly. Both Field Marshal Alexander and Field Marshal Wilson, when the operations against General Kesselring had succeeded, wished to press on to Vienna, to Budapest, the Balkans in general. And it had at one time been hoped to bring Turkey and Greece into a Balkan drive. It is not my business to write of military matters, but any diplomatic observer can see at a glance that such a plan would have far-reaching political consequences. In pushing back the Germans, the Allies would have prevented the Russians from invading and virtually annexing the Balkans. They would also have spared France, as Marshal Pétain was hoping. But "Uncle Joe's" aspirations and feelings had to be considered. He had been promised spoils at Teheran, and he must be allowed to take them. What would happen later in Europe was not considered.

Two capital blunders—without counting innumerable minor blunders—marked the campaign of the Allies: the prolongation of the war, until the paroxysm of fury and destruction could reach no higher, by the proclamation of "unconditional surrender" at Casablanca; and the diversion of the Allied troops to France instead of to Central Europe, for the sole benefit of Russia. It would be difficult to decide which of these major blunders was of the greater assistance to Bolshevism. They were both unnecessary and pernicious presents, which may well ruin us and our civilization.

In fairness to Russia—and to the Allies—we should however admit that Russia had furnished by far the greatest military effort. What was the apocryphal phrase attributed to Churchill? "English patience, American arms, Russian blood." To be sure, patience counted, and England had paid her blood tribute too; arms and money counted and, as in 1918, America would come in to deal the final blow like the gold-spangled matador who dispatches the weary and dying bull; but Russia had borne the brunt of the fighting, the bloody fighting in which men fell not by thousands or hundreds of thousands but by millions, for three long years. It was logical, if blood be the price of victory, that the country which had been put to fire and sword while the others were preparing to launch the final assault should dictate the terms. . . . The terms, however, made nonsense of our original intentions. The terms were such as the world could not support for long. They were far worse than Versailles and left the greater part of Europe, which we wished to save, and the hundreds of millions of Chinese at the mercy of a power under a régime which, in our hearts, we feared and hated.

A crowning mistake of the Allies was their treatment of defeated Germany. Seemingly, they had learned nothing from the example of the disastrous effects of the Versailles

Treaty. The Casablanca formula of "unconditional surrender" assured that Germany would be utterly destroyed in a military way and all but demolished materially, leaving a vacuum into which Russia could penetrate unless Germany was permanently occupied by a large Allied force or rearmed in serio-comic defiance of the whole principle of the Casablanca decision. The division of Germany into zones of occupation was determined at Teheran, Yalta and Potsdam, and this made it virtually certain that a large portion of eastern Germany would remain rather permanently under Russian domination. But this was not all; the notorious Morgenthau Plan to destroy German industry and transform Germany into a pastoral and agricultural country, even if it involved the starvation of millions of Germans, was approved by Roosevelt and Churchill (after brief opposition by the latter) at Quebec in September 1944. It was approved and applied, with slight changes, by the Potsdam Conference of July 1945. This led to further demoralization and destruction of the German industrial plant and the transfer of much which remained to Russia, Britain and France.

German recovery was thus long delayed and the support of the helpless and semistarving Germans cost the Allies, mainly America, billions of dollars. The results of this incredible folly are detailed by the American publicist Freda Utley in her book *The High Cost of Vengeance*. When the menace of possible Russian expansion in Western Europe was belatedly recognized, it was apparent that Russia could only be held back through providing a strong German army. Hence, the Allies, who had earlier publicly decreed the perpetual disarmament of Germany, were ignominiously compelled to reverse themselves and seek to induce Germany to rearm under the extremely adverse and weakened conditions which the Allies had themselves needlessly brought about.

As for France, she had been out of the war for four years, and neither the discourses of De Gaulle, nor the Maquis pitted against the Militia, nor the civil strife of which Frenchmen were the victims, nor even the little armies of Juin and Leclerc constituted a contribution that really counted. Of course, the French would deceive themselves, as they had done after 1918, and would be ready to affirm that they had done it all. . . .

When the end was in sight, Pétain emerged from the silence he had been compelled to observe, and went like a missionary on a tour of France to proclaim the glad tidings and to warn the French to be ready for events that would give them another opportunity to prove their mettle. Often, he had gone to cities in the South, had comforted the populations by his presence, and had invariably spoken heartening words; he had received mayors and innumerable delegations, had reminded Alsatians that they were still French, had cheered the potential soldiers of a new France, and had displayed an unusual gift of kindly and paternal speech. Now, he decided that he would visit the occupied regions, Paris itself, as a messenger of better days.

Recently, I was asked by an Englishman, who was ill-informed: "Why did the French suddenly change their opinion about Pétain?" I replied that never did the French, the bulk of the French, look on Pétain as other than he was, the man who had stood between them and the invader, who saved them from hardships far greater than those they had to bear. It was the politicians, those who returned with the Anglo-Americans, and particularly the Communists, who could not forgive him for telling the truth to France, and who turned on Pétain. And I pointed for proof of my assertion to the Marshal's visit to Paris in the spring of 1944. There exist photographs, which cannot be refuted, of the enthusiastic crowds that clustered around him, that thronged the streets, that made his passage in their midst a continuous exhibition of thankfulness and veneration. He came unheralded, unarmed, and unprotected. There was no whipping up of the multitudes to organized demonstrations. He entered the capital after a prolonged absence, simply, unostentatiously. Yet never, in the palmiest days of Hitler, in the most triumphant days of Stalin, has a chief been better received than Pétain was in Paris in the spring of 1944.

The word spread like wildfire that he had arrived, and all Paris was agog. The Parisians, as a single person, leaped and cried and rejoiced as they greeted the herald of Liberation.

Could he have announced, with the Germans in occupation, more clearly that deliverance was at hand? Listen to his short improvised address from the Hôtel de Ville to the immense crowds that surged to catch a glimpse of the man who had flown the flag of France through good and evil days. "I am come in unhappy circumstances to relieve the miseries that press upon Paris." (He did not then regard the occupation as an excellent thing? He did not treat the Germans as the friends of France?) "It is the first visit that I make, but I hope I can soon come again without being obliged to give notice to my guardians." (His guardians? He was then a prisoner. Come again without asking permission? Then he was anticipating the departure of the guardians, the restoration of his freedom, the freedom of Paris? Be sure that no one misunderstood his prediction.) "Today, my visit is one of thankfulness. When I return we shall have much to say to each other." (Without the presence of the Germans.) "That will be an official visit." (That is, in a liberated France.) "Soon then, I hope." (Soon? Their trials were nearly over. The dark days were passing.)

Many men in the Fourth Republic have been admitted to the highest honors for having written clandestinely, or for having spoken from a safe place, in England or in Africa, no more than the marshal dared to speak in the occupied city. To announce the defeat of Germany so plainly, to exhort the French to rally in anticipation of their release from the stranglehold of the enemy in their midst, was a bold deed that was acclaimed by the whole of Paris—and by the whole of France. It was thus, I imagine, that the marshal had rallied the men of Verdun. . . . Churchill could have done no more. Roosevelt could have done no more. De Gaulle could have done no more. Nobody could have done more in such conditions with such dignity and simplicity. Those who are embarrassed by the marshal's attitude, who have founded their fortune on the legend of his treacherous "collaboration" with the Germans, may wish to forget, but the people of France do not forget. . . .

The struggle that began on the coast of Normandy on June 6, 1944, when the English landed near Caen and the Americans at Sainte-Mère-Eglise (De Gaulle was not invited to participate in the Liberation of France), did not leave us long in doubt.

France had been bombed from March onward with an appalling intensity. Some 268,000 tons of bombs were dropped on Normandy, causing frightful havoc. The bravery of the Anglo-American troops was beyond praise. It was clear that, unless they could be thrown into the sea in the first few days, the forces they could put in motion, with a material equipment that far outweighed the resources of the Germans, would push back the enemy with irresistible rapidity. The race was to save Paris from destruction, either by the Germans or by the insurrectionists who, with romantic ideas, aimed at the liberation of the capital without the assistance of the Anglo-Americans. The Communists, it was rightly feared, would take advantage of the confusion to seize the city and to install themselves in power. An illuminating example of the strength of the Resistance is furnished by the estimate that 3,000 men took an active part in the Paris upheavals but, a few months later, no fewer than 125,000 applications were made for official certificates of the F.F.I.—*Forces Françaises de l'Interieur.* General Koenig, who had been placed at the head of these forces, cabled instructions that they must not act without orders. The moderate elements in the Resistance, afraid that premature movements would result in the annihilation of the capital—the Germans, under General Von Chotitz, had 20,000 men, 58 heavy cannon, 60 airplanes and 80 tanks, could have smashed the city, and killed thousands of Parisians, and, indeed, had orders to destroy Paris before leaving—declared against any uprising. What purpose would it serve to reduce the city to ashes? The Americans were on their way, and the inhabitants had only to wait a few days longer.

But the peaceable surrender of Paris by the Germans did not suit certain elements in the Resistance. For them, it was important to provoke an insurrection that would compel the Germans to make reprisals. That the Germans might shoot hundreds of hostages, direct their artillery against the principal buildings, blow up the sixty-odd bridges of the Seine did not trouble them. Only on the smoking ruins of the capital could Communism hope to triumph. So Paris was doomed, both by Hitler, whose orders were peremptory, and by the insurrectionists, to complete destruction.

Happily, Paris was spared the fate which threatened, first because the masses refused to revolt: they were wise enough to keep to their houses until the storm had passed; second, because De Gaulle and his staff at London multiplied their appeals for calm; third, because the provisional governor of Paris, General Chaban-Delmas, supported by the more responsible members of the Resistance, opposed the extremists; fourth, because Taittinger, the president of the municipal council (virtually the mayor of Paris), expostulated earnestly with General Von Chotitz on the shame which would attach to the demolition of Paris; fifth, because the consul of Sweden, Nordling, arranged a truce; and sixth, because General Von Chotitz was the best type of German officer and considered it his duty, for once, to disobey orders on humanitarian grounds.

Von Chotitz, according to my information (which has never been denied), proposed to Eisenhower that he should remain in the capital until the Americans approached, and should leave as they—or a regular French detachment—entered the city, in order that no interval should be allowed to the revolutionaries to set up a Commune, as in 1870. It is, of course, absurd to suppose that a few hundred revolutionaries could have held out against the troops of Von Chotitz had the German general chosen to act.

The truce was proclaimed by cars carrying loud-speakers —German cars and French cars. They announced that the Germans had agreed not to attack buildings in which the insurrectionists had taken refuge, not to shoot hostages, to release all prisoners, to treat French patriots as regulars, provided that order was maintained.

The truce, naturally, did not suit those who romantically wanted street battles with barricades that the lightest German tanks could have broken; they wished to claim the honor of having liberated Paris, even if it was demolished in the process. It has been suggested that the German S.S. actually gave arms to them with the Machiavellian purpose of creating disorder and leaving France in the hands of the revolutionaries. The moderates, after holding out against the extremists for a few days, sent emissaries to the American armies begging them to hurry. General Leclerc was authorized by the Americans to push on rapidly, since the main American forces had for their objective not Paris but Berlin, and it was better that a French detachment should first enter the city. It was agreed that the troops of Von Chotitz should evacuate Paris and that the few who remained for tactical reasons should surrender to the regular troops.

Legends die hard, but the truth is that Von Chotitz behaved with remarkable discretion, and only when his troops were fired on were a few persons killed. Whatever his motives, it is primarily to him and to Nordling, and afterward to the swift advance of Leclerc, that Paris owed its salvation.

Apart from sporadic street incidents, the transfer of Paris from German hands to French hands was effected in a comparatively orderly manner. Such insurrection as there was did only harm. The responsible members of the Resistance must be given full credit for their opposition to any action that might wipe Paris from the face of France.

The heroes of the barricade, however, took a small revenge. They stripped naked all women who were suspected of having consorted with the Germans during the four years of occupation, painted Nazi signs on their naked bodies, cut off their hair, and paraded them through the streets of Paris. Thousands of so-called "collaborators"—many of whom had not collaborated half as much as their captors—were thrown into prison.

It was not until later that De Gaulle arrived. He found that the divergences of view among the members of the Resistance were considerable and that the movement was in danger of breaking up. But the quarrels were for the moment appeased, and a provisional government of all the parties, including the Communists, was formed. Maurice Thorez, the leader of the French Communists, was recalled from Moscow, an amnesty pronounced for his conviction as deserter, and a place found for him at the side of De Gaulle as vice-president of the council of government.

The fate of Paris and the fate of France, in the critical interregnum, might have been much better or much worse. Had the Communists and those who were ready to associate themselves with the Communists been a little more audacious, had the militants of the party been more numerous, they might easily have succeeded in proclaiming a Soviet republic. Had Nordling, Taittinger, Von Chotitz, and the moderates among the Resistants been less intent on sparing Paris, had the march of Leclerc been a little slower, then Paris might well have been destroyed and the Reds installed before De Gaulle. But, on the other hand, attempts were made to transmit power legally to a new government. Laval, for his part, called Herriot, the president of the old Chamber, from his retreat, where he was living under German surveillance. Herriot, who certainly had played a prominent part in the election of Pétain but was now incensed against him, was asked to convoke Parliament. If the former Parliament did not exist, nothing representative existed in France. In my view it should have met, if only to nominate De Gaulle, whose pretensions to govern had no solid base. Whatever might have come of the Laval-Herriot conversations, is purely a matter of conjecture. The Germans intervened. They took Laval, carrying him off to Belfort, protesting. They deported Herriot.

But the marshal, too, had not been inactive. Admiral Auphan, as his delegate, entered into pourparlers with Teitgen, representing the responsible Resistance. It was also arranged that Taittinger, with General Brécard, the grand chancellor of the Legion of Honor, should officially receive De Gaulle and formally, in the name of the marshal, surrender all authority to him. Auphan was further charged with the function of establishing contacts with the Anglo-Americans and of seeking with De Gaulle a solution which would avert further civil war. The union of De Gaulle and Pétain would have symbolized the union of the French, and much bloodshed and unjust imprisonment would have been avoided. De Gaulle had, of course, no status whatever. He had neither been elected by the people nor been charged with a mission by an elected body.

He refused to enter into any discussion. He derived such rights as he might possess from himself—from his proclamations from London, from Brazzaville, from Algiers. "I sent away the messengers," he afterward haughtily said, "and where is the civil war?" He need not have looked far to discover the civil war. It was all about him, it was everywhere in France, in the few *départements* which he controlled, and in the many more where he had no authority.

Certainly the Parisians received him, in the joy of the Liberation, with enthusiasm. They would have received anyone who symbolized the end of the occupation. But they had received Pétain before the victory with even greater emotion. The thesis that Pétain was a usurper had become an article of the Gaullist creed. But if Pétain, despite the vote of the National Assembly, was a usurper, President Lebrun was still in office, and it was for him and not for De Gaulle to decide. Another article of the Gaullist creed was that the armistice was unnecessary and was a betrayal of France. That contention cannot be upheld by anyone who is acquainted with the facts. It served propagandist purposes during the occupation, but it should have been instantly dropped at the Liberation.

A little more generosity, a little more care for the future of the country, a little less preoccupation with parties and persons, in short a political truce, would have united all Frenchmen in recognition of the services of Pétain and of De Gaulle, would have rallied all Frenchmen in the gigantic task of reconstruction. One section of the French would not have proclaimed to the whole world that a much larger section was composed of "traitors." The best of France's servitors, in every department of national life, parliamentary, administrative, literary, artistic, would have continued their services, and France would not have been deprived of many of her generals, admirals, industrialists, and more humble officials. Hundreds of thousands of good citizens would not have been ruined in the Revolution, families who had committed no fault would not have been driven to despair, the hideous Terror would not have been let loose, the prisons would not have been filled, the glories of France would not have been tarnished, and the nation would not have been held up to opprobrium as harboring of at least a million active antipatriots.

The Germans took a hand in the game of dividing the French. They kidnaped the marshal to prevent any reconciliation. They deported him, as they had deported so many Frenchmen. (Odd, that nobody ever weeps over the deportation of the head of the state, though everybody sheds tears over the deportation of the politicians!)

On the 17th of August, Renthe-Finck, the marshal's guardian, ordered him to go to Nancy. He refused. He was told that Vichy would be bombed by the retreating Germans unless he obeyed. He called on the Apostolic nuncio and the Swiss minister, who were still accredited to Vichy, to protect him and, if that was impossible, at least to be witnesses of the violence of the Germans. He prepared a message for distribution and I received a copy.

Although I knew the whole story of the end of Vichy, I will refer the reader to the irrefutable testimony of the Swiss minister, Stucki, who has written a book in which he not only faithfully records precisely what happened but testifies to the dignity of Pétain in the most trying circumstances of deportation. It is strange that the legend of the marshal voluntarily leaving the country he had sworn never to desert still persists in face of the well-established truth.

On the 19th of August the Hôtel du Parc was surrounded, the marshal again refused to leave, doors and windows were broken by his captors, and the old man was dragged off by the Germans (ironically enough in a Cadillac which had been presented to him by Admiral Leahy!) to Belfort, and then to Sigmaringen on the Danube, where he was held in captivity until the advance of the Allies procured his release.

He immediately returned to France by way of Switzerland. De Gaulle would have preferred that he remain abroad and that he be condemned *in absentia,* since his condemnation alone would appear to justify De Gaulle. But Pétain declined to remain in safe and secure exile: he reentered France and was impeached before a special tribunal composed exclusively of Partisans, a tribunal which could have no legal existence whatever, a tribunal utterly unknown to the constitution (the only existing constitution was that of the Third Republic, which provided for the legal irresponsibility and the inviolability of the head of the state, who in any case could only be tried before the senate, that is, the senate of 1939). After a hasty mock trial, in which he properly declined to recognize his judges, Pétain was condemned to death. But the sentence was later commuted to life imprisonment. Admiral Leahy sent a letter attesting to his firm belief in the marshal's integrity and sincere devotion to the security and interests of France. Churchill expediently refrained from any tribute to the marshal, presumably for fear of offending Stalin and the Communists.

The imprisonment too was a smashing moral victory for the Russians: Pétain in prison, all who followed him and obeyed him persecuted, Thorez sitting at the right hand of De Gaulle, and the Communists in the key posts of France.

Marshal Pétain died in the summer of 1951 at the age of 95, after six years of solitary confinement in the harshest of fortresses on the Ile d'Yeu. Only just before his death had he been transferred to a government hospital, this too a prison.

22

Liberation and Sequel

I HAD received, when other means of communication failed, the mimeographed messages from Vichy, and now the last declaration of the marshal was delivered to me in Monaco. He stated that he was no longer even partially free, that he was about to be made a prisoner by the Germans. He explained that, having decided to remain, he had considered every day what was best calculated to serve the permanent interests of France: "If I could not be your sword, I could be your buckler." Sometimes, it may be, his acts or his words had surprised the French. They had hurt him more than they had hurt anyone else. But he had managed to spare the French greater suffering. Today, the enemy carried him away. There was only one France, the France of our ancestors. Therefore, he exhorted the people once more to unite. It was not difficult to do one's duty, though it was sometimes difficult to know where one's duty lay. The duty of the French was now simple: to group themselves around those who would conduct them in the ways of honor and of order.

Thus, the last message of Pétain was tantamount to an exhortation to accept De Gaulle and his companions, provided they would assure "social peace, without which no national system can be established. Those who speak a language which will lead to reconciliation and the restoration of France, by the reciprocal pardon of wrongs committed, by the love of all, are the true French chiefs. They continue my work—stand by them!"

I know nothing nobler than these parting words of the marshal who was being led into captivity by the Germans, and calumniated by the *émigrés* for having done everything that lay in his power during four of the most difficult years that France has ever endured: "I am separated from you, but I do not leave you in spirit. I hope that your devotion to France will restore her grandeur. I undergo the hardest trial that any man can suffer, but it is with joy that I accept it, if it is the condition of our salvation . . . if my sacrifice helps you to find again the path of union for the rebirth of the Fatherland."

That was the marshal's message as he was hurried away by the Germans. No word of reproach, no word which would divide; only words that would heal the wounds, that would aid his successor in obtaining the unanimity of the citizens. He was not placing personal prestige, pride, ambition before the cause of France. He was not promoting civil strife. He knew that France had need of all her children who had not willingly served the enemy, however divergent had been the methods they had adopted. Why was this message not published by those who had come to power, in every newspaper, placarded on every wall? Why was it not echoed by those who now had in their hands the destiny of the nation? It would have helped them.

In the South we were being bombed. Splinters of bombs were continually falling on the balcony of my apartment. The port below me was shattered. The Germans were rounding up all suspected persons. One of my closest friends was in prison at Nice for having written innocuous reminders that the French remained faithful to their former ideals. We were afraid lest he might be carried off as a hostage in the retreat of the German troops.

I was called to the French consulate by telephone. I went to see the consul. "It appears," he said, "that you have been sending letters to England, through Switzerland, using the diplomatic channel."

I tried to deny the accusation, but he stopped me.

"I am not complaining. The Germans are your accusers. They believe you are in the Intelligence Service. Nor do I want to be taken into your confidence. I know that whatever you have done has been in accordance with your conscience."

"Whatever I have done I have done without concealment. I considered it necessary to give certain information, not on military matters but on French sentiment. That is my function . . ."

"I do not doubt it. But the matter may be serious. I have just received a message from Marseilles that an order has been issued for your arrest. And an arrest at this time will be particularly serious. The Germans have their backs to the wall and they will not be tender. You will be treated as a spy. I beg you to make your escape."

"And you?" I asked. "Do you intend to escape?"

"No, it is my duty to remain."

"I have no liking for romantic evasions," I said. "I must take my chance—like you."

"I will not disguise the fact that the consulate is implicated in the charges against you," he declared. "We are placed in a difficult position. Yet we cannot run away. I implore you to go into hiding. It will be better not only for you but for us that the Germans should have no opportunity of questioning you."

In the end, I reluctantly agreed to leave my house and to go to a hotel, partly to save the consul from being compromised, partly to save myself from arrest, partly because my wife and I were tired of being in the area of daily bombing which had wrecked houses just below us.

There was another reason why we should stay in a hotel outside the usual range of the bombings. For some time, we had been almost without food. There was no bread in the shops. We had tickets but they were not honored. The authorities had set up soup kitchens in a number of centres, mostly in hotels, where people were given a ladleful of liquid with macaroni, and a piece of stale biscuit. We now went to live in one of these hotels which had one of the soup kitchens. There we were given our allowance without a long walk. We took with us the few tins of sardines that I had received from Portugal, saved up against such an emergency.

If the greater part of the war had been passed in relative comfort, the latter stages were exceptionally painful. I was pursued by the Germans, my friend was in prison, and his distracted wife came to us several times a day for consolation. We had far from enough to eat. A bomb had fallen on the water main and there was no water. The electricity had completely failed. . . .

In the hotel was a group of Resistants, among them a dancer from the ballet company, and we talked together of the war. The Resistants went out at night on strange missions, whose purpose I never learned. I began to wonder whether a hotel peopled by Resistants was, after all, the safest hiding place from the Germans.

And then I was disturbed by the tone of the Algiers radio, announcing that soon two million heads would fall in

France. Two million! The astounding threat made me fear for the future of France where bombings, hunger, fanatical partisanship, delation, German exactions, imprisonments, executions had engendered a state of feeling of unexampled bitterness that would be hard to allay. The feeling in the North was nothing like so vicious and violent as in the South and in certain other regions, such as the Massif Central, Toulouse, around the Spanish frontier, Grenoble, and the Jura. Here, in the South, was a remarkably mixed population, largely Italian in origin, and some of the Italians had Fascist sympathies, and others were more French than the French. Refugees from the Central European countries were ready to run amok. There were the Red Spaniards—though still more of them were in and around Perpignan and Montpellier. There were many thousands of homeless Jews, enraged by the sufferings of their fellows and their own. There were anti-Russians, and there were pro-Russians.

There were hundreds of private vendettas, husbands who had grudges against their wives, and wives who would seize the opportunity of injuring their husbands. Friends had fallen out and were waiting the chance to betray one another, storing up distorted reminiscences of conversations in which indiscreet words had been spoken. There were racial enmities. There were commercial jealousies. There were rivalries in the administrative services. There had been fraternization with the occupying troops, human and comprehensible, which would give a glorious (or inglorious) excuse to those who had not fraternized to wreak vengeance. Worse still, many of those who had fraternized with the enemy and had made money out of their relations with the enemy, having much to be pardoned for, would place themselves among the most zealous witch-hunters and patriotic *épurateurs.* There were the black marketeers, spivs, common criminals, who would be let loose and would add to the lawlessness. Where were the forces of law and order capable of coping with the forces of lawlessness and disorder, when once the hand of the Germans was removed? And now the *émigrés* from London and Africa were preparing, knowing nothing of the conditions of France, to come over with all the animosity of men who had long been in exile, to punish the wrongdoers and with the wrongdoers the innocent who were often denounced by the real wrongdoers.

I spoke of my apprehensions to a doctor, a friend of mine, a member of the Resistance, who was treating me for blood pressure. He grew grave. He acknowledged that my fears were not unfounded, but he believed that the sounder elements would prevail. The Resistance—the true Resistance which was neither vindictive nor Communist—would be called upon, not so much to harass the Germans as to maintain order. That was its task.

I expressed skepticism, but he assured me I was wrong. Was he not a typical Resistant? Did *he* stand for lawlessness? . . . He was soon to be disillusioned.

There were many like him. One day a group of men, one of whom was an ex-convict, burst into my room and demanded that I should deliver up any food I might have. I had nothing except a hambone with a few scraps of meat left on it. The ex-convict delivered an eloquent address on the "food hoarders" who starved the poor while they lived on the fat of the land. As the incident revealed the prospect of pillage, I thought it my duty to report it to the police. The officer asked me if I made any charge. I replied in the negative: I simply wanted him to be aware of what might happen. He told me that complaints were pouring in, but to his great regret he could do nothing.

The ballet dancer of the nocturnal expeditions, hearing of my misadventure from the hotel proprietor, called on me, and offered me his excuses. "Of course these men do not belong to our organization," he told me. "We have the strictest orders to respect persons and property. Pillaging is punishable by death. Give me a description of the men, and I will see that they are shot."

I was startled by the demand. Shoot a man—three or four men—for stealing the shank of a ham? It was grotesquely exaggerated.

"We are particularly anxious to keep the Resistance clean," said the ballet dancer. "We should never have taken arms without making sure that strict discipline would be observed during the transition period."

I thanked him, but refused any further information. He and others like him were armed not for the fight against the Germans but chiefly for the fight against the undisciplined members of the community who would take advantage of the interregnum to give free play to their antisocial instincts.

I was awakened on the morning of the 15th of August by an unnatural calm. There was an uncanny stillness in the air. Complete silence is so rare that it is frightening. Not a sound was to be heard. I went out into the streets, and was still more painfully aware of the cessation of all the little noises that animate a city. The air was deadened: nature herself was stunned. The absence of movement was ominous. I guessed at once what the vacuity meant. In the void of the dawn I knew, before it was announced, that there had been a landing in the South.

On the whole, I was glad, though from the viewpoint of Allied strategy I considered the landing in the South of France a mistake. The troops had been diverted from Italy and, therefore, from the Balkans where, in my opinion, they should have continued their advance to assure Central Europe freedom from Bolshevik occupation.

In the South, there were only a few divisions of Germans to defend over 400 miles of coast; and the fortifications in the South were nothing but bluff. The Germans were bound to retire, in any event, now that a breach had been made in Normandy, and when the Allies landed at St. Tropez, Ste. Maxime, and St. Raphael, the enemy fought little more than covering actions. The Allies pushed on to Toulon, Marseilles, by the Route Napoléon to Grenoble, and by the valley of the Rhône to Lyons.

At least I felt safe from arrest, and I hoped that the presence of the Allies would prevent the bloody revolution I foresaw.

Unhappily, the Americans did not repress the countless abuses that followed the retreat of the Germans. They left that business to the French authorities, and the French authorities in Paris were powerless, having no jurisdiction whatever in the South.

The Germans had received orders to blow up the port and, in the course of the next few days, there were explosions the smoke of which I saw from the bridge which separates the two halves of Monaco. But here, as elsewhere, the men on the spot chose to disobey orders, and the principality was generally spared. There was little attempt, on the other hand, to molest the German contingents as they went off to join the main columns. I went to the Hôtel de Paris and there saw flushed and bedraggled boys, fresh from the Maquis, caressed by excited women. Brassards were being handed out, and they were considered a sufficient proof that one had been in the Resistance. To my astonishment, the Red Flag was displayed on many houses. Never had I dreamed that Monaco, living as it did on the rich, could have harbored so many revolutionaries. When a cry of alarm was raised that the Germans were coming back, the flags disappeared as by magic, only to reappear when it was discovered that it was a false alarm. We waited anxiously for the American troops, and we were disappointed when it was known that Monaco was out of bounds.

I had long talks with a few English soldiers who visited the principality and who came to eat and drink in my hotel. They made me presents of tea and coffee which were very acceptable. How I loved to hear their stories, to listen to the old familiar tongue! What charming unspoiled young fellows they were! They belonged to a small detachment of aviators in liaison with the Americans.

The Germans had withdrawn, but they left, on the mountainside, batteries of cannon which were so placed as to be virtually inaccessible. British ships appeared before the hotel, and we took our field glasses to watch them firing broadside after broadside. The Germans, from time to time, replied; their shells fell into the sea around the British ships. The swish and whistle of the missiles hurtling over our heads were more impressive than the scores of air attacks we had endured, and when the battle began again at night, for the first time we deemed it prudent to descend to the vaulted cellar, where we sat, in the light of a few candles. Sometimes a shell fell short. There was one which crashed on the street stairway just behind us with a deafening clatter of broken masonry.

A small contingent of Germans had remained behind on Cap Martin, below Rocquebrune, and the attack on them was the most spectacular of all. The sky was lighted up by bright candles suspended in the sky: it was as if we were in broad daylight. The sight was uncanny; every tree, every house was picked out, and we watched the tiny figures of men scurrying like ants to and fro. Now and again, a fire was lighted by a bomb and blazed up redly. By the cool white light of the candles mysteriously hung in the heavens, we watched the landing of troops and hand-to-hand combats: we even fancied we could hear the cries of men mortally wounded. I was rather ashamed to look on at the set piece, as though it were a mere theatrical show put on for our benefit. Men like ourselves, whether Germans, English, or Americans, were killing and being killed on that narrow spit of ground before our eyes; within what seemed a stone's throw men were dead or dying in a wild nocturnal assault.

As I wandered about Monaco, shaking hands with all my acquaintances, exchanging expressions of relief that the long nightmare of war was nearly over, there came to me stories of what was happening in cities on the coast. Women were being paraded, as in the North, naked in the streets, their hair cut off, the Swastika painted in tar on their bodies; men were being arrested by the hundred, the Red Flag was flying over public buildings, the prefects appointed by Paris —or by Algiers—were being driven away, and other prefects, approved by the Communists, escorted by *mitrailleuses,* were being put in their place. Communists were seizing the municipal offices and acting as mayors. In short, a revolution was in full swing.

The new consul of Monaco placed himself under the protection of the prince, for he had been attached to Vichy, and that was an unforgivable sin. It was useless to argue that he had exercised a moderating influence, that he had publicly pleaded for a reconciliation, for the union of the "Armagnacs" and the "Bourguignons." As the representative of Vichy, now dethroned, he was in mortal danger, and it was questionable whether the authority of the prince, to whom he was accredited, could save him for long. The doctor who attended me, officially designated as the medical officer of the Resistance, and now wearing a superb uniform, with the rank of commandant, was troubled. For how long could the ordinary laws of civilized life be maintained?

I considered it my duty to write letters once more, to the American General, to a British minister with whom I had enjoyed forty years of friendship, pointing out the danger. But how were they to be reached? My new-found acquaintances, the British soldiers who had come to look at Monaco, undertook to deliver them or post them as soon as they got back to headquarters. I will not give in full these letters, which were long and in part personal, but I must quote the concluding passages, which express the thought that was then, as now, uppermost in my mind:

It appears to me particularly perilous to admit reprisals, to inaugurate the Liberation of France by wholesale executions and the division of France into opposing zones of citizens. There were two totally different problems for France after the defeat in 1940. The first and more immediate was the reorganization of the dislocated country. The second and more remote was the preparation of an eventual resistance. The two tasks were not incompatible and contradictory: rather were they complementary. In my view, it will be disastrous for France to allow differing conceptions of the urgency and priority of tasks to degenerate into expressions of hatred and pure partisanship. An effort of comprehension must be made; and any government which hopes to rally the citizens of France must appeal to all Frenchmen of goodwill by proclaiming a general amnesty. Otherwise, whatever the present results, there will be deep resentment, and the wheel of time will turn and vengeance will succeed to vengeance. I urge then that the first and most important act of statesmanship is the reconciliation of the French with themselves and with the Allies. . . . France, which has endured greatly and has remained faithful in tribulation, has now need of domestic peace and active sympathy.

I have good reason to stand by my reading of the situation in 1944. Sometime afterward, the Americans realized the truth of my plea and—belatedly—without intervening officially in French affairs, made representations, and even threats, that put an end to some of the worst features of the Liberation.

As for the English, though I must not mention names, since the letter was confidential, I think I may properly, after this lapse of time, record some phrases of a reply which reached me from a highly placed minister. After declaring that what I had written was of great interest, and that I had "very special qualifications for writing it," and after stating that the minister had "good reason to remember my helpfulness and acute judgment in the past," the writer continued:

As it happens, I had a conversation with the controller of one of the French regions the other day, and I ventured to urge that the real friends of France were perturbed at the lengths to which the pursuit of individuals on charges connected with their conduct in the war was carried. . . . So many people make grave political errors out of want of judgment rather than out of downright knavery. Punishment is inevitable for those who have deliberately sold themselves to the enemies of France, but this is quite distinct from the position of a citizen who, when faced with terrible difficulties in the crisis of his country's fate, makes an honest mistake as to where his duty lies. . . . The terribly heavy task of reconstruction and rehabilitation will need every honest Frenchman's active help . . . I will take the opportunity of showing your letter to one or two of my colleagues who are chiefly responsible for guiding Anglo-French relations. I yield to no one in the desire and the determination to promote Anglo-French solidarity.

One of my letters, or a copy, seems to have gone astray, and the conviction that I was a secret informer of the Anglo-Americans brought on me one of the most painful misadventures I had yet suffered.

23

Revolution and Terror 1944–1946

THERE has never been, in the history of France, a bloodier period than that which followed the Liberation of 1944–1945. The massacres of 1944 were no less savage than the massacres of the Jacquerie, of St. Bartholomew, of the Revolutionary Terror, of the Commune; and they were certainly more numerous and on a wider scale.

We shall here set down the facts, though we know that they may not correct the errors in public opinion. The mobs and murders of the French Revolution were honored and praised for more than a century, despite the repudiation of the Terror by great historians like Michelet, Carlyle, Mignet, Thiers, and Taine, long before the age of the rigorous scholars like Aulard and Madelin. The razing of the Bastille is still celebrated, although Madelin has shown that it was the work of a quasi-criminal mob eager to free their kind. But even Michelet, Mignet, and Thiers wrote from 50 to 75 years after the Revolution. We can now have the facts less than a decade after the Terror of 1944–1945. If we disregard these facts we do so at our peril, and for Frenchmen to disregard them will only postpone the achievement of that unity upon which the secure and happy future of France depends more than upon any other single item in French public life.

Authentic figures about the disorders and massacres of 1944–1945 are impossible to obtain but, in spite of belated official attempts to minimize the number of victims—in many cases innocent of any serious offense—the evidence points to a total of at least a hundred thousand persons—men, women, and even children—murdered (I can employ no other term) by individuals, by criminal bands, by irregular tribunals, by self-appointed bodies which proceeded, without trial, to what were euphemistically called "summary executions."

Obviously, there are no reliable statistics. No account was given of the killings. No reports were drawn up or, if there were, they remained in the possession of local groups. No attempt was made to deny these atrocities for several years. The attitude of the new masters of France toward them may be judged by the public statement of a minister of justice. He, it should be recalled, was referring only to official condemnations, and not to uncontrolled and lawless acts but he, nevertheless, revealed the temper of the time when, hard pressed by political opponents who accused him of undue leniency, he declared in the Chamber that Robespierre, Saint-Just and other sanguinary monsters of the Revolution were as little children compared with him. An extraordinary but accurate boast, which no doubt he has since regretted. This particular minister belonged to the moderate section of the Resistance, and I believe he tried to restrain the ardor of the more bloodthirsty camp followers of the Resistance. His endeavor to placate them is, therefore, all the more significant. They were screaming for vengeance; and whoever wished to remain in office had to scream as loudly as they.

Eight or nine years later, sentiment has changed. It is now thought desirable to explain away confessions of this sort. All decent citizens deplore the excesses of the *épuration* (purge); all genuine Resistants are ashamed of the blood bath into which France was plunged. There are, however, still a few unrepentant organizations which pretend that those who were not of their company were treated too mildly, that there should have been a greater slaughter, that there should be no revision of the ferocious sentences passed in 1944–1946 and later, that there should be no amnesty, that anyone sentenced, no matter how unjustly, to long terms of imprisonment should continue to rot in jail. In my view, their case is pathological; but the unhappy fact is that they have not yet ceased to exercise some pressure on those in authority who are afraid of being considered an inferior type of Resistant.

Let me make it clear that, great and lethal as their influence has been, they do not represent the vast majority of Frenchmen. The great majority of Frenchmen are not animated by such vicious sentiments; and, indeed, the real Resistance, courageous and disinterested, has paid many tributes to the courage and disinterestedness of the best of its opponents who, rightly or wrongly, but quite sincerely, held that true patriotism was expressed in the maintenance of order, the fulfillment of ordinary and unspectacular civic duties, in the face of an enemy occupation.

The real Resistance, free from fanaticism or mean political calculation, has unfortunately suffered from the ill fame into which the less worthy Resistance has fallen. I begged my friends in the Resistance—some of them high in its counsels and exceedingly honorable—to repudiate the baser elements, to remain an exclusive and relatively small company, with its escutcheon unblemished. One of them—a right-hand man of General De Gaulle—promised me that he would thus jealously safeguard the real Resistance from the riff-raff and scoundrels who used its name for their own ends; but the prevailing opinion was that the Resistance should be considered as a united bloc, and the mantle of Noah was thrown over the misdeeds of the more violent and irresponsible section.

One of my own difficulties, in my desire to tell the truth, is that, in "debunking" the false Resistance, I may be thought to be condemning a valiant and admirable (though always small) group of active adversaries of the invaders. Above all, I would not have it supposed that I wish to discredit France. I think France, on the whole, demonstrated her finest virtues in her passive resistance to the enemy, and behaved with sound sense; and I pay homage to the French people. That there should be heroic spirits who had not the patience to endure, who took bold (and sometimes premature) action, is not to be deprecated. That, on the other side, there should be heroic spirits (often misguided) who threw themselves too zealously into the fight against disorder and disunity was an inevitable consequence of the calamitous occupation; and it is lamentable that they should, patriotic though their motives were, have been forced into false relations with the occupying forces. Our indignation should be reserved for those who, on both sides, made war on the French rather than on the Germans, who engaged in a civil war, in which, after the Liberation, the weapons and the hostility were all on one side. The bulk of the French took a sensible middle course.

It is estimated that 20,000 persons lost their lives under the Reign of Terror; that 18,000 fell in the frightful butchery that followed the war and insurrection of 1870–1871. The American services put the figures of "summary executions" in France in the first months of the Liberation at 80,000. A former French minister later placed the figure at 105,000.

The Minister was M. Adrien Tixier, a Socialist, who in March 1945, when he was minister of the interior and, therefore, presumably acquainted with the facts, told "Colonel Passy," one of the chief agents of De Gaulle, that from August 1944 to March 1945 there had been 105,000 executions. The statement has been frequently made: there can be little doubt that it was repeated in good faith; and, of course, the executions were regarded as deplorable both by the minister and by the colonel. That there were many executions both before and after these dates is a matter of public notoriety.

It may also be noted that, on October 15, 1943, the Central Committee of the Resistance at Algiers addressed a circular to the metropolitan groups, envisaging the insurrection between the departure of the Germans and the arrival of the Anglo-American forces, thus "guaranteeing the revolutionary suppression, in a few hours, of the traitors, in conformity with the legitimate aspirations of reprisals of the Resistance," and "paralyzing the dispositions of the Vichy administration." The elimination of all officials should be accomplished "by authority." This order confined the revolution to "a few hours," and the time in which reprisals were to be taken, Vichy liquidated, and the functionaries eliminated was foreseen as of short duration. It is obvious, however, that such an operation could hardly be effected so quickly.

As the police records show, there were still sporadic killings at a much later date and, recently, there have been trials of "Resistants" who, for private reasons, were guilty of atrocious crimes in the tragic years after the Liberation. I myself narrowly escaped "summary" dispatch, as did my wife. The invariable excuse of those brought to justice in later years was that they were acting under orders of their superiors in the Resistance. Sometimes they were acquitted on this ground; sometimes they were sentenced to comparatively mild terms of imprisonment, even when the circumstances were abominable. It is noteworthy that, in every project of amnesty, there was particular insistence on the immunity of men who could show they were in the Resistance movement and were, therefore, presumed to be animated by the best of motives (while often mistaken in the choice of their victims)—and this immunity was extended to 1946, though the last of the Germans had left French soil many months earlier.

There were many kinds of executions. The mob, after the manner of mobs in all countries, joined in lynching parties without stopping to inquire what offense had been committed. There were professional criminals who had the chance of their lives to kill and rob with impunity and were responsible for many revolting happenings. Even more shocking were the crimes committed by normally respectable people whose sadistic instincts were aroused and given free rein. There were many cases of personal revenge with no public basis whatever. And there was a great deal of terrorism carried out with purely radical revolutionary aims: the opportunity for the suppression of political opponents was too good to be lost.

Bands of armed men, answerable to no one, their connection with the Resistance often dubious and of recent date, went from house to house in the cities of the South (of which I can speak with personal knowledge) asking the *concierges* whether there were any "Pétainists" or "collaborators" in the apartments. They proceeded to arrest, with brutality, whoever was so designated. The public, anxious to assure its own safety, preferred to remain silent, or, to be even more secure, joined the persecutors. Anyone with a grudge against his neighbor could safely work it off—and, at the same time, become a noble "Resistant"—by denouncing that neighbor. Those who had uneasy consciences, who had compromised themselves, perhaps in some innocent and inevitable way, were most inclined to rush to the aid of the *épurateurs*. Anyone who has read, as I have done, the French newspapers in the past few years, will have discovered that men who had been the auxiliaries of the Germans slipped into the ranks of the Resistants at the last minute and, having tortured on behalf of Germany, were now ready to torture in the name of French patriotism. What better alibi could be found? The Resistance was wide open to anyone who cared to join after the Germans began to decamp. The worst of these recruits of the eleventh hour had served on both sides—from Militia to Maquis, from Gestapo to Resistance—and were equally zealous and savage in both camps. Such is human nature, when the fitting conditions for the display of its darker side are furnished.

General De Gaulle was not yet recognized by the Allies as the new leader of France. He came on the scene when France was "liberated" and was acclaimed by the Parisians, as anybody who seemed to symbolize the deliverance would have been acclaimed—as Pétain had been acclaimed a few months earlier when he announced by his presence in Paris that the hour of deliverance was at hand. But De Gaulle had no constitutional or legal right to office. He had not been elected; in the absence of other authority he seized power. No body of representatives, chosen by the people, had given it to him, as such a constitutional body had given it to Pétain. Yet the word went forth that he was the "legitimate" chief, while Pétain was "illegitimate." I do not imply that De Gaulle would not have been elected—there could have been no other choice in the circumstances: I merely record the plain fact.

It was, then, only by accepting as associates the most undesirable parties and persons who were willing—temporarily—to march under his banner, that De Gaulle could hope to succeed. The link that loosely held together the most disparate elements was that of the Resistance, real or false; those who could pretend to exceptional "patriotism"—though the Communists, in particular, had a long history of antipatriotism, not only in the early part of the war but during their whole existence, and were soon to show that Russia was their *patrie*—were his momentary allies. Whether he intended and desired it or not—and I do not suggest that he did—his associates had to be given a free hand, which they used unsparingly against their "enemies," their "enemies" being French, not German. If one did not admit a special brand of patriotism, consisting of allegiance to De Gaulle and at least tolerance of Communism, then one was dubbed an "anti-patriot" and handed over, as it were, to the hangman.

The *épuration* was a political operation, in the manner in which it was carried out. De Gaulle, who could hardly have been less blind to the Russian peril than Churchill and Roosevelt (though they too chose to close their eyes), outspeeded them in making pacts and giving concessions to Stalin. In return for Russian support, he granted amnesty to Maurice Thorez, the Communist chief, who had deserted from the French army before the débâcle and had sought refuge in Russia; and Thorez was brought back as a hero to sit as vice-president of the council beside De Gaulle. It will be seen how equivocal was De Gaulle's position; many who had approved of the leadership he had given in England were now dubious of the leadership he gave—or failed to give—in France. Had he accepted, when it was offered, the legal transmission of power from Pétain, he would have been far stronger.

As it was, he was obliged to improvise in every domain, relying on men who were, in reality, his bitterest adversaries. The men who attached themselves to his movement, often in the last year, the last month, or even the last week of the struggle, claimed all the posts available, whether they had any qualifications for them or not and, to make more posts available, it was necessary to oust the civil servants who had quite properly carried on under the Pétain régime. It had been the only régime, and France had to be governed and administered, whether the Germans were in occupation or not. These faithful servants, against whom nothing disloyal could, in most cases, be fairly alleged, were dubbed "traitors," unless they had double affiliations or could turn a quick somersault. They were all "suspect," though some were saved. Communists and members of other radical parties seized key posts.

De Gaulle must, of course, be absolved from personal responsibility for the many illegalities perpetrated. But why should Pétain be held guilty of horrors committed by the Germans and pro-Germans, which he could not prevent and did his best to oppose? The deportees, indoctrinated, were ready to accuse Vichy of having deported them—which is absurd! Some of them were venomously vindictive. The prisoners of war, to whom the deep solicitude of the marshal was unknown in many cases, somehow blamed him for their sufferings. In my day—if I may use the phrase of a veteran —a prisoner of war was, *a priori*, suspect. Why had he allowed himself to be captured? Had he chosen an easy way out of the war? Had he really fought? That was an unduly stern view: the finest soldier may be taken prisoner. Yet, except in special cases, no war prisoner could claim to be a hero. That was how we thought in 1914–1918, but in 1944–1945 a prisoner of war came back as a great fellow, who had been betrayed by Vichy, though Vichy was not in existence when he was captured in 1939–1940. He was asked no questions about his conduct. He was useful for propaganda. He was a martyr and a victim of the marshal. He was inclined to take the adulation seriously, and I saw signs in ever so many shop fronts that the proprietor was a POW and, therefore, should have our trade. He sometimes took an active part in the *épuration* of those unfortunate Frenchmen who had not had the honor of being caught by the enemy, though he could know nothing about the conditions in a country from which he had, perforce, been absent for so long. My sympathy for POWs and deportees is immense; but I cannot see that it is blasphemy to question their blanket credentials as heroes. Certain deportees were common criminals; and in several cases I knew they had indulged in foolish talking in public places such as cafés.

There was an almost unlimited field—an "open season"— for the *épurateurs*. Everybody in France was a "collaborator," in the sense that he had at some time or other come into contact with the Germans. The workers were necessarily so since, to earn a living, they had to work in factories which helped in some degree to supply German demands. The industrialists were, against their will, "collaborators," for, unless they closed down their factories and threw out their workers, they could not refuse to obey German commands. Indeed, it was later decreed that an industrialist who had given Germany no more than 60 per cent of his total output was not liable to prosecution. This came some time after 1944 and did not save honest industrialists, against whom workers had a grudge, from being killed before the decree. Newspapermen were all "collaborators," inasmuch as they had to handle German communiqués. Should France have been left without news? Or should it have been left to the Germans to establish their own newspapers? Actors and singers and entertainers of all sorts were "collaborators," because they had played or sung before Germans in the audience. Therefore, any actor or singer who had incurred the dislike of his colleagues was a marked man.

Painters had sold pictures to artistically inclined Germans and could, if second-rate artists so decided, be barred from the galleries. Shopkeepers had sold goods to Germans—they could not do otherwise. Civil servants had been compelled to cooperate with the Germans. The looser kind of women did not shut up shop for the duration of the war—and ran their business neither on patriotic nor antipatriotic lines. Young men and young women are much the same the world over and, in the course of four years, there was plenty of time for purer idylls. Civilians generally had to apply to the Germans for various facilities, such as visas and permits to travel from one zone to the other. I do not know what the *émigrés* imagined—that no one should pursue his vocation, that no one should marry or beget children, or even dare to die, since these acts obliged him to have dealings with officials who were ultimately under the authority of Pétain or Hitler?

A policeman who, in the normal performance of his duties, had arrested a criminal who happened to be a Communist or a Gaullist was almost sure to be arrested at the Liberation. I met a number of them myself; they were dismissed from their posts and imprisoned. An individual who knew the German language and consented to act as an interpreter might be charged with "intelligence with the enemy"—a crime punishable by death. Widely differing views were taken on this, as on many other points. In the South, I saw interpreters thrown into jail; in the North, I was told that they had rendered great service to the population—which indeed is obvious.

In practice, the *épuration* was purely arbitrary. Some generals who had served under Pétain, who had played a part in the condemnation of De Gaulle, who had negotiated with the Germans, who had resisted the North African landing—were condemned; others who had done the same things were honored. Most of the big industrialists who had helped to build fortifications and walls for the Germans and, incidentally, made billions of francs, went scot free; while minor businessmen were convicted. One foreigner, who had collected metal for the Germans, was virtually immune, because he had financed a resistance group in the police. The axe fell or did not fall according to no set rules—but often where it fell it was fatal.

Writers, and particularly journalists, who were not "Leftish" were the hardest hit. Charles Maurras, one of France's foremost thinkers (with whose views one may not agree), had spent his life fulminating against the "Prussians" and had a morbid hatred of all things German. He took his paper—the *Action Française*—into the unoccupied zone of France; he refused the subsidies from Vichy that most papers were allowed; he declined to mention the name of Laval, whom he thought pro-German; he wrote not a line in favor of the German occupant. But he was a Monarchist, anti-Republican, anti-Communist and, in spite of his great age (the "oldest prisoner in the world," after the marshal), he received a life sentence. Henri Béraud, France's ablest polemicist, a brilliant writer who was intensely anti-German but was opposed to Gaullism, was sentenced to death and spent some weeks in irons, before his death sentence was commuted. It is said—but I cannot vouch for it—that England intervened in his favor, paradoxically enough, for Béraud was anti-English. Several members of the *Académie Française* were condemned. Robert Brasillach, a young poet, was executed for his writings, and is now regarded in the same light as Chénier, who fell under the guillotine in the Great Revolution. A truly remarkable aged scientist was condemned. Alexis Carrel, who left his handsomely paid job in the United States to share the sufferings of France, in the hope of alleviating them, while others were seeking refuge overseas, went into hiding and died of a broken heart. On the fate of many foremost men, whose patriotism cannot be doubted, a discreet silence is maintained.

As I never tired of pointing out, this wholesale condemnation of the *élite* of France, described as "traitors," was propaganda in reverse. Those who have done most harm to France are the *épurateurs*. For years, they held up France as a country in which a considerable percentage of the population—and among them the most distinguished citizens—danced with glee on the downfall of the nation and rushed forward to help Germany fasten her yoke on an afflicted people. The picture is not true. It is utterly false. Yet it is the picture painted by many of the so-called ultrapatriots. There were traitors, real traitors, torturers, informers, the dregs of society, such as you will find in any country in time of trouble; but let it not be supposed that those whose hands were stained with blood would have obtained the grace of Pétain had he continued to rule. Before the Germans occupied the South, he was as rigorous as the men of the Fourth Republic against the spies and traitors who fell into his power and, after the Liberation, he would have ordered an *épura-*

tion. An *épuration* was necessary. There were men who deserved the heaviest punishment. The complaint is that the *épuration* was carried out wildly—and in some cases with cunning political calculation—often against the wrong persons, often by the very persons who should have been incarcerated, and with a partiality, a lack of control, a spirit of vengeance, that constitute an abominable scandal.

I watched the working of the courts of justice, which were not the normal tribunals, composed as they were of juries chosen from a panel of professed partisans. The verdict and the sentence were frequently—I am tempted to say, usually—fixed in advance by committees, with Communists in a majority. The proceedings were conducted amid cries of "Death! Death!" Any judicial hearing was impossible. The lawyers rarely ventured to put forward arguments as to the nullity and illegality of the trials. These courts were instituted under decisions taken at London or in Algiers, at a time when there could be no legal authority or legislative assembly outside Vichy. Therefore, I think that their validity—like the so-called High Court of Justice—ought to have been challenged. However, I suppose that such a challenge would have been without the smallest effect, and would have only worsened the case of prisoners

Death sentences, life imprisonment, twenty years, ten years, for newspaper criticism, were pronounced; trivial lapses, such as fraternization, were punished as though they had seriously imperiled the State. I examined the dossier of a French relative of mine: it merely contained articles discussing various aspects of Syndicalism (radical trade unionism). He was sentenced to eight years. After three years he was released, and then had to start his career over again —a very difficult task for a man left penniless in changed conditions. A friend of mine was sentenced to ten years for perfectly proper comments on foreign policy. Happily, he escaped to Switzerland and, after some years, came back and asked to be tried again. This time he was acquitted—there was not the smallest case against him.

How many persons were arrested in France? It is hard to say. The official figures mean little. They acknowledge somewhere about 120,000 prosecutions—already a prodigious number of presumed "traitors"—but they are only a fraction of the truth. The *Figaro,* which took the orthodox view of the *épuration,* although the Catholic writer François Mauriac occasionally shed an unavailing tear on the injustices of the period, did not exaggerate when it acknowledged one million incarcerations. Many thousands who were arrested and spent months in prison were never charged with anything and, when they were released, generally ruined in health and pocket, they were not included in the official count. The prefects, appointed by Algiers or Paris and sometimes placed in office by an irresponsible group of Communists armed with *mitraillettes,* were given power to order "administrative detention," that is, internments in which there was no semblance of formal justice, no preliminary investigation, no attempt at justification, or no specific accusation, usually on a vague denunciation; and many of these "administrative internments" often lasted for a year or more.

I speak not from hearsay but at first hand. A full month after the landing, I too was arrested by as ruffianly-looking a band of fellows with machine guns as you can imagine; and the next day my wife was arrested, and my house and belongings sequestrated. Nobody signed any warrant at any time, no accusation was brought, there was not even an "administrative order." It was just like that—anybody could arrest anybody on any pretext—or without pretext. I do not regret this incident, which was ended by the intervention of the representatives of General Eisenhower and of the British ambassador; and General de Benouville, acting for General De Gaulle, also came to my rescue. I was fortunate in having highly placed friends; without them I might have fared badly. I know the private reasons which dictated this attempt—there were certainly no public reasons—and despicable indeed they were. My activities, such as they were during the war, were directed to informing the British authorities of the situation in France, and I ran great risks. I do not propose to talk of them, but certainly they should have commended themselves to the Resistants.

To forestall any malevolent misunderstanding, I would add that, not content with our release, with suitable excuses, I considered it my duty to launch an action for arbitrary and illegal detention before the highest tribunal in France—the *Conseil d'État,* one of the few bodies that maintained a judicial spirit in the tragic years. The government spokesman admitted the mistake, and the court condemned, in the most unequivocal terms, the "gross blunder" committed by its "agents." The administration was ordered to pay me and my wife substantial damages. It will be seen, therefore, that I have little to complain of personally, nor do I harbor the smallest resentment. On the contrary, I pay my tribute to the impartiality and fairness of ordinary French justice. That I should have come off so well, however, cannot blind me to the terrible injustices of the "exceptional" procedure. I was fortunate, but many thousands of victims could not hope for redress.

I say that I do not regret this experience, painful though it was, since it enabled me to see for myself how honest citizens were treated in the 1944 revolution. Although I was warned—by a member of the Resistance—not to write of what I had seen for "at least two years" (the direst retribution was threatened if I did), I immediately wrote my book in French, *Terreur 1944,* and found a courageous publisher. I pleaded not only for a return to humane conditions but also for a reconciliation of the French, whichever side they had taken in what was tantamount to a civil war. The way back to civilized jurisprudence has been long and hard—

longer and harder than I had anticipated—but at last I am glad to say that normal conditions have returned and, if I am proud of anything in my life, I am proud to have, as I hope, contributed something toward the restoration of the traditional virtues of France.

I will not repeat what I have already written in the book mentioned above, but I will briefly recall that where I was temporarily confined there were five of us in a narrow, exceedingly dirty cell in which it was impossible to walk about, and barely room to sleep on the cement floor. Our food consisted of two bowls of thin soup a day, and a loaf of almost uneatable bread. For the natural functions of five of us, there was provided a tin receptacle, emptied once a day. Among my fellow prisoners was a retired commandant, a major of the French army who was shopping for his invalid wife, when a woman whom he had never seen before shouted: "He belongs to the Gestapo." He was seized by half a dozen hooligans. When he pointed to his medals won in the 1914–1918 war, they cried: "we don't care about your paltry little war—this is the only war that counts." He remained several months in jail, and was then released. There was a tax collector, who had held aloof from politics, and had not the slightest idea why he had been arrested. He, too, was eventually released. There was a well-to-do Dutchman, whose wife was of German origin; they had lived quietly on the coast without participating in public events. He too was released, but not before he had lived in the squalid conditions I have mentioned for months. There was an Italian baker, who had (for aught I know) sold a little bread on the black market, though this was not charged against him. Thus, of my immediate companions not one figured in the official list of accused persons. Hundreds of such cases came within my personal knowledge, but these may be taken as typical.

The wife of the tax collector had been stripped naked

and paraded through the streets, her head shaved, the Swastika sign painted in tar on her back. The baker told me that the cart in which he and a number of companions were conveyed to prison by men armed to the teeth, ready to fire if anyone tried to escape, halted several times, forced prisoners to alight in a wooded region—and no more was heard of these prisoners. Were I to narrate all the stories which I heard from eyewitnesses, I should fill another volume as large as this. I refer the future historian to an admirable publication, *Écrits de Paris,* in which, month after month, M. Jean Pleyber devoted many pages to succinct accounts of crimes in the different *départements* of France. Let me give a few examples (omitting the names, which would mean nothing to my readers):

Allier: M. ———, farrier at Sauvigny, was savagely beaten in August 1944, and shot in the wood near Cordeliers.

Alpes-Maritimes: On October 8, 1944, M.C., horticulturist at Cagnes, was arrested and has never since been seen. He had previously been the victim of extortions.

Corrèze: the *Journal Officiel* of 29 February contains the judgment of a tribunal of Tulle regarding the "absence" of M. ———, who "disappeared December 12, 1944, following his arrest by members of the F.F.I." At Brive were "slaughtered" in the spring of 1944 MM. [here follow four names], as well as a girl of 22 years, the chauffeur of Dr. ———, and a police officer whose names I do not possess. In August 1944 were assassinated at Brive MM. [five names], at Tulle MM. [five other names], at Egletons, Dr. ——— and Mademoiselle ———, 18 years of age, at Lagraulière, M.G., at Cublac M. ——— and M. ———, who died from his wounds two years later, at Saint-Setier, a shoemaker, at Bort-Les-Orgues, twenty persons, at Curement, H.N., at Chambert, M.B., at Eyrem, a woman whose name I do not know, at Ayem, M.G., died from injuries received in prison.

Corsica: In the *Patriote* of Bastia (9 September, 1944) there is a declaration of a certain M. ———, member of the Consultative Assembly of Algiers, and member of the *Comité de Libération Nationale:*

"The Front National contains patriots of all parties. It is sufficient for us to know that they were opposed to the Vichy régime." Is not that an excellent definition of "patriotism"?

Côte D'Or: The appeal court of Dijon having condemned thirteen inhabitants (including the Mayor and his deputy) for falsely accusing M. ——— of "collaboration," the Municipal Council of Paguy-la-Ville has resigned.

Dordogne: The public prosecutor has proceeded to the reconstruction of the assassination, 7 June, 1944, of M. ———, garage owner at St. Georges-de-Montclaie, by a group of "liberators," led by a certain F. and Captain B.

Drôme: The military tribunal of Lyons has sentenced to five years' imprisonment the sailor P., "Captain" in the Resistance, who ordered the strangulation of Mlle. L. The "executioners," four in number, were acquitted. P. was the "*Commissaire du Gouvernement*" at the court-martial which condemned to death Colonel T. and Captain G., who were both shot.

Eure: At Louviers, M.C. was assassinated in August 1944, falsely accused of having denounced an American aviator.

Finistère: The Assize Court has sentenced to two years' imprisonment N., who, in 1944, pillaged several farms "on behalf of the Resistance."

Morbihan: The military tribunal of Paris has condemned to ten years' hard labor L., who, in August 1944, assassinated at Bresch, Mesdames B. and L., who, in his turn, said he only carried out the orders of his superiors.

Nièvre: The military tribunal of Lyons has condemned to twenty years' hard labor B., who killed (25 August, 1944) near Cosne, a Dutchman V. Der H. He declared he executed the order of "Lieutenant" P. But another "lieutenant" C. affirmed that B. entered the Resistance "in order to rob and kill." His accomplices were acquitted, but they admitted that they only "entered the Maquis when the Germans were leaving."

Puy-de-Dôme: The Minister of Ex-Combatants has rehabilitated the memory of M.M. assassinated in August 1944 and has allowed a pension to his widow.

Pyrénées-Orientales: Assassinated in August 1944, MM. [here follow twenty-four names, including a priest, a colonel, and two women]. Shot after court-martial: [here follow twenty-nine names, including a major, and a priest who "suffered the most cruel torture before being shot"].

Rhône: The military tribunal has sentenced to ten years G., former "Chief" of the Montcorin Fort, who was responsible for the torturing and execution of [five names] on 28 August, 1944. He said he had received orders. The same tribunal sentenced to ten years the "Resistant" T., who was, while in the Resistance, a Gestapo agent.

Var: At Toulon, on "Liberation Day," a naval officer was murdered by a seaman belonging to a group of "Liberators." At Sainte-Maxime, in July 1944, the deputy Mayor was assassinated. A notary at Salernes, M.F., received in February 1944 a woman who said she was looking for a house to buy. She pretended to know the political opinions of a number of people in the district. The notary told her she was mistaken, and entered into discussion with her. At the Liberation, there was found in the quarters of the Gestapo at Draguignon a report of the woman, attributing to M.F. the information she gave. M.F., on the simple evidence of this document of a spy, was condemned to death and executed 27 December, 1944.

Haute-Vienne: According to reliable information, the Prefect of the *département* addressed to M. Tixier, Minister of the Interior, in October 1944, a telegram putting at 1,500 the number of "summary executions" in his *département*.

Monotonous though this brief list may be, it is necessary that I supplement my own observations by a reference to these reports. They are an infinitesimal part of the records already made public and, so far as I know, never denied. Scarcely a day goes by without its batch of new revelations. Some of them attract attention, others pass unnoticed. I myself knew of one murder of a man who had been acquitted (a notable event in these days, and proof, if proof there could be, of his innocence). I know of two cases where accused persons were taken from a hospital by a band of armed men and executed. I know of "hostages" in a southern fortress, presumably innocent, who were, on the orders of a "captain," taken out and shot. I know . . . but why continue? No one who had eyes to see and ears to hear could doubt that a wave of terror, such as France has never before known, followed (and preceded) the Liberation. I do not for a moment affirm that these and innumerable other incidents condemn the Resistance—I do affirm that, unless the Resistance was confined to well-disciplined adherents, carefully selected, it was inevitable that, in the confusion of the Liberation, the criminally minded and the fanatics would run amok and steal and slay in the name of the Resistance. I, likewise, affirm that the first and most important *épuration* should have been in the ranks of the Resistance.

One was a "collaborator," a "traitor," because a neighbor said so, because one possessed a portrait of the marshal, because one had (quite properly) regretted the Allied bombings, because one had uttered a word against banditry, because one had quarreled with an employee, because of anything or nothing. The truth about the terrible transition period, when France was without an effective government (the writ of Paris did not run far) and when nobody thought it his business to stem the tide of pent-up hatred, is that the Communists and the near Communists were in effective command: but it would be unfair to the Communists to put all the blame on them. Other parties, afraid of being thought less "patriotic," just as eager in the scramble for places, affected the stern figure of implacable Roman virtue and refused to see or hear of abuses and atrocities.

It will be observed that the military courts, which have now been substituted for the *cours de justice*, are at last inclined to punish the false Resistants guilty of crime. But their sentences are mild compared with those earlier inflicted on "Pétainists" and, too often, the claim to have acted in the interest of the Resistance gives the criminal right to an "amnesty," denied until 1952 (on any considerable scale) to those "collaborators" whose hands were unstained by the blood of their compatriots.

When I think that, not far away, in the Channel Islands,

which are under the British Crown, the Germans were in occupation almost as long as they were in France, that the population lived peaceably alongside the occupier, that there was just as much natural fraternization or collaboration, free or forced, as there was in France, and that, nevertheless, no one in the Channel Islands dreamed of an *épuration* of the population, I am afflicted by a consciousness of what political strife and personal manoeuvring can lead to in a land where it was held to be "patriotic" to arm lawless adventurers and irresponsible "Resistants."

When, after my incarceration, I met in the streets of Nice the "Commandant" (they loved the title of "Commandant!") to whom I owed what he called my "protection," he greeted me effusively and, after the usual silly reference to my supposed work for the "Intelligence Service," he told me that, as a delegate of Algiers, he had been given special instructions to repress any "popular" vengeance and to conduct the *épuration* in an orderly manner. I do not doubt it, and I bear no ill will against him. He was as courteous as I could have wished. He regretted that he had been overwhelmed by the rush of men—and women—bent on personal revenge or political profit. He spoke of persons whose assassination he had been unable to prevent—seventeen was the number he mentioned. We agreed that those who had deliberately betrayed France deserved punishment; that "Pétainists" and "Gaullists" should have been in accord for a "purge" of those who had fought against the French (on either side), who had denounced the Jews, the Communists, the Resistants, to the Gestapo, who had tortured and killed their compatriots, and who had acted as spies and agents of the enemy. But, to confound these unworthy citizens, small in number, with those whose only offense was to have obeyed the marshal, to have admired him and trusted him, or who had expressed opinions on the conduct of the war (opinions that now all informed and intelligent citizens accept) different from those entertained by the men in power after the Liberation, was a profound error which would long leave dire traces in France. Irresponsible men, though they had truly distinguished themselves in the Resistance (which was far from being always the case), should not have been allowed to judge others whose "patriotism" took another form. The *épuration* should have been carried out by competent and independent juridical bodies, not by committees which were both passionate and political.

We shook hands, and he left me with thanks for such assistance as I had tried to render, unconvinced, I am afraid, that I had not acted in cooperation with an organized service, British, American, or French. Like most people in the Resistance, he could not imagine that anyone might behave simply according to his conscience without attaching himself to a group or a party or a leader.

Among the *épurateurs,* as I soon discovered, were former members of the International Brigades (mostly Communist) which had fought in Spain. They were Hungarians, Italians, Bulgarians, and even Germans, and they were more unscrupulous—and therefore greater "patriots"—than the French. Many of those whom they called for questioning did not survive the ordeal. In the hotels which served for prisons, women of the street were called to gloat over victims, among them high officials, who were compelled to turn around in circles and to cry "Maréchal, nous voilà!" as they were beaten with bludgeons and cowhide whips. Some of the victims were cut with razors or burned with cigarettes—the breasts of women were thus disfigured. Others were made to kneel on three-edged rulers, or were plunged head foremost into cold baths to the point of suffocation. There were fiendishly ingenious applications of electrical apparatus, both external and internal. Some of the torturers delighted in scorching the soles of their victims' feet. There were many cases of rape. The first time I heard an *épurateur* say: "We are not the Gestapo," I was surprised; the second and third and fourth time, I realized that he had an uneasy conscience and, although not personally guilty of cruelty, was trying to hide his shame at the practice of his fellows. Men were forced to dig their own graves. Those who died under torture were tossed from windows and were said to have committed suicide. There was, of course, no inquiry. My wife was to have been removed from Monaco to Nice at two or three in the morning, and I am convinced that only the timely appearance of my American friend in uniform saved her from being thrown into a ravine. Now and again we read in the newspapers of common graves discovered in lonely places and, as tongues are loosened, more and more horrors come to light.

Naturally all this is quite outside official knowledge; the authorities were, and are, ignorant of many of the misdeeds, and I am willing to believe that they are as distressed as anyone. But there are many reasons, besides the reluctance to acknowledge how badly the revolution turned out, why they should not immediately press for the most searching investigations. Legends had been manufactured and had to be preserved. There must be no quarrels within the Resistance movement. The more vindictive elements of the majority were the most vociferous. Any attacks on the régime were held to be "antipatriotic," "anti-Resistant," "anti-Republican," inspired by Vichyism, Fascism, pro-Germanism; they were the criticisms of "traitors" who had been overlooked and were now daring to raise their heads again. The Resistance, long after the Germans had gone, had to be kept in existence, though there was now nothing to resist; it had become a vested interest, a passport to success, to posts and prebends. To venture to expose not the Resistance as such, but the methods of many who had disgraced the Resistance, was to put oneself outside the pale. Therefore there was little protest, little plain speaking; an independent and impartial press did not exist, and publication in book form was difficult.

Nevertheless, from the pulpit of Notre Dame, the principal cathedral of France, the burningly eloquent Lenten preacher Père Panici raised his voice against the régime. He was not allowed to continue. He disappeared into a monastery, and his place was taken by a preacher who had been interned in a German camp and was more orthodox. Père Panici's sermon, which had been printed, was censored. I obtained a copy of the original text, and I read:

> Since the beginning of the century we breathe an air of trouble and of war, an air of folly, of cruelty, an air that excites a horrible thirst in men, the desire to inflict sufferings, to watch blood flow, to contemplate death. . . . We awaited our liberation and the joy that would accompany it. We awaited with no less fervor the cessation of German tyranny. . . . But we are far from being freed. Illegal arrests, massacres without judgment, indefensible imprisonments, tortures, breaches of justice . . . these facts are above all shameful in France! [He spoke of private and public vendettas, of sequestrations of citizens by persons without any public function, without proper cause; he spoke of the "special courts" in which errors committed in good faith by irreproachable citizens were confounded with the crime of treason; he spoke of verdicts of an incomprehensible severity, assassinations even in prisons, of delation encouraged, denunciations demanded, in offices opened to receive them.]
>
> These wounds to the respect of the human person cannot be denied. The evidence abounds. Have the French been transformed? We do not recognize as French of the true France, of the humane France, of the liberty-loving France, of the France worthy of love for her high civilization, we do not recognize as French the torturers and the murderers who cover us with blood and shame. We do not defend the traitors, nor the infamous profiteers, but we remind ourselves that even in these men we must respect the dignity of man. If they have compromised that dignity, it is not for men without mandate to compromise it still more for the abominable pleasure of watching their fellows suffer and die. What a horrible future these sadists, these men of blood and death, will bring upon us! Years of legal and private assassination,

of tortures and hatred, a régime of the slaughterhouse! A climate in which we feel, perpetually, a disgust of living, a desire to disappear from a world where, amid tigers with men's faces, we are tormented in spirit, an impoverishment as a result of carnage, though France needs all her children to rebuild her substance—a future lost by the loss of so much of value when we want every man of value, by an enormous hemorrhage when we need all our blood! Yes, a frightful future, a slaughterhouse régime, men become sanguinary; in the prisons, in the camps, a feeling grows, hatred! We do not consider the political aspects of these facts, the disregard of State authority, the rights that certain parties arrogate to themselves as though they alone held power, but we have the duty of examining the moral aspect and of denouncing frightful tendencies. What tendencies? The total absence of love, the existence of hatred, of fearful hatred. . . .

I have translated these broken sentences as literally as possible. It is apparent that this priest was speaking under the stress of violent emotion, perhaps not wisely, perhaps with rhetorical exaggeration. No wonder that he was driven from the pulpit of Notre Dame! Yet, it would have been well had his words been heeded. France might then have recovered from the shock of war, occupation, revolution, a one-sided civil war, at a much earlier date. As it was, the "courts of exception," which the French normally held in horror, functioned for six years; trivial and venial shortcomings were treated as "intelligence with the enemy," or as "injurious to national defense"; the death sentence was sometimes carried out after the condemned man had been kept for more than a year with his feet in irons, chained up like a dog, expecting every morning to be taken out and shot. Finally, as I write, I understand that an amnesty is shortly to be proclaimed. It is certainly not too soon; the maximum of mischief has been done; God grant that it may not be too late!

I am bound to refer to an innovation reminiscent of Nazi or Soviet legislation: the institution of what was called "national indignity" by the committees of Algiers at a time when they had no possible claim to the status of a legislative body. Sometimes it was impossible to find, even by straining the law, that a punishable offense had been committed. Therefore "civil courts" were given the right to impose disabilities, depriving "bad citizens" of the vote, of official occupations, of employment in the law, the press, the cinema, the teaching profession, and so forth. Nor could such persons obtain passports, and, unwanted at home, unable to earn a living, they were forbidden to go abroad. The most famous cantatrice in France, denounced by a servant with whom she had some dispute, was thus reduced to silence. She could no longer sing at the Opera, and she could not accept engagements in the foreign countries that wanted to hear her. For all I know, she may have possessed the wherewithal to live; humbler persons thus stigmatized were condemned to misery. In her case, music lovers lost a pleasure; in many other cases the whole community was the poorer for the nonexercise of the talents of trained workers. In an old phrase, France was cutting off her nose to spite her face. The sum total of individual human suffering and the impoverishment of French life were considerable—they made all the difference between speedy recovery from the wounds of war and a lingering purulence in the body politic. Sometimes I thought that the greatest punishment of all was the infliction of a disabling "indignity"; it did not at once kill but it was a festering sore.

Nor was this the whole story: self-appointed censors in the professions, usually the second-rate, the envious, the embittered took it upon themselves to ban their colleagues, mostly of a higher degree of skill, from pursuing their calling. Their colleagues had not been condemned by the courts of justice, they had not even been arraigned on the vague charge of being "nationally unworthy," but they might still be debarred by their fellows. A friend of mine, perhaps the most erudite journalist I have known, was summoned to appear before a self-constituted jury on which sat two reporters whom he had once discharged for unprofessional conduct, on the ground that he had deplored the bombing of priceless monuments: he died in poverty. Nearly all the best-known painers were forbidden to paint, at least for the public. Actors were forbidden to act. Dancers were forbidden to dance. Radio speakers were forbidden to speak. Singers were forbidden to sing. Cinema favorites were forbidden to appear in films. The second-raters were thus given the opportunity to take places they had been unable to earn on their merits. The ban, however, broke down fairly soon. The public insisted on seeing and hearing talented performers who happened to have entertained Germans as well as French. Again, I will not mention names, but there is one "star," known throughout the world, who is now more popular than ever after a period of ostracism: the "crime" for which it was sought to exclude him from his profession was that of visiting a camp of French war prisoners in Germany in order to cheer up his compatriots. Writers had the hardest struggle: they were gagged by mediocrities for several years.

As for the politicians, I have failed to understand the tests applied. In principle, anyone who voted for the investiture of Pétain was declared ineligible for public office; but, in fact, some of the most prominent figures now in French assemblies not only voted for Pétain but enthusiastically called on the members of the National Assembly to vote for him, while others, far less compromised, are prevented from sitting in the Chamber and in other elected bodies, though a majority of voters persistently plump for them. It is difficult to explain why anyone who honestly cast his vote in fulfillment of his parliamentary mandate should have been declared ineligible. Again, it was decided by Algiers that anyone who had served under Pétain was automatically pronounced unfit to serve the public in future. Yet, there are today ministers in office who, for the highest motives, did serve under Pétain; while there are others (Flandin, for example), actually exonerated from all blame by the High Court of Justice, whose candidature is yet prohibited. How could the Fourth Republic hope to start off well, when it refused the assistance of experienced politicians of the former régime—unless these experienced politicians had somehow managed to climb onto the band wagon in time and were prepared to repudiate what they had once commended?

Among the newcomers were, naturally, men of doubtful character. One of them, who took some part in the preparation of the trial of Pétain, is now in jail. Another, who was elected to the Chamber and helped to condemn the ministers of Pétain, is likewise in jail for stealing government bonds and for burglary. The latter was an authentic hero in the Resistance, but he had become so accustomed to illegalities and violences normally regarded as crimes in any civilized society, but glorified when committed in the name of the Resistance, that he continued his disgraceful career when Resistance no longer furnished an excuse. He well illustrates one of the dangers of condoning—or even praising—illegalities and violence in certain circumstances: for many others, far humbler, have found it hard to conform to the ordinary rules of disciplined communities. They too are victims of the teachings of the troubled years.

It would be wrong to bear ill will; when it was still dangerous I preached forgiveness to both sides; I pleaded for a reconciliation; I held, as I held throughout the war, that unity was essential, that France has need of all her citizens, whether they held this or that view of policy, whether they were or were not mistaken as to the path of duty.

I trust, then, that bitterness will be forgiven, that the future and not the past will occupy French minds. But I do not think that the lesson of the revolution (to which we are still reluctant to give its rightful name) should be lost. It is dangerous, in no matter what conditions, to divide a nation;

it may be fatal to arouse passions, to provide opportunities for wrongdoing, to encourage personal ambitions; it is suicidal to advocate disobedience, to pour contempt on the constituted authorities, to loosen the moral laws, to permit brutal action under any pretext, to cry for vengeance, to unchain the forces of evil, of lawlessness, of anarchy. Yet, if I have suffered disillusionment, if I have discovered that cruelty, injustice, ingratitude, intolerance are not confined to this or that country but are inherent in our human nature, I have also witnessed in France extraordinary patience in distress, mutual helpfulness, compassion, good sense—all those virtues which are not accounted heroic but are better than heroism—in the common people who make up the real France. For that real France, after the tragic ordeal, my sympathy and my love are unabated.

24

Fourth Republic

"How wonderful was the Republic . . . in the days of the Empire!" That was an epigrammatic criticism of the Third Republic in its early years. When Napoleon III fell, in the débâcle of 1870, it was hoped that the dreams of a republic in which men would breathe the air of freedom would at last be realized, and that concord, equality, and justice would be attained by the brotherhood of Frenchmen. Alas, the dreams that had been entertained under the Empire were not realized under the Republic. The character of men, their customs, their institutions, cannot be changed by a simple change of régime. When Rochefort wrote that France was peopled by thirty million subjects—not counting the subjects of discontent—he thought of the Empire, but when the Republic was founded, the nature of the subjects of discontent may not have been precisely the same, but the number was certainly no fewer.

So it was with the Fourth Republic, which was established in 1946, after the interregnum during which De Gaulle was virtually dictator. During the darkest days of the occupation, the Resistance, imitating in this the government of Vichy, had been engaged in drawing up plans for a better France. All the defects of the Third Republic, which were so obvious that ever since I have known France there have been periodical talks of a complete recasting of the constitution, were to be remedied. There were blueprints for everything.

Apart from real militants in the Resistance, apart from the outlaws who attached themselves to the movement, the principal preoccupation of the Resistance was the renovation of France by the establishment of certain parties in power.

The Resistance, in its confabulations in France and more particularly in Algiers, arranged a program. The instability of governments was to be remedied, for the instability and brevity of governments had been the curse of the Third Republic. The press was to be purified, for the French press before 1939 had been a by-word for irresponsibility, not to say corruption. Social justice was to be achieved by the raising of the workers' standard of living and the nationalization of banks, industries, insurance, and such services as gas and electricity and railways. In short, there was to be a revolution, not in the bloodier sense but in the political and social sense.

Well, we can now, eight years after the Liberation, see how it has worked out. Most of the members of Parliament were debarred from the Chamber, were considered ineligible because they had voted for Pétain. (As though anybody is entitled to punish elected representatives of the people retrospectively for the votes they thought fit to cast!) Generally speaking, the members of the Chamber and the successive prime ministers were new and untried men. Without experience, they made a sorry mess of things. The finances, which had been kept remarkably sound under the occupation, collapsed. On paper, the franc which was worth, at the end of the occupation, about 175 to the pound, fell to 1,000 to the pound and, in fact, its purchasing power was much lower than these rates indicate. In terms of the dollar it fell to 224 francs and then, in a further devaluation to 263, and finally to 400, which is much higher than the free market rate. The gold reserves, which were handed over practically intact, dwindled from 1599 tons to 464 tons, though much gold remained in private hands. When I first knew France, the annual budget was of 5,000,000,000 francs; today it stands at over 4,000,000,000,000 francs. The fiduciary circulation often jumps by 20,000,000,000 a week.

Wages have been a constant subject of dispute since 1944, and the workers think they have been cheated, inasmuch as large sections of the population have to live on less than the acknowledged minimum living wage. Social insurance is incredibly mismanaged, with the result that the employer pays for labor a third more than the wages received by his workman, while the workman is compelled to hand over sums that are greatly in excess of the benefits he receives. On the other hand, while old folk obtain utterly inadequate pensions, relatively large premiums are paid for the birth of children, and family allowances, which sometimes amount to more than wages, are accorded in a country which cannot, for many years to come, properly house its present population.

Taxation has reached what is agreed to be the breaking point, an intolerable burden for the artisan and small shopkeeper. The nationalized industries, which paid their own way before the war, which gave profits to their shareholders, show huge deficits, and the cost of electricity, gas, and transport is going up continuously. The *Cour des Comptes*, which belatedly checks government expenditure, issues reports which reveal the gravest dilapidation of public funds, amounting not merely to waste but to malversation. Functionarism, which was already a blight before the war, has grown enormously, and the huge army of useless officials is a problem which no one dares to tackle.

As for the press, which was illegally taken over, largely to the profit of the Communists, it sank, by general consent, to the lowest depths of partisanship, allied with vulgarity. There are, of course, certain newspapers which are dignified and well informed, but the press cannot compare, in the bulk, with the press of 1939. I need not name the most scandalous sheets, filled with suggestive stories, lewd pictures, intimate revelations of the lives of more or less prominent persons. The whole tone of the press has lamentably fallen. It is almost needless for me to state that, with few exceptions, the whole subject of the crimes of "Resistentialism" has been avoided, and the lying legends have been ardently defended. It is in vain that you will look for the truth about the war, the occupation, the *épuration* in the ordinary French newspapers. There have been scandals beside which the scandals of prewar days are trivial, beginning with the wine scandal in which the first prime minister after De Gaulle was, rightly or wrongly, implicated, and continuing with the scandal of the divulging of confidential reports on Indo-China and the traffic in piasters. They could not be excluded from the newspapers, but they were allowed to fizzle out, without any logical conclusion.

As for government stability, I will give a list of the earlier successive ministries since the liberation. There was first the government of De Gaulle, lasting from September 10, 1944, to November 6, 1945. It then resigned but took office again in a Constituent Assembly on November 20, and then retired, it has never been explained why, on January 20, 1946. Then came the government of Félix Gouin, which lasted five and a half months. It was followed by the government of Georges Bidault, which managed to remain in office for five months. Bidault was again designated, and presented himself before the Chamber, where he received far fewer than the constitutional number of votes. Léon Blum stayed only one month, resigning when Vincent Auriol was elected president of the Republic on January 16, 1947. Paul Ramadier remained for ten months, which was, apart from the De Gaulle government, a record, but it should be noted that, in reality, there were two Ramadier governments in this period, for the Communists who had, until May 1947, formed one of the parties in the ministry, retired, and Ramadier had to present a fresh cabinet to the Chamber. Léon Blum then was put up again and was beaten. On November 24, 1947, Robert Schuman was elected and stayed on for eight months. André Marie was in office as prime minister for less than a month. Robert Schuman came again and managed to stay for two days. Henri Queuille, one of the older school of politicians, then established another record, succeeding, by sheer force of inertia, in remaining for the comparatively long period of thirteen months. Jules Moch was then invested with the office of prime minister, but was unable to form a cabinet. The same mishap was experienced by René Meyer who, although prime minister for a few days, found he could not get together a team that would survive. Almost in despair, the President asked Bidault to form a government. He was in office for just over three months when the Socialists retired. He then formed a second cabinet and, if the two cabinets are taken as one, he stayed for eight months. When he was overthrown, Queuille once more formed a cabinet, which lasted a day or two. René Pleven, after an interregnum of several weeks of "crisis," that is to say, after several weeks without a government, struggled along. Queuille "made" the general elections in June 1952. You can count as you please, but with the immediate defeats, and the changes due to the retirement of Communists or Socialists, I cannot make the figures less than seventeen or eighteen cabinets or designated prime ministers in, say, 70 months; an average duration of four months. The long intervals in which France had no government at all, besides the periods in which Parliament did not sit, might also be noted. The Third Republic, with all its faults, did rather better than the Fourth.

The French, disgusted with the insincerity and ebulliency of parties, should at last have been given an opportunity of expressing their real opinions at the polls in the 1951 elections. They were thwarted. The electoral law was again twisted in the favor of the so-called middle-of-the-road parties. It not only was based on proportionalism, by which the seats were allotted to the various parties according to the percentage of votes, but the parties were allowed to make temporary alliances, to profess "affiliations" which enabled them to pool their total votes and then divide up the seats between themselves. Obviously, Socialists, M.R.P.'s and Radical-Socialists, who had really little in common with each other, could thus, by counting their votes as though they were one party, obtain an advantage over the Communists and the Gaullists, who had to stand on their own feet; and they also enjoyed all sorts of incidental benefits. The parties which appealed to the electorate as an entity were, in fact, deeply divided, and an anti-Socialist might find that he had voted to put in a Socialist, or vice-versa.

So strong, however, was the feeling against the "affiliated" parties that many Independents ran and were elected; not as many as would have won had the "affiliations" not been allowed, but sufficient to give a new turn to French politics. The public asked for something new. It wanted to close the unhappy chapter of the postwar muddle, with its *épuration,* its ostracisms, its misgovernment. The Independents were not enough to form a government, but they were strong enough to make their voice heard in the formation of a government. The swing was undoubtedly away from Socialism and Christian Democracy, away from the tyranny of the parties. At first, the change was not noticeable in practice.

Pleven and then Edgar Faure were chosen as prime ministers.

When another "crisis" came, the finances of France touched rock bottom. In despair, the president called on an inconspicuous Independent, a modest businessman, Antoine Pinay; he, strangely enough, though a genuine Resistant, had certain associations with the Pétain régime, and for this he had at one time been disqualified. It was thought that he might tide over the difficulties which were making government impossible until a combination of the old parties could again be formed. He was a stop-gap, quite harmless. But, to the astonishment of the parties, Pinay displayed precisely the qualities of commonsense and honesty that pleased the public. He was unexpectedly popular. He inspired confidence. It would have been bad tactics to throw him down at once in the face of the many manifestations in his favor. His very simplicity and frankness helped him.

General De Gaulle was alarmed. If Pinay succeeded where so many had failed, he would not only disrupt the party system but would cut the ground from under the feet of the Gaullist "Rally." Pinay went quietly on his way, halting the rise in the cost of living, stopping the flight from the franc, launching a loan designed to bring gold from its hiding places back into the Bank of France, preparing to open the doors of the prisons wider and wider, and bringing fresh hope to the country, much as Poincaré had done nearly thirty years before. Poincaré had great personal prestige, Pinay was virtually unknown; yet, the results were equally magical.

Let us take one more glance at the checkered history of the Fourth Republic. Why, it will be asked, the Fourth? It had been pretended, without the slightest truth, that Pétain was a usurper, though he had been duly placed in power, first by President Lebrun and second, after the armistice—I repeat, *after* the armistice—by a virtually unanimous vote of the National Assembly, that is, the Senate and the Chamber sitting together in accordance with the constitution. But if Pétain was a usurper, then it is clear that the Third Republic had never legally ceased to exist, and it was not De Gaulle who should have been a provisional president. President Lebrun should have been restored to office in 1944, and the deputies and senators of 1940, the only constitutional Parliament, should have sat pending new elections. But such a course would not have suited those who had effective power within their reach. Instead, President, Senate, and Chamber were liquidated, many of the members forbidden to offer their candidature, and a Constituent Assembly of the Fourth Republic was installed.

For support, De Gaulle was obliged to rely on the political elements of the Resistance which had, at Algiers and in the Interior, decided how they would share the spoils of office when the Anglo-Americans opened the way to Paris. These elements were the Communists, the Socialists, and the Christian Democrats (M.R.P.). Once installed, they could arrange to stay there. They must, for this purpose, not fall out. The Communists, the most active and the most numerous party, obtained the principal posts. How far they secured control may be illustrated by a comparison of the figures of the daily newspapers they were allowed to take from their rightful owners. Before the war, the Communists had four daily papers; after the Liberation they had 52. The Socialists possessed four daily organs; after the Liberation they were allotted (or took) 32. The M.R.P. had two; now it had 27. All opposition papers were suppressed: first, because newspaper plants had been taken over; second, because authorization to appear had to be obtained from the government; third, because newsprint was distributed by the authorities. Weekly and monthly organs were likewise suppressed or transformed. The radio naturally fell into the hands of the three parties, the Communists taking their full share. Communist propaganda was not merely permitted; the other parties tried to approach as nearly as they could to Communism. The Communists were praised as the chief Resistants, and they claimed to be the only real patriots. Socialists and M.R.P.'s lagged in the rear. We have seen since how such a situation—notably in Czechoslovakia—resulted in complete domination by Communism. The *Confédération Générale du Travail* (C.G.T.), the Trades Union organization, was altogether Communist and could command strikes as it pleased in furtherance of its cause.

The Radical-Socialists, who are really traditionalist and conservative, in spite of their name, had for many years been the principal party in France. They were now almost eliminated. The Right was reduced to feeble proportions. In these conditions, De Gaulle, who was certainly not Communist or Socialist at heart, depended on the parties which vilified and persecuted and, as far as possible, "liquidated" the Frenchmen who might otherwise have supported him.

It was a short-sighted policy. For, if the Communists were ready to use him as a banner in order to silence the anti-Communists, they soon had no further use for him. They had planted their men everywhere and, aided by their confederates, had classified as traitors all who could not squeeze into the Resistance; therefore De Gaulle, a military man with dictatorial dispositions, was now superfluous. The Socialists also repudiated him. The M.R.P., in spite of its protestations of fidelity to De Gaulle, felt obliged to stick to the tripartite accords. Neither the army nor the police were Gaullist. De Gaulle was forced to go.

But the mischief was done. The Senate had been suppressed, and France was governed by a single Chamber. In the plebiscites for a constitution which succeeded each other, the three parties agreed that the Senate should not be revived. That meant that the Communists had only to get the upper hand in the Chamber for their final triumph to be certain. After a first draft of the constitution had been rejected, the voters, heartily tired of the appeals to them, consented by a narrow majority (with a third of the electors abstaining) to a ramshackle constitution which was to prove wholly unworkable. It did, in fact, provide for a second body, called a Council, without any power to check legislation passed by the Chamber.

Then the Chamber proceeded to elections on a system that inevitably gave a majority to the three parties, Communist, Socialist, and M.R.P., as long as they held together. The public was not invited to vote for a given candidate in a specified circumscription. It was presented with party lists which it might not change, in which names counted for nothing, and had to be taken in the order in which they were presented by the parties. Then, by a system of complicated proportionalism, the parties sorted themselves out. It was, therefore, impossible to defeat any candidate who was a party leader. Even if his list received so few votes that it was eliminated, he could still be brought back in the national shuffle of seats.

It may properly be said that never did the level of parliamentary life fall so low, never before had there been such disgraceful scenes, free fights, uproar, obscene invective, as in the first years of the Fourth Republic. The intellectual quality had never been so poor. I think of the men I have known, the Caillauxs, the Clemenceaus, the Poincarés, the Tardieus, the Briands, the Herriots, and then think of the men who succeeded them! There have been, since the Liberation, at least ten thousand laws and decrees, contradictory, confused, inapplicable, useless, or downright detrimental, unjust, or illegal, and it would be impossible for any lawyer to find his way through such a maze of measures. What is legal and what is illegal today is doubtful, and it is probable that everybody in France almost hourly breaks some law or other. The task of the administrators, particularly of the mayors, who are overwhelmed with questionnaires to be filled and signed, is incredibly heavy, and delays in securing the recognition of one's rights are longer than has ever been known.

Good government is, of course, in inverse ratio to the number of laws.

Communists, Socialists, and M.R.P. contrived to form their tripartite governments until May 1947, when the Communists broke away. They had obtained all they could get from participation. They could now do better in opposition. The new line-up, though not anti-Communist for some time, was called the Third Force. It consisted of Socialists, M.R.P.'s and smaller groups of Radical-Socialists and others. But the Third Force was a mere minority of the French people. The Communists represented not far from a third of the electors, and when De Gaulle formed a new party (which he called a Rally, to which members of other parties might belong), it was proved that, in opposition to the government, it had the support of roughly another third of the population.

France was thus being governed by about a third of the electors, and that third was split up into groups which had divergent views. The Socialists stood for higher wages, whatever might be the consequences with regard to the nation's economy and finances, and insisted on the closing of religious schools. The M.R.P., on the contrary, professing Catholicism, stood for religious institutions. The rump of the Radical-Socialists and the Right, which made up the rest of the Third Force, were against the control of prices and rationing, which the Socialists were inclined to impose permanently on the French people—*dirigisme,* as they named it. Time after time, the Socialists upset the governments of which they were members, until all positive action became virtually impossible in France. Nobody dared to tackle the principal problems, and drift was the order of the day.

The control of prices was, in the end, so inefficacious that coal, for example, cost more than twenty times as much as under the Pétain régime, and the black market was the chief beneficiary of *dirigisme*. A more liberal policy, which brought down prices and restored plenty, was not due to governments but to the innate virtues of the French themselves. They began to ignore the multitudinous rules and regulations. They refused to give tickets for everything. The tradesmen decreed that they would not collect them. And so, as the restraints were thrown off, as *dirigisme* died a natural death, it was discovered that France, as before the war, was practically self-sufficing, and relative abundance returned as controls were abandoned.

France, while governments continued to waste her extensive resources, by her own efforts and American aid became fairly normal again. The governments which had sprung from the 1944 revolution can take little credit for France's revival. Politics hindered and delayed her return to better conditions.

It is rather piquant to observe that De Gaulle, who considered that he had the sole right to govern France, and that all who were not with him were traitors to France, appealed to the Frenchmen's discontent with the new governments he had called into being. He had joined hands with the Communists, had placed them in power: now he was implacably anti-Communist. He had begun, or at least permitted, the *épuration*, because it was only by sweeping away existing institutions and personnel that he could establish his own power: now he called for the release of Pétain and an amnesty which would assuredly not undo the harm that had been done but would limit the damage.

To De Gaulle might be attributed the disunity of the French; now he was the promoter of a Rally. He called for discipline, order, a strong army, French independence. But he forgot that he had imprisoned Weygand, who had formed the only real army that France possessed in North Africa, that he had imprisoned Admiral Decoux, who had kept Indo-China loyal to France, whereas Indo-China now, witnessing the division of the French, was in revolt. There were revolts in Algeria, anti-French movements in Tunisia, in Morocco, in Madagascar, in all the French dependencies which had been faithful to the marshal. Syria had been lost. France had been deprived of her *élite*.

France had made a pact with Russia. Both America and England were more than cool toward the general. Neither Communists, nor Socialists, nor M.R.P., nor Radical-Socialists, nor various smaller groups would admit his claims, and they denounced him as the leader of a faction, to be fought as a troublemaker. They would make no compromise with him. They were weak; they had committed grievous faults; they could not agree except on one point—that De Gaulle should not be allowed to return. The strength of De Gaulle in the country lay only in the weakness of the governments. Many Frenchmen were not so much for him as they were against the incompetent ministries, but hundreds of thousands of Frenchmen could not forget that he had brought these governments with him on his return from England, and that he was responsible for the failure of official France at the Liberation.

Patriotism is not a monopoly; it cannot be cornered like sugar or steel, and it may take many different forms. I am tempted to say that patriotism may be either the noblest or the vilest sentiment. Jeanne d'Arc was a patriot who saved France; Hitler was a patriot who ruined Germany; Stalin was a patriot who would chain the world to the chariot of Russia; the Communists are patriots—when it helps the cause of Bolshevism—and antipatriots when they are asked to resist a possible Russian invasion.

Patriotism is not enough, as Nurse Edith Cavell said. In the first place, it should be intelligently directed. Sacha Guitry, France's best-known modern playwright and actor, when accused of "intelligence with the enemy" because he had not thrown German officers out of his theatre but had behaved with courtesy toward them, rightly said that there was such a thing as "unintelligence with the enemy." Patriotism which leads to destruction and disunion in one's country is an inferior sort of patriotism. Patriotism must be based on love of one's fellows, on love of justice, love of freedom, love of peace. When patriotism degenerates into hatred, ambition, discord, intolerance, conquest, domination, it may become the most evil of human vices.

For my part, in surveying the past decade in France and in the wider world, I am chiefly struck by the good intentions which were often displayed by Frenchmen whether Gaullists or Pétainists, and I think that we should judge, if we judge at all, only the intentions of men. Unhappily, good intentions, as is well said, are the paving stones of Hell. Both Pétainists and Gaullists, in so far as their intentions were good, should forgive each other; they have both, even when their motives were good, wrought much harm. Tolerance of each other was never so necessary as today, when in many countries the meaning of the word has been forgotten.

To understand what has happened in France since 1940, we must employ a word more often used in France than in England or America: the word *mystique*. In 1940, Pétain possessed a *mystique*. Slowly, gradually, there grew about the name of De Gaulle another *mystique,* but it was never anything like so powerful as the *mystique* of Pétain and, reaching its height in 1944, it quickly declined, and has today largely disappeared. Both Churchill and Roosevelt enjoyed a *mystique*. So, undoubtedly, did Hitler. The *mystique* of Stalin was the greatest of all the *mystiques* of our time. A *mystique* is altogether beyond reason: it does not spring from superhuman deeds, perhaps hardly from words. It is a blind belief in the exceptional qualities of those who possess it. They can do no wrong. They are to be regarded with the eyes of faith. They are, while the halo surrounds them, demigods, infallible, moved by an intuition, a familiar spirit, which commands the worship of the masses.

They all committed the most disastrous errors, but their errors, however demonstrable, could not immediately shatter their *mystique*. In critical times, such a *mystique* is necessary for the leaders of mankind: and sometimes it is beneficial and sometimes baneful. In this book, I have tried to examine their decisions with a cooler judgment, not with an iconoclastic purpose but in the hope that we shall understand where we went astray and be kindlier in our appreciation of one another. When all is said and done, even the best of humans are but blundering mortals, and I know no man who has taken a prominent part in the events of the past decade who has not fallen into the most egregious folly.

The turning point in French recovery was the application of the Marshall Plan of financial and economic aid. Had America deserted Europe, had she not behaved with enlightened generosity, Europe would long ago have "gone Bolshevik." The Marshall Plan was the turning point for two reasons: first, because it furnished a material basis for reconstruction; second, because it forced France to make a choice. On the first point, it is unnecessary for me to expatiate. But on the second, I will add a few reflections.

France, in my view, had, after the disillusionment of the Liberation, lost hope. The tribulations of the war and the occupation, the violence and the injustice which accompanied the victory and left few families untouched, the mismanagement which followed the establishment of a constitution which was infinitely worse than the constitution of 1875, and might easily have resulted in one-chamber government, that is to say, in a dictatorship of the political parties which offered themselves at the elections and practically forbade any opposition, the malpractices, the scandals, the exactions, the requisitions, the spoliations of all sorts, the division of France into two groups of citizens, the ultrapatriots and the near traitors, the restrictions, the controls, the excessive functionarism, the toleration, if not the encouragement, of a black market worse than any that flourished during the war, the suppression of independent opinion, the refusal to pass a generous amnesty bill, the shameful exploitation by the false Resistants of their privileged position, the lawlessness that declared itself in every domain of daily life, the continual rise of the cost of living, the steady depreciation of the currency, the inadequate wages, the gross immorality reflected in the press, the pusillanimity of the politicians, the partiality of the radio for the Communists, the constant strikes of a frankly revolutionary character, all these things and more that I might enumerate discouraged the better citizens of France, who could be heard to say (how many times have I heard them say it!) that France was better off under the occupation than under the succeeding governments!

France felt that she was alone, helpless, having lost her rank among the nations, fallen into decadence, no longer a nation, and with nothing to indicate that she could ever be a nation again. Communism actually offered to many an escape from the feeling of frustration. In these conditions, the Marshall Plan was received with joy. It had a salutary effect. It stimulated the French. It was fought ruthlessly by the Communists, who rightly saw that it would prevent France from turning completely to Bolshevism. They described the Plan as an attempt to make France a satellite of America, when they far preferred her becoming a satellite of Russia. The choice had to be made, however reluctantly, by the governments. Materially, they were compelled to choose the American Plan, whatever its consequences, and soon they had, by the sheer force of Communist opposition, to choose it morally as well. The breach between Communism and (may I call it?) Americanism grew wider every month. The good effects of the Plan were soon felt, and any immediate return to Communism was at last improbable.

The pact with England concluded at Dunkirk, the port by

which the English left France, paradoxically regarded as a symbol of mutual help and of union, though it passed without much notice, operated in the same sense. The Atlantic Pact, which definitely linked up France with America, carried the process a step farther. But I am bound to state that these measures seemed to come too late and were always insufficient to create the full sentiment of the unity of the Western world. The menace of Bolshevism was hardly appreciated for years, though it was obvious from the commencement. The Socialists, in particular, without whom no government could live, were slow to understand that an absolute severing of all relations with Communism was essential: they looked on the Communists merely as rivals for political power. No drastic laws against a mortal enemy have yet been taken, though it is apparent that there is a Fifth Column in France bent on sabotage, declaring openly that, in the event of war, the Communists will refuse to fight, or rather will fight against their own country. If it were not tragic, it would be comic to watch the attempts to fashion European unity. Three or four competing bodies have been formed which seem chiefly designed to serve the political ends of European "leaders," and some of these European "leaders" do not in the least see that the first step to European unity is the unity of their own countries. France is not yet united; there is no full appeasement of old quarrels, no firmness in dealing with dissidents. Nevertheless, there is at last hope, and it is a hope which has its roots in the Atlantic Pact.

On the military side, the outlook is uncertain. France is, in the opinion of the most authoritative experts, without adequate arms, without enough men, without competent officers. The NATO plan of international armies has yet to be tried, and the skeptics, who doubt that men will fight enthusiastically for a vague geographical expression and an abstract ideology instead of for their country, side by side with their traditional "enemies," cannot be lightly brushed aside.

One might have thought that the first thing that those Frenchmen who were ready to pronounce the word treason in 1944 would have done would be to reconstruct the army, to enlist everybody who professed to be in the Resistance. In 1939, there were 5,000,000 men mobilized: today, the machinery of mobilization is out of gear. The fact is that France has not known for what she might have to fight. The Communists dropped the mask of patriotism: they did their best to stop a small army from being sent to Indo-China, and returning soldiers told me that they could never rely on the effectiveness of the inadequate arms furnished them.

But, say the pessimists, did not England and America disarm, while Russia was arming? Did they not shrink from realizing the plain fact that you cannot leave a big blank space in Europe, notably Germany, who alone might have been strong enough to hold back Bolshevism, without inviting Russia to fill the empty unarmed space? Had they not refused to heed warnings such as the blockade of Berlin, representing their *tour de force* of carrying provisions by air as a proper reply, when in truth it was no reply at all and left Russia indifferent? Why reckon on France to provide an army?

Alas, the years of sterile dispute demoralized France, wiped Germany off the military map, left nothing in Europe to oppose the Russian armies, should they be set in motion. And to be "liberated" once more, after three or four years of Russian occupation, would be mere mockery, for France would have ceased to exist. Such was the pessimistic view, induced by the foolish conduct of a civil war bent only on disruption, without regard for the future. France had seen enough of fighting and was inclined to refuse to furnish cannon fodder. She was tempted by the false security of neutrality. Her government at one time proposed, on the outbreak of war, to abandon the country, and to carry the army with it to North Africa, since it had been laid down that the heroes are not those who stay to protect their country, but those who desert it. Happily, wiser counsels have prevailed, but it will be a long and hard task to make France even as strong as she was in 1940.

Nor can I conclude without a word about war in general. We still despise the peacemakers, and exalt the warmakers. Should the first war have been avoided? Did it not inevitably lead to the second war? And was not the second war so pursued that it made a third war likely? War can only lead to war. War has definitely worsened the world since 1914, and after untold misery we again live in fear.

In a scholarly article on the Second World War, *Larousse* estimates that among the belligerent nations some 33 million persons lost their lives: 14 million in the military services and 19 million civilians. Many more millions died in prisoners' camps. It is difficult to estimate how many among belligerents and non-belligerents died of starvation, exposure and disease as a direct result of the war. The material losses and wastes have been conservatively estimated at 500 billion dollars. The cost of war has enormously increased. One scholar estimates that whereas it cost only 75 cents to kill a soldier in the time of Julius Caesar, it cost over $20,000 in the First World War and $50,000 in the Second. The best estimates of the total direct costs of the Second World War run between three and four trillion dollars, and experts tell us that ultimate war costs run to about four times the direct and immediate costs. It is reckoned that about 150 million persons were rendered homeless as a result of the Second World War. To these figures must be added the victims of the conquest of China by the Communists, the extensive massacres in China since the conquest, and the victims, civilians and soldiers, of the Korean and Indo-Chinese wars. What an incredible sum of human slaughter and misery!

The money spent on war would have given every family in America, Russia, England, France, Germany, and many other countries a fully furnished house and a substantial capital. Moreover, every city of 200,000 inhabitants could have been provided with new schools, sport grounds, hospitals, and libraries. I do not need to verify these assertions: they are, as we all know, essentially true. I made some such calculations after the First World War, and I have seen, with my own eyes, immeasurably more suffering since 1944 than after 1919. I think of the "displaced persons," as we euphemistically call them, of the millions of prisoners still in concentration camps, of the millions of homes wrecked, of the millions of families broken up and ruined. I think of the ravages in France, multiplied to infinity in many other countries, I think of the men and women deprived of their means of livelihood. I think of the resultant hate that is more explosive than any atomic bomb.

To die is nothing; we must all die. But to live in affliction, amid the follies and crimes of a topsy-turvy world, in which all we had been taught to prize is scorned, and all we had been taught to abhor is raised to a pinnacle of adoration, in which the warmakers and the destroyers are acclaimed and the compassionate and the imaginative are derided, in which gentle women applaud the slaying of Beethoven by Bill Sikes (as Bernard Shaw puts it), and material wreckage and moral degeneration are the lot of victor and vanquished, in which only the stupid, the selfish, the cruel, the narrow-minded and the utterly callous can escape an emotional strain that shatters the nerves and numbs the brain, that is distressing almost beyond endurance. How is it possible for men to talk of war when they have seen and felt its horrors?

For France I retain my affection, without bitterness, without regret for the grievous losses which were the price of my allegiance to her. I realize that the period of suicidal madness through which we passed was the result of the war, in which France suffered in some ways more than the countries which were actively engaged. My affection for France is unimpaired, and I recognize that, if she has been the prey of turbulent political forces and fallacious doctrines, the common people, the ordinary Frenchmen, have the same virtues that endeared them to me forty years ago. They are normally kindly, sensible, tolerant, understanding, and have learned the art of happiness. That is the greatest of all arts. But is happiness compatible with so-called greatness in these strenuous days? Must not France choose between might and happiness?

Auguste Detoeuf, an important industrialist, declared before the war that France was no longer "great," in the sense of being able to impose her will on the world by violence, or by the threat of violence. The French are content to live on a generous soil, in a delightful climate, as comfortably as may be in the short passage from birth to death. "Believe me," he wrote (and I quote from Montgomery Belgion's excellent book *News from France*):

> On the material plane France is *not* a great country: she is merely a country where people are happy . . . France, if we wish it, may yet remain the country where people are happy, where unemployment is rare, where the peasantry is peaceable and sound, where thinking is free, a country whose spirit radiates over the world . . . We must decide whether we want to be mighty or happy. We must decide whether we would terrify or attract. If we decide to be mighty, we shall have to live on a war footing. We shall have to give up talking, laughing . . . we shall have to welcome war and the civil wars that succeed it, and poverty, and perhaps famine, in a Europe fallen into anarchy.

Willingly or unwillingly—unwillingly as I think—France was forced to welcome war, and the civil war that ensued. She endured hardships, poverty, anarchy, in a chaotic Europe. She tried to play a rôle that was greater than her strength allowed. Relative happiness has returned. In my village, in Paris, in the provincial cities that I know, even though the scars of war remain, the old gaiety, the old *savoir-vivre* are once more reappearing. There is again plenty and a smiling philosophy prevails. God grant that France will not have to choose between an elusive greatness and her charming and contagious happiness!

25

The Marshal Dies

On July 23, 1951, the last of the great marshals of France—perhaps the greatest and the noblest of them all—Henri Philippe Pétain, died in his ninety-sixth year. He was the "oldest prisoner in the world" for, despite a general and persistent clamor for his release, in France and in all enlightened circles abroad, where it was realized that his condemnation was one of the many flagrant injustices of our time, he was indeed a prisoner until death released him from his jailors.

How harshly he was treated by the men of the Fourth Republic has been revealed by Maître Isorni, one of his devoted lawyers, in a book entitled *Souffrances et Mort du Maréchal.* It will remain for posterity to judge the attitude of the authorities who showed such complete lack of respect for the extreme old age of one of France's ablest, most devoted, and most unselfish public servants. Maître Isorni has indelibly branded on the forehead of certain public men the deep shame of their inhumanity.

It might be imagined that the fortress of the Ile d'Yeu

was as comfortable a place of detention as could be found. On the contrary, it was actually a spot of an appalling rigor. Difficult of access, exposed to the inclemencies of the Atlantic, off the Vendean coast, it was quite unsuitable as the habitation of a nonogenarian. He was entirely cut off from any society except that of his aged wife, who was eventually allowed to see him for a short time each day, painfully defying her rheumatism to drag herself from the little hotel on the island to the insalubrious prison.

The marshal was confined to a narrow cell, most summarily furnished and, for his daily exercise, had to descend thirty or more steps to the courtyard, always accompanied by his guardians. Neither from the cell nor from the courtyard could be obtain even a glimpse of the sea and the outside world. His food was of the most unsuitable character—food only fit for healthy young guardsmen—until it was supplemented by parcels sent to Madame la Maréchale by admirers who remained faithful to her husband and could not forget what France owed to him—at Verdun, the most fiercely fought battle of the 1914–1918 war; in quelling the mutiny of 1917; in Morocco, where he defeated the revolt of Abd-el-Krim (whom it was actually proposed to lodge in the marshal's private house, now confiscated, at Villeneuve-Loubet!); in Spain, where, old as he was, he was sent by the 1939 government to persuade General Franco to observe strict neutrality; and, in my opinion, at Vichy, where he made, in response to the plea of the government and the people, the sacrifice of his person and of his renown, in the hope of alleviating the miseries of France, defeated and bewildered, by interposing himself between the occupant and the nation.

I had thought of including in this book some account of the trial of Marshal Pétain before a tribunal specially instituted and so composed that, in the mood of the new masters of France, a condemnation was, for *raison d'état,* inevitable. Every word that was spoken is before me. The proceedings lasted from July 23 to August 14, 1945, and the *compte-*

rendu is published *in extenso* by the *Journal Officiel*, filling 336 closely printed three-column pages. I discovered that it would be impossible to summarize the evidence within reasonable compass, but I affirm that no impartial reader, in the light of what I have written, and in the light of subsequent disclosures, can have the slightest doubt that the marshal acted to the best of his ability while at Vichy. The task was, of course, superhuman, and that he failed is not surprising; but that he succeeded in the measure that he did is surprising.

It is monstrous to suppose that the old soldier, after an illustrious career, sought the supreme post in a defeated country with the intention of betraying it to the enemy. No well-informed person, free from fanaticism and political hatred, thinks that the marshal turned traitor somewhere between 85 and 90 years of age! Let us assume that his policy was mistaken, that he often chose his ministers and agents badly, that he was ill-advised, that he had strange lapses to be attributed to his failing faculties—let us assume anything we please, though it be unsubstantiated by the evidence and rebutted by the facts and their proper interpretation, it is still impossible, for any judicious student of contemporary history, or even for any student of human nature, to imagine for a moment that, after a glorious past of absolute devotion and loyalty, the aged man, on the threshold of the grave, could deliberately stultify his whole life of exceptional service to his country. Yet, such was the incredible accusation. Even if we assume that his mental capacities had sadly declined—which in my view was not the case—surely he should have been treated with kindness and compassion. Alas, kindness and compassion were qualities which were also among the predestined victims of the war and of the civil war in France!

There is still another consideration: was it wise, from the national viewpoint, to hold up France to the mocking yet shocked gaze of the world, as a country in which the marshal, the generals, the ecclesiastics, the members of the *Académie,* the members of the Chamber and the Senate, the prefects, the officials, the ministers, the writers, the intellectuals, the artists, were devoid of love of their country, and were ready—or in fact did—"sell out" France to the "hereditary enemy"? Was it wise to pretend that large sections of the French people were traitors or near traitors, and that only the *émigrés* and a relatively small number of active (and sometimes imprudent) Resistants were patriotic? Against these self-interested calumniators of France, I maintain that the bulk of the French people, obedient to the constituted authorities, whether they expressed their sentiments or not under the occupation, were just as much animated by patriotic emotions as the Gaullists and the Communists. Was it wise to disunite Frenchmen?

Pétain was born on April 24, 1856, and, the conditions of his detention slightly ameliorated, he was just strong enough to take notice of the celebration of his ninety-fifth birthday in the fortress. He was, nevertheless, a dying man. For a long time, it was intended to bury him secretly in the fortress, to prevent pilgrimages to his tomb. But, at last, the protests were so strong that his transfer to a small villa, transformed into a "military hospital"—but still a prison—on the island, was permitted. Politics, however, could not be kept out. The announcement was delayed until "after the general elections" on July 17, 1951. Then, there were doubts as to whether he could be removed, and a few days more elapsed before a medical man assumed the responsibility of taking him out of his cell. He died on July 23.

Stringent measures were enforced after his death, but at least one point—two points—were gained. He was allowed to be buried in his uniform of marshal, and he was accorded a private grave outside the citadel. Masses were said for him in many of the churches of France, including the Cathedral of Notre Dame. His last wish was to be interred at Douaumont, with the soldiers who fell under his command at Verdun. I do not doubt that permission will, eventually, in happier days, be given to the surviving veterans of Verdun to escort his ashes to their last resting place, and that all France will watch their passage with bowed heads.

"A marshal of France asks nothing," said the old man proudly; and then, with touching abnegation: "Release first, before you think of me, the faithful servants who obeyed my commands." I could fill pages with the petitions of authentic Resistants—to whom I render the most profound homage—for an annulment of the verdicts of the tragic years. Let me quote a few passages from one of these appeals, signed by a number of deportees, sectional chiefs of the Resistance, leaders of the Maquis, who claim no other title than that of "combatants."

They ask that an end should be made "of the divisions of the French caused by grave political divergence during the years of occupation and accentuated by a so-called *épuration.*" They declare that a study of the facts, sometimes ignored at the Liberation, now permits the establishment of a more humane and historical truth: "Some who were described as traitors were citizens who, having chosen ungrateful tasks without glory, contributed to the *maintenance* of the nation for which they had an ardent love. Their names and their work should be rehabilitated."

The actions of others may seem to have been contrary to the interest of the country, but political errors should not be confounded with common crimes and in no way affect honor: "It is the duty of those who risked their lives in clandestine warfare, and who never associated themselves with an enterprise of vengeance but fought at the Liberation for the triumph of justice (the ideal of the true Resistance!) to protest with energy against the persistence of a partisan spirit injurious to the country. We dissociate ourselves completely from the attitude adopted by various groups whose objectives are opposed to the aims of the Resistance. We hope for a reconciliation and for the renewal of French unity (a word on which the marshal insisted!) which, if now achieved, will lead to a rebirth of French genius, in all its purity and force, as it has appeared in the course of the centuries. We call on all Resistants who still have faith in the cause for which they fought to join us in our appeal."

That, I think, is the *real* sentiment of the *real* Resistance, so different from the spirit which animated the assassins and profiteers of the Resistance. It does the highest credit to those who profess it, and discredits those who do not. There, and there alone, is the Resistance which I admire, a Resistance which does not arrogate to itself alone all rectitude and righteousness, which admits that its adversaries (or rather those who honestly felt compelled to choose a different rôle) might also have been right and have rendered valuable services, while even those whom they still think mistaken were nevertheless good citizens.

I do not doubt that the memory of the marshal will be absolved of the grievous and unfounded charges brought against him, that he will be recognized as one of the noblest figures of a tragic epoch, and that there will soon be a reconciliation of all good Frenchmen and of all who love France.

Index

Abd-el-Krim, 348
Abetz, Otto, 150; diplomacy of, 151; urges "collaboration" be voluntary, 232-33
Académie Française, 307, 350
Action Française, Royalist newspaper, 77, 306
"Administrative detention," 309
Adowa, defeat of Italian army, 145
Advance to Barbarism, 244
Afrika Korps, 180
Alexander I, 81
Alexander, Field Marshal Lord, 63, 149, 271
Algeria, occupation, 179
Algerian Committee, 223
Algiers, 215-27; Communists, 222-23, 224
Alibert, minister of justice, 77, 102
Allier, 312
Allies and Bolshevism, 269; mistakes, 272-73
Alpes-Maritimes, 312
Alsace-Lorraine, problem, 102
America, demands withdrawal of Japan from China, 161; enters the war, 153-69; events heralding entry into war, 158-59
America's Second Crusade, book, 271
Angély, Félix, 263
Anschluss, 12
Ark Royal, ship, 62
Astrakhan, 218
Atlantic Charter, 159, 160, 161, 270
Atlantic Pact, 341
Atlantic Wall, 218, 219
Attentiste, 132, 151, 193, 205, 206
Attlee, Clement, quoted, 155
Auchinleck, General Claude J., 180
Auphan, Admiral, 175, 280
Auriol, Vincent, elected president of France, 329
Ayem, 312

Back Door to War, book, 8
Badoglio, Marshal, 225, 227; miscalculation of, 149
Baku, 218
Balkan States, 11; and Bolshevism, 269
Bandol, 173
Barnes, Harry Elmer, 9
Barré, General, 151, 175
Barthète, Du Moulin de la, 77
Bassorah, 218
Bastia, 312
Battle of Britain, 76
Batum, 218
Baudouin, 66, 102
Beard, Charles Austin, 162
Beck, Colonel, 15
Belfort, 280
Belgion, Montgomery, quoted, 345
Beneš, Eduard, 12
Benjamin, René, xv, xxiv
Benoit-Méchin, 115, 150, 151; asks for liberation of General Giraud, 151
Benouville, General de, 309
Béraud, Henri, 307
Berchtesgaden, 13, 117
Bidault, Georges, 328
Bizerte, North Africa, 118
Black market in France, 123-24
Blitzkrieg, 26
Blockade, slackening, 86
Blum, Léon, 5, 328, 329; quoted, 55

Bock, General von, 28
Bogomolov, Russian Ambassador, 222
Boisson, Governor-General, 78, 180; arrested, 222; eliminated, 221
Bolshevism, 268; and the Allies, 269; in China, 269; in the Far East, 160; growth, 266; Japan barrier, 268; menace, 341
Bonnefoy, René, 228
Bonnet, Georges, Foreign Minister, 4, 16
Bort-Les-Orgues, 312
Bossuet, Bishop, 202
Bouthillier, French finance minister, 77, 102
Boulangists, 164
Brasillach, Robert, 307
Brazza, Savorgnan de, xxi
Brazzaville, 90, 280
Brécard, General, grand chancellor of the Legion of Honor, 280
Brest-Litovsk, 96
Bretagne, airplane carrier, 62
Briand, Aristide, 93
Brinon, Fernand de, 93, 103
British, bomb Beirut, 118; bomb Palmyra, 118; bomb Renault works, 152; place embargo on Italian trade, 53
British Empire, liquidation, 138
Brive, 312
Bruening, Chancellor, 259
Bullitt, William C., xxiv; opinion of Pétain, 108; report, 108
Byrnes, James, 134; opinions, 135

Cachin, Marcel, 232
Cadogan, Sir Alexander, 87
Caen, 276
Cagoule, 93
Cagoulards (Hooded Men), 93
Caillaux, Joseph, xvii, 93
Cannes, 243
Cap Martin, 292
Carlyle, Thomas, 168, 296
Carrel, Alexis, 307
Casablanca, 221, 272
Catroux, General, 119, 121
Cavell, Edith, quoted, xxii, 337
Central Committee of the Resistance, 300
C.F.L.N. *See Comité Français de Libération Nationale*
Chaban-Delmas, General, 277
Chamberlain, Arthur Neville, 7, 13
Chamberlain, William Henry, 271
Chambert, 312
Channel Islands, 315-16
Chantiers de Jeunesse (Labor Camps), 183
Chapelle, Bonnier de la, 187
Chateldon, home of Laval, 105, 106
Chautemps, Camille, 40, 41
Chénier, Marie Joseph, French poet, 307
Chevalier, Jacques, 87
Chiang Kai-shek, 269
China, Bolshevism, 269
Chotitz, General von, 277, 279; proposal to Eisenhower, 278; truce, 278
Christian Democracy, 330
Christian Democrats (M.R.P.), 224, 332, 333, 334, 335, 337
Churchill, Randolph, 115
Churchill-Rougier accord, 212
Churchill, Winston, 155; appreciation of Pétain, 129; declaration on Germany, 137; declarations, 130; meeting with Professor Louis Rougier, 84, 85, 87; offers to form a Franco-British Commonwealth, 38; quoted, 15, 57, 226, 272; and Roosevelt meet off Newfoundland, 158; Russia as against Germany, 156; sees Colonel Groussard, 129; strategy, 133; takes over government in England, 29
Ciano, Galeazzo, Mussolini's son-in-law, 25, 225, 226
Claudel, Paul, 204
Clemenceau, Georges, vii, 7, 89; quoted, 9
Clermont-Ferrand, 240
C.N.R. *See Conseil National de la Résistance*
"Collaboration," 81, 185
Cologne, 243
Colson, General, 182
Comédie Française, 204
Comité Française de Libération Nationale, 221, 222, 312
Commandant Teste, ship, 62
Committee of Algiers, 222
Committee of De Gaulle, 129
Communism in America, 267; in England, 267; menace to civilization, 139
Compulsory service, 238-39
Communists, 232, 276, 315, 332, 333; activities, 240; claims, 236-37; distrust of America, 165; in France, 4, 5, 96, 185; and press, 332
Conseil National de la Résistance, 238
Consultative Assembly, 312
Cooperative Congress, 154
"Conscientious objection," 46
Conseil d'État, French tribunal, 310
Conseil de l'Humanité, 244
Constituent Assembly, 528, 332
Corap, General, 32
Corrèze, 312
Corsica, 312
Cot, Pierre, 55
Côte D'Or, 313
Counterresistance, 254-66
Cour des Comptes, 327
"Courts of exception," 320
Courts of justice, 308
Cours de justice, 315
Creyssel, Paul, 228
Cublac, 312
Cunningham, Admiral Andrew, 180
Curement, 312
Cyrenaica, 179

Dakar, 10, 118, 157
Daladier, Edouard, French Prime Minister, 13, 20, 22, 24, 27
Danzig, 2
Danzig question, 14, 15
Darlan, Alain, xx
Darlan, Admiral François, 46, 63, 102, 108-21; agrees to help Germans, 117; in Algiers, 187; ambitions, 112; criticizes Pétain's New Year's message of 1942, 150;

demands, 114; fears, 187; French call him career man," 111; murder, 187; in North Africa, 173; ordered to defend North Africa, 175; promotion, 114; Radicals' regard, 111; and the radio, 114; relations with Pétain, 212; succeeds Laval as "Dauphin" in France, 110
Darnand, Joseph, 259; behavior, 264; heroism, 263; outstanding figure in Counter-resistance, 262-63
Darrien, Admiral, 175
Daudet, Léon, xvii
Déat, Marcel, 91, 92, 103, 259, 262
Decoux, Admiral, 336
Deloncle, Eugen, 94
Dentz, General, 37, 120, 130; arrested at Liberation, 120-21; honors of war awarded, 120
Design for War, book, 154
Detoeuf, Auguste, 345
Digne, 216
Dijon, 313
Diktat, 110, 150
Dirigisme, 335, 336
Doriot, Jacques, 92, 103, 259; killed by machine gunner, 262
Doriotists, 164
Dorrien, Admiral, 219
Doumergue, Gaston, xvii
Draguignon, 314
"Drôle de guerre," phony war, 21
Drôme, 313
Drummond, Sir John C., 231
Du Gard, Martin, quoted, 179
Dulles, Allen W., 13
Dunkerque, battleship, 62
Dunkirk, 31, 32
Dupuis, Pierre, 86

Eckart, Dietrich, 201
Écrits de Paris, publication, 312
Egletons, 312
Eisenhower, General Dwight D., 309
El Alamein, 180
Emerson, Ralph Waldo, 168
Émigrés, animus, 119
Énergie accrue, policy of, 24
England, alarmed at possibility of French fleet falling into power of Germans, 60, 61; declares war on Japan, 162; pledges support to Poland, 14; policy, 10
Épurateurs, 301, 307, 317
Épuration, purge, 223, 236, 288, 298, 303, 304, 306, 308, 315, 316, 317, 328, 330, 351
Ethiopia, 52
Essays, 202
Esteva, Admiral, 175, 219
Eure, 313
Eyrem, 312

Faure, Edgar, chosen as prime minister, 331
Fay, Sidney Bradshaw, 9
Feder, Gottfried, 201
F.F.I. *See Forces Françaises de l'Intérieur*
Fifth Column, 341
Figaro, publication, 78, 309
Finistère, 313
Finland, defeat, 24; surrender, 23
Flandin, Pierre-Étienne, 24, 93, 115, 323; acquitted, 116; arrested, 222
Foch, Marshal Ferdinand, 8, 19, 29, 89
Forces Françaises de l'Intérieur, 276
Fourth Republic, 325-46, 347; Constituent Assembly installed in, 332; establishment, 325; history, 331-33
Franc, devaluation, 326-27
France, 3, 4; bans, 321, 322; Bolshevism, 267; budget, 327; conditions, 304-5; control of prices, 335-36; corruption, 253; effect of war on morality, 252-53; elections, 330-31; enters the war, 16-17; government, 335; governmental stability, 328-29; inadequacy of preparation for war, 6; incarcerations, 309; mobilization, 342; occupation, by Germans, 181; organizations, 164; prepares for peace, 256, 257; press, 328; recent history, 163; revival, 336; social insurance, 327; taxation, 327; under the occupation, 164; wages, 327
France, South of, bombings, 286-87; conditions, 123-24, 126-27, 146; Germans, 147; Italian military record, 145; living conditions, 126-27
Franco, General Francisco, 11, 29, 348; reluctant to enter into bargain with Germany, 82; stalls off Hitler, 79
French and Communism, 4; dislike of *émigrés,* 44; double character, 89; and Italians, attitude compared, 147-48; resentful of Italy, 53
French High Command, 25
French Legion of Volunteers against Bolshevism, 259
Functionarism, 327

Galerie des Glaces, 7
Gallacher, William, quoted, 154
Gamelin, General Maurice, 20, 29, 32; dismissed, 26
Gaulle, General Charles de, 19, 37, 45, 46, 56, 57; acclaimed by Parisians, 302; arrives in Paris, 279; calls on Governor-General Boisson, in Dakar, 78; consents to come to Casablanca, 221; and épuration, 336; grants amnesty to Maurice Thorez, 303; misrepresents French intentions, 64; pacts given to Stalin, 303; quoted, 65; reception by French, 281; reproaches French government, 64; safeguards real Resistance, 298; stipulations, 90-91
Gaullist Resistance, 184
Gensoul, Admiral, 62
Gestapo, 50, 124
German Armistice Commission, 183
Germany, 11; armistice with, 55; attempts to seize port of Toulon, 184-85; champion of anti-Bolshevism, 267; declares war with Russia, 133; declares war on the United States, 162; enters Paris, 37; incorporates Austria, 12; negotiations, 15; plans to traverse Spain, 79; plans to wrest Gibraltar from British, 79; and Poland, 15-16

Germans, in Crete, 116; in Greece, 116; in North Africa, 116-17; in Yugoslavia, 116
Gillouin, René, 78, 87
Girard, Louis-Dominique, 46, 83, 115, 151; bravery, 172; chosen to succeed Darlan, 187-88; escapes from North Africa, 171; installed in the Midi of France, 172; meeting with De Gaulle, 221; proclaims Montoire a "diplomatic Verdun" for Nazis, 83
Glières, 265
Godesberg, 13
Goebbels, Joseph Paul, denounces Pétain, 151; and Hitler, 151, 152
Goering, Hermann, 22, 55; counsels Laval, 171; opposes Hitler's attack on Russia, 136
Gort, Lord, 30
Gouin, Félix, 378
Gran Sassa, 226
Grand Council, 225
Grandi, Dino, 225
Graziani, Marshal, 179
Grenoble, 288, 290
Grosny, 218
Groussard, Colonel, 128; arrested by Darlan, 131; authorized to organize a liaison between the war ministry and the Gaullists in France, 131; mission to London, 128-29; negotiations with Churchill, 130
Guderian, General Heinz, 26, 27, 28
Guitard, Louis, xi, xxiv
Guitry, Sacha, 337, 338
Guizot, François, 208

Halifax, Lord, 87
Halifax-Chevalier accord, 212
Hamburg, 243
Hankey, Lord, 25
Hart, Captain Liddell, quoted, 154
Haute Savoie, 265
Henriot, Philippe, xx, 259, 260, 261; enemy of the Resistance, 261; killed by Resistants, 262
Herriot, Edouard, 55; deported by Germans, 280; recalled by Laval, 280
Hervé, Gustave, 54
Hess, Rudolph, 117
High Cost of Vengeance, The, book, 273
High Court of Justice, 323
Hitler, Adolf, 8, 11, 13, 16; annexes Bohemia, 14; armies, 141; and armistice, 48; attempts negotiations in Spain and Sweden, 75; concessions of, to Russia, 134; dealings with France, 52; decision of, in France, 138; demands return of Sudetens to Germany, 12; doesn't wish Mussolini to enter war, 52; and France, 47; and Franco-German collaboration, 102; and Goebbels, 152; invades Czechoslovakia, 14; judgment of successes, 143; meeting with Pétain at tomb of Aiglon, 103; Molotov's demands, 136; and Napoleon compared, 141-42; occupies Denmark and Norwegian ports, 25; offers to Stalin, 136; plan, 218; recalls Abetz, 233; relies on Hess's mission to influence England, 137; strikes at Russia, 132-43
Hoare, Sir Samuel (Lord Templewood), 86
Hood, ship, 62
Hoover, Herbert, 161
Hopkins, Harry, goes to London, 158
Hull, Secretary Cordell, 161
Huntziger, General Charles, 102, 105, 128, 183

"Ideology," 140
Ile d'Yeu, fortress, 283, 347-48
"Imperialism," British, 4
In My Time, book, 9
Indignité Nationale, 138
International Brigades, 317
Iraq, rises against English, 118; Syrian war material sent, 118
Ironside, General, 30
Isorni, Maître, 347
Italian Social Republic, 226
Italy, 10, 25; allied advance, 271; armistice with, 55; assault on Menton, 54; conduct of, in the war, 149; declares war on the United States, 162; events, 225-27; Italian soldiers' attitude toward fate, 148-49; Spanish demands alarm, 79

Japan, 163; barrier to Bolshevism, 268; negotiations with, 161; walks out of League, 161
Jeanneney, President of Senate, 44, 55
Jeannequin, Monsieur, 70
Joffre, Joseph, 89
Jour de la Grande Peur, The Day of Wrath, 28
Journal Officiel, 312, 349
Journaux d'information, national newspapers, 94
Journaux d'opinion, 94
Juin, General, 151, 180, 187, 263, 274; objects to Darlan, 175

Kai-shek, Chiang, 269
Kasprzycki, General, 20
Kesselring, General Albert, 227, 271
Koeltz, General, 151
Koenig, General, 276-77
Königstein, 172
Konoye, Premier, 161
Krauss, General, 219

Laborde, Admiral de, 184, 186
Lacaille, General, 183
L'Action Française, newspaper, 94
L'Humanité, 55
La Chronique de Vichy, 179
La Dépèche de Toulouse, newspaper, 265
Lagraulière, 312
Langer, William L., 9, 20, 201
Larousse, 343
Laval, Pierre, xix, xx, xxi, 44, 77; arrest, 106; carried off to Belfort by Germans, 280; comparison, with Pétain, 99-100; flies to Berchtesgaden, 175; insults Pétain, 106; motives, 171; and problem of Franco-German relations, 104; recalls

Herriot, 280; returns to Vichy, 106, 171; unfitness as second in command to Pétain, 101; unpopularity, 99
League of Nations, 8, 161; condemns Russia, 23
Leahy, Admiral William D., xviii, xix, 91, 153; contacts Flandin, 116; nominated Ambassador of the United States, 108, 109; relations with Pétain, 212
Lebrun, Albert, President of France, xviii, 36, 40, 46, 48, 55, 64, 281, 331, 332
Leclerc, General, 120, 180, 221, 274, 278, 279
Leeb, General von, 28
Leeds, Stanton B., quoted, 202
Le Figaro, newspaper, 94
Legion, 73, 182
Legion of Former Combatants, 263
Le Livre de Saint Pierre, book, 131
L'Humanité, newspaper, 95, 96
Le Mythe de la Liberté, book, 190
Leningrad besieged, 141
Leopold III, quoted, 31, 32
Le parti des fusillés, 140
Le Play, Frédéric, 202
Lequerica, de, Spanish ambassador, 43, 91
Le Soulier de Satin, play, 204
Les Arcs, 216, 217
Liberation, 94; period following, 296
Libya, 179
Life, magazine, 167
Little Entente, 12
Lloyd George, David, 7
Louis XIV, 3, 111
Low Countries, fall, 157
Luce, Henry R., 167
Luchaire, 103
Luftwaffe, 118
L.V.F. *See* French Legion of Volunteers
Lyautey, Marshal, 54
Lyons, 215, 216, 290; Gestapo, 216, 217; Resistance, 216

MacArthur, Douglas, 271
MacDonald plan of armament, 10
Madariaga, Salvador de, xiii
Madelin, 296
Maginot Line, 17, 19, 20, 21, 26, 28
Maikev, 218
Mandel, Georges, 43, 265
Manstein, General von, 28
Maquis, 125, 230, 231, 263, 265, 275; creation of, 239; elements, 240; life in, 240; made by Germany, 239
Maréchale, Madame la, 348
Marie, André, 329
Marion, Paul, 228; quoted, 229
Marine, Ministère de la, 111
Marseilles, 79, 242, 290
Marshall, General George, 157
Marshall Plan, 168, 339, 340
Massilia, ship, 44
Massis, Henri, 78
Mauriac, François, 309
Maurras, Charles, 55, 306
Mein Kampf, 136
Menelik, King of Ethiopia, 145
Ménétrel, Dr., 78, 259
Menton, Italians annex, 144-45
Meredith, 89
Mers-el-Kebir, 59-70, 63, 74, 130
Meyer, René, 329
Michelet, Jules, 296
Mignet, François, 296
Militia, 182, 231, 263, 274; atrocities, 264
Mitraillettes (Sten guns), 237
Mobile Guards, 263
Moch, Jules, 329
Molotov, V. M., 37; announces Russia's intentions in Bulgaria and her designs on the Straits, 95; demands, 134; interview with Hitler, 134; quoted, 20
Monaco, 51, 292, 293; Jews, 51; living conditions, 50; revolutionaries, 291
Mont Agel, fortress, 53
Montaigne, Michel de, 202
Montcorin Fort, 314
Monte Carlo, 49-50
Montgomery, Marshal Bernard, 180; march, 220
Montoire, 71-83, 108; meeting of Hitler and Pétain, 79, 80; significance, 80, 81
Montpellier, 242, 288
Monzie, Anatole de, xvii
Morbihan, 313
Morgenstern, George, 162
Morgenthau Plan, 273
Morocco, occupation, 179
M.R.P. *See Movement Républicain Populaire*
Movement Républican Populaire, 222
Mun, Count Albert de, 202
Murphy, Robert, 109; places his consuls in North Africa, 110
Muselier, Admiral, 120; eliminated, 221
Mussolini, Benito, 10, 25; arrested, 225; assumes policy of nonbelligerency, 53; begins war against Greece, 96; criticizes Hitler, 146; driven into Albania, 96; meeting with Hitler, 52, 226; mistake of, 145; murder of, 226; rescue of, 226
Mystique, 54, 338, 339
Myth of Liberty, xxii

Napoleon III, 81, 325
National Assembly, 55, 56, 108, 112, 257, 281, 322, 332
National Council, 116
"National indignity," 320-21
NATO, 341
Near East, revolt, 118
"New Deal," 153
News from France, book, 345
Nice, 243, 316, 318
Nièvre, 313
Nîmes, 240
Noguès, General, 151, 180, 187; eliminated, 221
Nordling, consul of Sweden, 277, 278
North Africa, 40, 43, 170-88; army, loyal to Pétain, 57; feeling, 172; Italian soldiers, 96; landing of Americans, 170, 171; preparation, 159
Notre Dame, 319

Occupation, 122-31; informers, 127; restrictions, 128
Oradour, 240
Oran, 59-70; French fleet, 62
Our Vichy Gamble, book, 201

Paguy-la-Ville, 313
Palace of Nations, 1
Palmyra, fall, 122
Panama Canal closed to Japan, 161
Panici, Père, driven from Notre Dame, 320; quoted, 319-20
Pantelleria, 225
Pareto, v., 201
Paris, attitude, 71; destruction in, 243-45; distinction between Vichy, 72; during Liberation, 95; effects of bombing, 248-49; living conditions, 246; press, 94, 95; saving, 263-83; surrendered by Germans, 277; transportation, 246; treatment of Jews, 247
Paris, Comte de, 187
Pas-de-Calais, 77
Passy, Colonel, 57, 233
Peace Through Federation, book, 154
Pearl Harbor, 158; attacked, 161-62; position of England, Russia, and Germany before, 162-63
Pearl Harbor: The Story of the Secret War, book, 162
Péri, Gabriel, 55
Perpignan, 288
Pershing, General John, 19, 108, 109
Pétain, Henri Philippe, xviii, xix, 18, 19, 29, 30, 35, 42, 58, 62, 203, 271; accepts "principle" of collaboration, 81; accusations against, 112; action against German spies, 181-82; and Admiral Leahy, 171; admits Laval to his cabinet, 171; gives Laval post of commander-in-chief, 171; asked to form a cabinet, 42; association of Leahy and, 109; attacks launched against, from London, 73; attitude toward Laval, 99; case against, 56; death of, 347; decides to break with Laval, 101-2; demands resignation of Ripert, 104; description, 204; dies in fortress on Ile d'Yeu, 283; disavows Darlan, 175; establishes National Council, 116; home at Saint-Pierre, xxii; hopes of evacuation of German forces from France without fighting, 256; impeached by special tribunal, 282-83; judgment of Darlan, 110; intervention, 39; issues note of protest, 176; last message, 284-85; literary ability, 100; loyalty of African countries, 180-81; loyalty of Frenchmen, 72; meets Goering in St. Florentine, 150; messages, 67; motives in naming successors, 113-14; *mystique,* 54; New Year's message of 1942, 150; policy, 95; quoted, 205, 206, 207, 208, 209, 210, 212, 213, 275; reenters France, 282; sent to Belfort, 282; sentence commuted, 283; suspicions, 102; tours France, 274; views about "collaboration," 105; wishes to be interred at Douaumont, 350-51
Peyrouton, Marcel B., 102, 105; arrested, 222; eliminated, 221
Picquedon, General, 183
Pinay, Antoine, 331
Platon, Admiral, 102
Pleven, René, 329; chosen as Prime Minister, 331
Pleyber, M. Jean, quoted, 312-14
Poincaré, Raymond, 93
Poland, 269-70; and France, 2, 3
Polish Corridor, 15
Potsdam Conference, 273
Pound, Sir Dudley, 62, 63
Prague, 2
President Roosevelt and the Coming of the War, 1941, book, 162
Production Industrielle, 190
Protocols of Paris, 118
Provence, battleship, 62
Pucheu, Pierre, 115; arrested, 222
Punch, magazine, 141
Puy-de-Dôme, 313
Pyrénées-Orientales, 313

Queuille, Henri, 329
Quisling (yes man), 98

Radio, use of forbidden, 258
Radical-Socialists, 333, 335
Ramadier, Paul, 329
Refractaires, 263
Reichstadt, Duc de, 102
Rémy, Colonel, 89, 233
Renan, Joseph, 44
"Reply to Montone, The," 85
Resolution, ship, 62
Revolution, great, 163
Reynaud, Paul, 18, 19, 24, 26, 29, 30, 31, 41, 42, 44; goes to Notre Dame, 37; quarrels with Weygand, 38; reforms his cabinet, 37
Resistance, 57, 197, 228-40, 233, 238, 263, 315, 318; beginning, 125; code, 186; ineffectiveness, 149; feeling about, 236; liquidation of men and women, 235; in Lyons, 216; men of, 230; plans a better France, 326; politics, 140; program, 326; real, 298; responsible for action to save Paris, 279; sentiment of real, 352; spirit of, 58; strength, 276; task, 289, 290
Resistants, 239; in France, 233, 234, 236, 237; in South of France, 287
"Resistentialism," 328
Rhône, 314
Ribbentrop, Joachim von, 258
Rocquebrune, 292
Rochefort, Victor, 325
Romier, Lucien, 78, 259
Rommel, General Erwin, 117, 133; promises to take Alexandria, 180
Roosevelt, Franklin D., 153, 157; agreement with Churchill, 156; and De Gaulle, 221; denounced for concessions to Stalin at Teheran and Yalta, 137; hopes of converting Stalin, 269; partisan of China, 161; refuses to support De Gaulle, 221-22; sends Harry Hopkins to London, 158

Roque, De La, 164
Rothfels, Hans, 13
Rouen, 243
Rougier, Professor Louis, 84, 86; explains French proposals, 87, 88
Runciman, Lord, 12
Rundstedt, General von, 28, 176
Russia, attacks Finland, 23; and Germany, 4; and *la terre brûlée*—"scorched earth," 142; failure of Germans, 142; and pact with Germany, 133; resistance, 162; treaty with Germany, 16; victories, 270; wins war at Casablanca, 270; wins war at Teheran, 270; wins the war, 266

Saar, 2
St. Florentine, 150
St. Georges-de-Montclaie, 313
St. Jean d'Acre, 120
Saint-Just, 297
Saint-Pierre, xxii
St. Raphael, 290
Saint-Setier, 312
St. Tropez, 290
Sainte-Maxime, 290, 314
Sainte-Mère-Église, 276
Salernes, 314
Salle de l'Horloge, 14
Salter, Alfred, quoted, 155
Sanborn, Frederic R., 154
Sauckel, Fritz, 239
Saurraut, Maurice, 2, 265
Schuman, Robert, 93, 329
Second World War, cost of, 343-44
"Septembrisards," 233
Service d'Ordre, 263
Shaw, Bernard, 344
Sicily, attack, 225
Sigmaringen, 282
Sirius, 268, 269
Skorzeny, Major, 226
Smuts, Marshal Jan, 165; speech before British Parliament, 166
S.O.L. *See Service d'Ordre*
Souffrances et Mort du Maréchal, book, 347
Speaking Frankly, book, 134
Spears, General, 45
Stalin, Josef, annexes piece of Finland, 95; cause of two-front war waged, 136; friendship with Hitler, 95; instructions of, to Molotov, 135; in Stalingrad, 219; takes Bessarabia, 95; takes East Bukovina, 95
Stalingrad, 218, 219
Stark, Admiral, 158
Stimson, Henry L., Secretary of State, 161
Strasbourg, battleship, 62, 184
Stresa Conference, 10
Stucki, French minister, 282
Sudetens, 12
Synarchists, 262
Syndicalism, 308

Taine, H. A., 296
Taittinger, president of Paris municipal council, 277, 279
Tansill, Professor Charles C., 8
Tassigny, De Lattre de, exploit, 181
Tardieu, André, xvii
Tchad, 180
Teheran, 272; surrender, 266
Templewood, Lord. *See* Sir Samuel Hoare.
Temps, newspaper, 94
Terreur 1944, book, 310
Terror of 1944-1945, 296-324; atrocities, 297; loss of life during, 299, 300
Tête de Chien, fortress, 53
These Men Rule France, book, 202
Thiers, Louis A., 296
Third Force, 335
Third Republic, 326, 330, 332; collapse, 55
Thorez, Maurice, leader of the French Communists, 5, 45, 92, 203
"Three D's," 260
Thuringia, 239
Tixier, Adrian, Minister of the Interior, 299, 314
Totalitarianism, 157
Toulon, 79, 184-85, 290
Treaty of Versailles, 2, 11
Trohan, Walter, 271
Truman, Harry S., 157; peace terms accepted by, 271
Tulle, 240
Tunisia, 179, 180; fight, 219
"Twenty-five Points," 201

Union Sacrée, 164
Utley, Freda, 273

Valiant, ship, 62
Var Bridge, 243, 251
Veale, F. J. P., 244
Vercors, 265
Versailles Treaty, 273
Vichy, bird's-eye view, 189-202; description, 194, 195; displaced persons, 77; "double game," 175; legality, 49-58; newspaper attacks, 91; perplexity, 174; Resistance, 191, 192, 198; sponsors movement of resistance, 74; in state of siege, 105; unoccupied, 198, 199
Villeneuve Loubet, 204, 348

War, causes, 9
War of ideologies, 139
War Unless . . . , book, 154
Wavell, Archibald, 119, 180
Wehrmacht, 20
Wellcock, Wilfred, quoted, 154
Welles, Sumner, 155
Weygand, Marshal Maxime, 18, 19, 42; accusations against, 37; arrested, 176; consults with Churchill and Eden, 37, 38; denounces Darlan, 118; first Resistant, 36; goes to North Africa, 73-74; influence, 175; quarrels with Reynaud, 39; quoted, 86
Weygand-Murphy pact, 171
Wilson, Field Marshal, 271

Wilson, Woodrow, 7, 153
Wilson's Fourteen Points, 8, 159
Winter, General, 141
Woodring, Harry H., Secretary of War, resignation, 158

Yalta, 269; concessions, 270-71
Yugoslavia, policy, 25

Zay, Jean, 265